BEN JONSON AND KING JAMES

BEN JONSON

Engraved by R. Vaughan. Frontispiece to the 1616 edition
of his works

BEN JONSON AND KING JAMES

Biography and Portrait

BY

ERIC LINKLATER

KENNIKAT PRESS
Port Washington, N. Y./London

BEN JONSON AND KING JAMES

First published 1931
Reissued in 1972 by Kennikat Press
by arrangement with the author
Library of Congress Catalog Card No: 74-168250
ISBN 0-8046-1689-2

Manufactured by Taylor Publishing Company   Dallas, Texas

CONTENTS

ILLUSTRATIONS

NOTE

MOST of the preliminary reading for this book was done during my tenure of a Commonwealth Fellowship in the United States of America. I record this fact not merely in acknowledgment of my indebtedness to the Founders and Committee of the Commonwealth Fund, but also for the pleasure it gives me to recall my residence in America.

I owe, and proffer, my thanks to Mr. Sidney Cockerell for leave to reprint the Latin verses on page 273, the manuscript of which is his property; to the Clarendon Press for permission to quote the letters on pages 148, 149, and 150; and for the use of certain illustrations to His Grace the Duke of Devonshire, and to the Keeper of the National Portrait Gallery of Scotland.

I am also grateful, for their courteous assistance, to the librarians of Cornell University, the National Library of Scotland, and King's College, Aberdeen.

For omissions in the index, failures in proof-reading, and opinions expressed in the text, I have only myself to congratulate.

CHAPTER I

THE BRICKLAYER'S BOY

BRICKLAYING, though useful, is a tedious occupation. One brick is very like another, and however attractive may be the houses which ultimately emerge from the untidy chrysalis of scaffolding, those who build them rarely meet those who go to live in them. For more bricks are waiting to be laid elsewhere; endless bricks, timelessly patterning the first brick of all that was thumped squarely out of shapeless clay and set in the indifferent sun to dry; brick to be set on brick and next to brick, tapped into alignment, sealed with mortar, in dull pedantic movements so that no one can repeat under his breath even the stateliest hexameter without setting his bricks awry, while if one turned to Pindar chaos would come quick between strophe and antistrophe. A dusty life, in which hands become hard and stony and heart dry, even though one's head is full of the grandeur of dead Rome that has found new garments in living Italy, of the tall white ghosts of Greece that come out of haunted medieval forests, of strange islands somewhere between Ireland and Cathay that look to sea-weary voyagers like an earthly paradise, and wash down gold in their streams, and hide silver in their mountains. . . . But the barrow creaks, the hod comes over the wall,

9

and here are more bricks exactly like the last, while the Thames carries soldiers to the Lowlands and sailors to the Indies, and apprentices are cheering mad Hieronimo, and tavern-talk swaggers over the menace and the riches of Spain. . . . Hands stiff with mortar and bruised with innumerable bricks, a mind that lingers with lame iambics, and at the end of the day a stepfather who praises bricklaying as a means of livelihood, bids one consider what bricklaying has done for him, earning him respect from honest artisans and craftsmen – a fig for scholars and poets – and enabling him to keep in decent comfort a widow-wife that a grave minister of the gospel had left penniless. . . . The minister's wife says nothing, but looks grimly at the master-bricklayer she had married eighteen years before because she was too poor to live alone and too much of a woman to wish to; he has grown garrulous with age, and brickdust has not sweetened his temper or hers; but she keeps silent now (though some years ago she had spoken her mind and insisted that Camden have his way and Ben go to Westminster to learn Greek and Latin if he could) and glances from her husband to her tall ugly son, hoping that another quarrel may somehow be averted. . . .

Two years earlier the Armada had sailed slowly into the Channel while the sunset gilded the white stern-wash of the galleons and threw long shadows at England. Two years ago, or a little less, the beaten ships had staggered back into the sunset with Drake at their heels, and behind him the arrogant Queen safer than ever before in her invincible island. That year Edward Alleyn, the actor, had taken a new play called *Tamburlaine* to the Theatre beside Finsbury Fields and, with the echo of Spanish guns still in their ears, Londoners had heard a stage thunder, as no stage ever thundered before, to the progress of a poet-king 'riding in triumph through Persepolis.' While English ships were on every sea, and every strange topsail meant another prize for England, Marlowe put his Scythian king on the London stage and made of English speech such mighty music as befitted the conquest of the world. When Tamburlaine's chariot was pulled across the stage by captive monarchs it was easy to recognize a good Englishman under the Scythian disguise, and a very proper conveyance for any Englishman, thought the 'prentices. And again, while English scholars pored on palimpsests and scientists stared at the new skies of Copernicus, while every student's nose quivered at the dusty smell of a library more greedily than a beggar's in front of a pie-shop, Marlowe left his bloody Tamburlaine 'drooping and pining for Zenocrate,' and contrived in Faustus a fresh manifestation of the passionate soul of Elizabeth's England, the soul which dared declare its faculties could comprehend

'The wondrous architecture of the world
And measure every wandering planet's course,
Still climbing after knowledge infinite. . . .'

Ships from Russia and Holland and Italy came up the Thames, and Genoese artificers, Dutch merchants, and Russian sailors stared at the steep-roofed houses on London Bridge, at the great church of Paul's to the north, and with even more anticipation at the long row of bawdy-houses on the Bankside. On either side of their ships white swans sailed sedately, and a multitude of small boats trafficked to and fro. In Gresham's Royal Exchange business was negotiated that touched every shore from Riga to Cyprus. And in Paul's Church, that looked so great and godly from the river, masterless men and swindlers crowded the middle aisle; players and country squires and soldiers and pimps and courtiers swaggered and hitched up their cloaks, swore a new oath or two, heard the gossip of the day, protested their friendship or readiness to fight, and went off to dine if they had money or to find a citizen's easy wife if their pockets were bare.

Ships and soldiers pass and leave no memory when a poet's playthings, with words for bones and ink for their blood, may live for ever. And in the year after the defeat of the Armada a new company of fictitious immortals came gracefully out of Ireland to jostle their countrymen at court. For nine years Spenser had been living with naked Irish for his neighbours and now, out of the wilderness, came Una and the Red Cross Knight, a very English lion, a Duessa taught by the Medici, a Guyon and a Palmer that the Reformation had made possible, an Arthur that the spirit of Sidney, Raleigh, and Spenser himself made not quite incredible, and a Gloriana that all men knew was a red-headed elderly virgin throned superbly in England's heart. Virgil and Tasso and Ariosto were Spenser's teachers, but Spenser was English, his knights were Devonshire men, and the Faerie Queene was Elizabeth.

So England grew, and was the last place on earth where youth could happily carry a trowel or ambition find comfort in trundling bricks. And this was the second time that Ben Jonson had tried to make his living by building walls.

His father had died in 1572, a poor man, stubborn in defence of his church and scantly loving the world. He had forfeited an estate which he could have kept by modifying his faith, and righteousness had not prospered. His wife controlled her grief at his death for fear of hurting the child eight months old in her womb. The last weeks of her pregnancy, bitter with unshed tears, were tortured with such anxiety for the future that the agony of her labour was almost a relief. It was a well-made child that she bore. His limbs soon promised strength but his face did not follow with a pledge of comeliness, for its symmetry was marred by one eye being slightly bigger than its fellow.

The bricklayer who presently married the minister's widow was good to the boy and let him go to a grammar school for some years. But when he was old enough to mix mortar Ben was set to work in his step-father's trade. He followed the bricklayers here and there through the town, despising (with a schoolboy's assurance) his masters' stupidity, and enjoying (with a small boy's love of dirt) the muddy business of building; until he somehow attracted the attention of

William Camden, who was then second master at Westminster and a man wiser than the majority. How he and the bricklayer's boy became acquainted we do not know. It may have been through the intermediacy of a snowball. It may have been that Ben, when he wished to annoy the men about him, found that the best way to do it was to recite a little Latin, a jingle from the grammar-book, a '*Neque lux, neque crux, nisi solum clink,*' or some such line; for a snobbish affectation of learning will immeasurably reinforce any small boy's rudeness, and the bricklayers, hearing this unfamiliar stuff, would naturally conclude that it meant something too gross for English words and lose their tempers. It may have been that such wrangling between dog Latin and the common tongue reached one day the ears of Camden passing by. A Latinist's occasions for field-work being rare, perhaps the schoolmaster stopped and spoke to the boy, and found his intelligence alert and his memory retentive. Ben would be ready enough to display his knowledge, and Camden found this zest for conjugation and declension – in a wild-looking boy whose hands and boots were grey with mortar – sufficiently entertaining to accompany the phenomenon to its home in Hartshorne Lane.

There he would learn that the boy's stepfather thought well enough of bricks as a foundation for life, but his mother had loftier notions to which the smallest encouragement lent words, and when Camden said 'Let him come to school again,' she gave the bricklayer no peace till he consented. So Ben went to

Westminster, and there he stayed till it was time for him to go to Cambridge.

By then, however, the stepfather's patience was utterly exhausted. He had small sympathy for schools and none at all for a university. His wife, grown old and lean in her anxiety, found so great a piece of fresh persuasion beyond her powers. Flatly the brick-layer refused to keep in idleness a lad strong enough to earn his own living. 'Let him work,' he said. And when Ben and his mother explained how the years at Westminster would all be wasted if Ben were to do nothing more than lay bricks with his Latinity, he replied that he had always known they were being wasted.

With the town full of clever young men newly down from the universities there was, indeed, nothing very brilliant for a Westminster schoolboy to do. But new houses (though the Privy Council forbade them) were being built in plenty. London was growing fast, and the bricklayer, who needed a new apprentice, grew more and more noisily insistent that Ben should earn his keep in the way that both opportunity and common sense dictated. And Ben, sixteen or seventeen years old, had no counter-arguments stronger than a surly hatred of his step-father's trade and a tender belief in his own capacity for some higher employment, vaguely conceived and obstinately refusing to materialize. So scant a defence as this was bound to fall, and when to importunacy was added bread-and-butter pressure – for the brick-layer had it in his power to starve as well as to beleaguer – Ben surrendered and took up a hod as bitterly as a beaten soldier might carry out a flag of truce. He and his mother knew that a truce was not peace, but the bricklayer had no subtlety. He treated Ben heartily, as one convalescent from a long sickness, and talked interminably of his trade, and thanked God that the boy's head was no longer to be occupied with Latin tags and ideas got by candle-light out of heathen Greek, and bade him keep his angles square and build his walls straight and true. Contemptuously he spoke of books and ever more complacently of bricks. Daily Ben worked, and nightly, in the house by Charing Cross, the air grew more ominous. The widow of the forfeited clergyman looked grimly and anxiously from Ben to her husband, waiting for the storm. She said little. She was proud of her son and felt it unjust to be angry with the honest workman who had married her and fed her bad-tempered clever child.

CHAPTER II

INTERLUDE IN THE LOWLANDS

FOR a year or so Ben endured his servitude, but the situation was impossible, for the longer his stepfather talked the more certain Ben grew that he himself was half a scholar and half a gentleman; and therefore doubly unfitted for building chimneys. His grandfather had been a gentleman – though of Scotland, which was a needy country – and a gentleman's grandson should be either a soldier or a scholar. Scholarship, it seemed, was out of the question. But there were English soldiers on the continent, where England guarded among the dykes of Holland a frontier against Spain almost as wet as the frontier she had thrust out to the Azores. There were gentlemen – so they said in the taverns – who trailed an honourable pike in the Netherlands, and found profit there, and the satisfaction that comes of living as a gentleman should. When he was eighteen years old Ben had the broad shoulders, the tall gaunt frame, and the long legs that were later to carry, without distress, the mountainous belly of his middle age to Edinburgh and back. At eighteen his wrists were strong, his temper was both quick and stubborn, and he hated bricklaying. Clearly, at eighteen, there was nothing more suitable for him to do than to join the army.

Before going farther it must be admitted that Jonson's early history is like a basket which has to be filled with a certain number of undated eggs. We know that he was born in 1572 and that he produced *Every Man in his Humour* in 1598. There are the dimensions of the basket. And we know that during those years he survived his childhood (no small feat in Elizabeth's London), went to grammar school and Westminster, laid bricks when he was not otherwise engaged, fought in the Low Countries, married and begot children, became an actor and a dramatic author, suffered a revolution in his own mind, and led – though he did not inaugurate – a revolution in the theatre. There are the eggs. Now opinions differ as to how they should be placed in the basket. Some, of course, can be dropped in without discussion. Clearly he went to school before he wrote presentable tragedy. One is a definitely ancient egg, proper to the bottom of the basket, and the other a new-laid one which claims the top layer. But many eggs are notoriously inscrutable. When did he join the army, when did he lay the majority of his bricks, when did he marry, and when did he turn to his proper craft of the theatre? These are the silent enigmatic eggs which guard their secret age. There are here, as in the market, new-laid eggs, fresh eggs, eggs equivocal, and mere eggs; some may suspect a faint mustiness where others find only freshness, or what you think new-laid I may fancy eggs equivocal.

And (for the basket is temporarily in my hands) I choose to put the egg of Ben's flirtation with war in the compartment marked 1590. The younger one is, the more naturally one thinks of soldiering as a possible career, and to adolescence especially does warfare promise relief from the humdrum care of a peaceful existence. Ben's adventure in the Low Countries almost certainly took place at the first possible opportunity, before his brain had begun to look for mental battlefields, before the idea of marriage crossed his mind – and that did not tarry long – and before he had weakened his pride in the sweat of his stepfather's trade. If, then, 1590 is the year of his brief campaign, the circumstances were possibly as follows:

On the first day of March of that year, a canal-boat apparently loaded with peat entered the harbour of Breda. There was broken ice in the river and the harbour was half-choked, so that the boat had difficulty in getting to the quay. But the Spanish guard threw ropes aboard and hauled her in. The master, Adrien de Berghe, was grateful but nervous, and in the 'tween-decks, under a roof of peat, forty young Dutchmen shivered as silently as they could – the boat was leaking fast – in the icy water that crept up to their knees. For two days they had lived in this chill darkness, nursing their pikes and halberds and muskets, and now, with Spanish voices overhead, they must endure a little longer. One of them sneezed suddenly, a loud country sneeze, and Adrien de Berghe felt his forehead grow sweaty in spite of the snow that fell swiftly from a colourless sky and settled thick on black Spanish armour and Spanish morions. But the Spaniards were unsuspicious, for sneezing has no accent and there were Castilians about who also suffered from an itchy rheum in that cold land. So the Dutch volunteers waited patiently, undiscovered, till night-fall, when stiffly they crawled out of their hiding-place and fell stiffly on the Spanish guard. Then, having killed them, they opened the city gates and Prince Maurice rode in with Count Hohenlohe, Sir Francis Vere, and seventeen hundred soldiers. The garrison woke from warm sleep and were dismayed by sudden invasion in the chill and friendless night. Panic attacked the Spanish veterans and Breda fell.

News of the romantic episode reached London and – so we drop this egg into the basket – Ben made up his mind. His forbears of Annandale would have loved such cold and bloody strategy. Vere was a gallant commander, trained under Prince Maurice, and Prince Maurice was the best soldier in Europe. The Spaniards sent their finest regiments to the Netherlands, and the English mercenaries did them the honour of copying their armour and organization and tactics. The Spanish troops were superbly proud of their traditions and efficiency. One of their regiments, the Tercio Viezo, had men in its ranks who had fought under the great Captain Gonzalo de Cordova in the time of Charles V. The pride of this battalion became so overbearing that even Spanish commanders found it intolerable. These were enemies worthy of a Westminster schoolboy with Border blood in his veins and his head full of a private view of the Renascence.

Ben crossed to the Netherlands with reinforcements. His pike, which the Spaniards called *la señora y reyna de las armas*, was eighteen feet long, a tall enough lady for any fiery voluntary to worship. He also had a sword and a dagger, and his pay was ninepence a day. Three pints of beer cost twopence.

The allied troops marched into the Betuwe, which is the country between the Waal and the Rhine, because a Spanish army under Count Charles de Mansfelt was advancing with the idea of counterattacking and retaking Breda, and it was considered advisable to divert their attention. This was done by throwing up entrenchments on the banks of the Waal opposite the city of Nymegen. Sir Francis Vere had been taught by Prince Maurice to believe in trenches. He also believed in quick cheerful exploits which took the enemy by surprise. But for serious warfare there was, he had been told, nothing like trenches, and so he would stand on the parapet between shovelfuls of earth thrown up from under him and bullets from snipers across the river, and direct with real enthusiasm the excavation of bays and galleries and saps. He was often wounded. But the next day, with a bandage round his head or perhaps limping a little, he would be back on the parapet, pointing here, bidding a sweaty soldier dig deeper there, seeing that a traverse was neatly finished and the fire-step left high enough. This, Ben found, was modern warfare as Queen Elizabeth's generals knew it.

For months he dug in wet heavy clay until there was a trench system that guarded the Betuwe from aggression and another that threatened the city of Nymegen. He saw no Spaniards. But the people of Nymegen, who were partisans of Spain, had organized the young and warlike men of their town into a company called Knodsendragers.

The Knodsendragers never offered battle, but in a score of ways harassed the patient trench-diggers. Muskets barked across the river and often a soldier who had taken off his morion – no man can delve in comfort with an iron pot on his head – fell sprawling in the mud and had no more need for armour. Ration parties were cut off. If a man strolled forth at night to a nearby farm where the girls were said to be friendly, he was likely to find three or four Knodsendragers waiting in the barn for him. And so his fellows had more work to do. Trenches were neatly revetted and sumps dug for the water that oozed up under every spadeful of clay. Then, in the intervals of digging, halberdiers drilled recruits in the proper exercise of their pikes, as the City bands were drilled on Finsbury Fields. War, that had promised riotous adventure, became as drab as bricklaying and ten times as uncomfortable. By and by Spanish artillery arrived in Nymegen and their round shot fell heavily into the wet trenches, so that every day there was more digging. One at least of the English pikemen grew tired of war, for it seemed to Ben that service in the Low Countries meant nothing more than ceasing to be a bricklayer in order to become a bricklayer's labourer.

But the Knodsendragers, with Spanish guns behind

them, became insolent and walked openly on the walls of Nymegen, and shouted insults across the river. One of them had a loud voice and a mixed reputation, among his friends, for swordsmanship and wit. His bawdy comments profaned the peace of evening and in the rain-washed air his broken English was intolerable. A voice as loud as the Knodsendrager's went back across the river as Ben – whose beard was beginning to grow – bade the Dutchman keep his mouth shut, or come down and fight. Trulls and cripples can talk. Let men fight or hold their peace – and so forth.

Such, it may be, was the prelude to the duel so cloudily famous in English literature. Ben fought in single combat between the armies: that we know. But with whom did he fight? There is another unmarked egg. His opponent may have been one of Gonzalo's men, a veteran of harsh experience and prodigious skill in arms. But we should probably know more of the matter if his enemy had been distinguished, and Drummond's bald recital may well conceal the fact that he whom Ben killed was only the lusty cock of some city dunghill. To argue this probability does not depreciate Ben's courage; it merely avoids the temptation to make a Cockney d'Artagnan of him. But having deprived him of a romantic foe, let us give him a romantic stage. Let us imagine a little silence following the challenge – few of the Nymegen men would understand English. Let us picture a bridge across the river, for a bridge is more romantic than a field, and calls up memories of

23

Horatius, and Artegall, and Isumbras who lacked one. The boy deserves a good setting for his maiden fight, for it was the first of many – some that drew blood and more that pricked into bile – and he never gave ground. A brave fighter whose mistress, later on, was often only a spare and angular lady called Truth, whose caresses, though always virtuous, were sometimes a little cold; a soldier – not seldom in a private and solitary army – from boyhood to old age; and this is his début.

Now, then, armed with sword and dagger, he climbs out of the trench and stiffly walks to the bridge that spans, on boats, the sluggish river. The pioneers (let us suppose) have but newly made it, so that the boards are still white between muddy footmarks and the edges are rough with splinter-prickles. There, on the bridge, Ben shouts again to the silent Knodsendrager. The pikemen on guard cheer him and laugh, rousing gladly from their routine of dull watchfulness; and either their laughter or their cheering, whichever was louder, summons the rest of the English from their huts. They come as happily as if bears were to be baited. The Dutchmen argue on the wall in broad and vehement outline against the sky until a Spaniard, weary of such sluggish allies and punctilious in his attitude to a challenge, settles their dispute, and presently through a city gate the swordsman comes, very red and angry, with half the garrison behind him. They line one bank of the river and the English press forward on the other. On the bridge – it swings beneath them and the river

chuckles to the anchored barges – Ben and the
Dutchman stare at each other while each considers
such things as his opponent's reach, how close
his gorget fits, the look of his dagger-arm, and the
uneasy boards underfoot.

Then, swaying and hitting, thrusting and guarding,
they fight. The boards creak beneath their feet.
The soldiers on the banks crane forward, muttering.
Steel meets steel, hard and briskly. The first fury
passes and they fence more cautiously. Then anger
grows again. Parry leaps into cut and returns to
parry thrust.

Now the Dutchman overreaches himself, and
before he can recover Ben's point goes through his
face to meet, with a jerk, the solid wall of his skull
behind. What was, a moment before, a countenance
all lively and angry, sweaty and intent, becomes in a
second a mask of inanity with a bloody split in it.
As Ben withdraws, the soldier's weight hangs on and
follows his sword. The Nymegen man falls forward,
dead, with a dull crash on the bridge. For a moment
his arms twitch and his body is convulsive under its
partial armour. Blood flows on the raw new planks,
running darkly into muddy footprints.

The English cheer and smack their thighs, and
laugh uproariously to see this rough cockerel of
theirs blooded so finely. But Ben, exultant, breathing
harshly, does not idly stand and watch the Dutchman's blood drip into the river and make red streaks,
quickly washed away, on the tawny water. He
remembers something that Camden taught him,

25

something about *spolia opima* that the Romans took when they had fought and won; and perhaps there is a subconsious memory of the canny ways of Annandale, where fighting was commonly followed by an increase in wealth. So he puts back his sword and, working quickly, with his dagger cuts off the Knodsendrager's armour, and finds a ring or two on his fingers, and some little things of interest in his pockets, and a very good belt round his middle. These he stows away or tucks under his arm, and for the first time feeling pleased with war, goes back to the English bank. The Dutchmen, indeed, make a move to prevent this unmannerly classicism, but a dozen pikemen run on to the bridge and maintain a growling peace.

For a day or two Ben would be half a hero; but only half a one, for the English were more inclined to laugh at an enemy's downfall than to be surprised at a comrade's victory. And Vere was away, taking a holiday from trench-digging, and news came in of his swift, cheerful, romantic, good-humoured exploits at Recklinghausen, and Büderich, and Zutphen. He had dressed his men up like countrywomen going to market, and persuaded a Spanish garrison to open its gates to them. And then the wolf had shed its wimple and bitten. This was a better joke than settling young game-cocks on to fat Knodsendragers. The siege-force thought kindlier of war, and hoped that they too would see more lively action than tramping up and down the marshy banks of a dull river.

But instead there came a rumour that the States had decided to build a new dyke across the lower part of the Betuwe. Such a dyke might indeed have some tactical value. But a suspicious mind could also see, behind this plan, an astute desire to use good soldiers as labourers, and employ an idle army in agricultural improvements. And no soldier is interested in alien agriculture. The English began to grumble more seriously than they generally grumbled, and the thoughts of a dissatisfied mercenary turn naturally to desertion. It is something of an adventure to desert on foreign soil. . . .

In London poets were writing. All the world walked down London streets. From the lips of Alleyn, that stately actor, fell Marlowe's gorgeous lines. At night men talked of books, and surely there was more life in books than in this dull soldier's drill? And worse than drill was the prospect of more digging, endless digging, back-breaking spade-work beside men who, though good companions in battle, were easily exhausted in talk and knew nothing of Horace, and thought of Sir Philip Sidney as a soldier, not (which was much more important) as the author of *A Defence of Poesie*. If this is war, a pox on it! thought Ben, and joined two or three more who were tired of the Low Countries, and without advertising his intentions left the army behind him and found his way back to London.

CHAPTER III

ELIZABETH'S LONDON

THE swans bent their heads to see themselves in the clear Thames water that ruffled their ivory reflexion. The watermen bent their backs and pulled steadily towards the Bankside. A land breeze carried across the river a strong smell of bears and the harsh barking of dogs. The watermen pulled into the landing stairs and their passengers disembarked. Harry Hunks was going to be baited by mastiffs from a new kennel, and there was no time to be wasted, and twopence was not too dear for a good seat from which blood could be seen clearly.

The Bear Garden, like a wooden drum, echoed the terrible roaring of Harry Hunks as he tossed and tumbled with a dog clinging to his shoulders, another to his ears, and another in his arms that he speedily crushed the life out of. Presently he freed himself and stood upright, shaggy and black and huge, shaking his head, his face all blood and slaver, and his nose a pretty pink in the midst of dark hair. The audience shouted their delight. Harry Hunks could always be depended on for pleasant sport.

He was coaxed out of the ring to make room for a bull and more mastiffs. The bull stopped to snuffle at a pool of blood. A mastiff, crawling on his belly, slowly approached. The bull charged, head down, and the dog was tossed high into the air. Now another dog comes, creeping close to the ground, and before the horns can get under his body his teeth are in the bull's nose. Furiously, without a sound, the bull tosses its horns, flinging its head this way and that, stamping the ground. But the mastiff hangs on till his teeth break and he is thrown with a thud against the wall, and promptly the bull's fore-feet pound in his ribs. But the next dog holds his bull till it bellows loudly, and that, for a bull, is the ultimate admission of defeat.

Now comes comedy. A pony with an ape strapped to its back gallops into the ring with a dozen vicious curs behind it, that bark loudly as they leap to the pony's shoulders and try to tear down the ridiculous-looking foreigner. The noise increases, and the good Londoners are weak with laughter at the ludicrous panic of the pony and the tortured monkey. . . .

The following day some gentlemen who had watched with the liveliest interest this rude entertainment, heard at court a play called *Endimion*. Lyly's fantastic conceits gave them as much pleasure as the monkey had given them. Poetry and myth and lines that were damascened with bright similes delighted them as the strong rough bear and the fearless dogs had delighted them. Mellifluous antithesis and all that air of graceful education, which was Lyly's privilege, enchanted them as the blood of bulls and the smell of kennels had. For they were Elizabethans.

And that night the news reached London that Sir Richard Grenville was dead, and Spain had two galleons less than yesterday; and thirteen others would need patching and mending; while every Spanish sailor in fifty ships was silent at the thought of the black-avised Englishman whom nothing could dismay. Nothing, they said. Not even visible death, for had he not drunk a last health in the Spanish admiral's cabin and then crushed the beaker between his teeth, breaking glass instead of bread for the viaticum?

Waiting for trials that would be as unjust as their arrest, the Puritans in London prisons heard this story of the *Revenge* and gave thanks to God who had made them Englishmen. Courtiers learning Italian by Florio's method – who provided bi-lingual discourses on chess, fencing, and the thirty beauties of a woman's body – called for another bottle and remembered their raddled but excellent Queen. At the Curtain Theatre beside Finsbury Fields a lesser playwright of the time (waiting to act in a comedy of his own making that gave pleasure to the vulgar by a clown called Launce, who suffered for his dog) listened to one speaking of the gunner of the *Revenge*, who had wished to sink his ship and drown with her, and found his thoughts whirling into lines that should sing again and again this sceptred isle of England, whose sons, made famous by their very birth, grew renowned for their deeds as far from home as is the sepulchre in stubborn Jewry of the world's ransom. . . .

Sir Walter Raleigh forgot for a while his pretty Throckmorton, and Drake, cursing afresh his Queen's distrust, smelt the sea and the burnt smell of powder blowing and the smell of spice-islands. . . . While in the taverns men compared, speaking professionally over their ale, this action of Grenville's with a fight last Easter day, in the Straits of Gibraltar, when the ship *Centurion*, under Mr. Robert Bradshawe, repelled the attack of five Spanish galleys. Each galley had a company of some five or six hundred, whereas the *Centurion* carried only forty-eight men and a boy. But the boy blew gallantly on a trumpet to cheer the forty-eight and warn them of new attacks, and presently, dolefully regarding their dead and miserably holding their wounds, the galleys cut loose and rowed away. . . . But the Privy Council was in mortal dread of a Spanish invasion, and the Lord Mayor slept poorly, being troubled by thoughts of cutpurses, and rowdy apprentices, and butchers who would not keep Lent properly.

This was the London to which Ben Jonson came home from war. A city of velvet cloaks and open drains; of plague and poetry and great news from sea; of stews that paid rent to a Bishop and fanatics who would hail a man to trial on the whisper of agnosticism; of Shakespeare in his early manhood, and of Bacon in his; of Whitgift and Hooker; and of the river with its ivory multitude of swans, and ships that went back to sea with dreams of Manoa beneath a gold horizon.

But even in the high noon of history the little

business of living may be difficult. Indeed, when wealth is a commonplace poverty becomes brutal. With a schoolboy's knowledge of the classics, a brief apprenticeship to bricklaying, and a private soldier's intimacy with war, Ben was a pauper in this London of scholars, empire-builders, and admirals. And life is hard for a pauper who has notions of high destiny. Poverty and ambition are uneasy bedfellows, especially when ambition is unspecific, when it bids a man do something and cannot tell him what. So far Ben found himself directed only by negative signs. He did not want to lay bricks; he did not want to be a soldier; and because he had no money he could not go to Cambridge and acquire there the endless learning which greedily he desired. Pride and the knowledge that his gifts were not commercial kept him from trade. What then could he do? He felt a vague hereditary itch for preaching or teaching tickle his mind. But he was too ragged for a tutor, too lusty for a Puritan. He felt the need for action, a need that gave him no peace. But what kind of action? Not yet did he recognize the imperative 'Create!' in his restlessness. His need was blind as Cupids on the Bankside and gave him no help. He was tall and strong, he could write and read as quick as the Queen's Secretary, so that by hanging round the Middle Aisle at Paul's he might have found service with a gentleman from the country who wanted a scribe, or a debt-ridden gentleman from court who wanted protection. But Ben, who had difficulty enough in treating the world with civility, found nothing to attract him in the prospect of eating broken meats and living a life of finical servility. In all London, it seemed, there was nothing for him to do.

His mother had been glad to see him again, and appeared to think that he had done well in killing the Knodsendrager. His stepfather also behaved agreeably and was willing to let bygones be bygones, assuming that the air of the Lowlands had taught Ben sense. By sense he meant a proper reverence for bricklaying. He really believed in bricks and had a genuine regard for their solidity. With indisputable accuracy he pointed out that London itself was a monument to his trade; as indeed were the cities that Israel built in Egypt; and other cities too, in all probability.

'The land of bondage,' thought Ben, and lived miserably in the twilight of dark streets, looking for he knew not what. At last he gave in – this was his second surrender – remembering, like the Israelites, the fish and the onions and the cucumbers of Egypt, and laid bricks day after day, and watched the full hod come over the wall, and the boys tramping mortar, and the gentlemen go by with pages attending them.

Camden lent him books to read. 'That writer Ovid, and that writer Metamorphosis,' as the clown said. Quintilian and Catullus and Chaucer and Montaigne; Plautus and Seneca; Terence and Homer and the first cantos of the *Faerie Queene*. Camden himself was a rare scholar, interested in everything from

Welsh grammar to the wine-dark sea past Mytilene; and his disciple had a wolfish appetite for letters.

His bricklaying suffered, of course. His stepfather lost his temper, of course. And, of course, Ben went off again to the taverns and alleys of London, as if looking for a friend he had lost in the crowd. Then he met an actor. There were actors everywhere, in satin suits, sworded, page-attended like gentlemen, and very often worried to death by the custom of acting a different play every day. A satin suit did not always mean that its wearer was at home with polysyllables; and God knows the playwrights stuffed their lines with hard words as thick as a pie with plums. The actor, when Ben saw him, was studying a manuscript full of improbable expressions and making small headway. Ben, with contemptuous assurance, read it for him. Astonishing words behaved easily on his tongue, and every syllable he pronounced loud and clear, mouthing it as if relishing the taste. The actor was grateful; paid for their dinner; swore that Ben was a master of speech; brought presently other manuscripts and more actors. They were busy men, and a good reader was worth something to them.

In some such way as this, it is probable, was Ben's association with the theatre established. Casual at first, it gradually became regular. Then from reading parts he may have been promoted to copying them. And from the copying of old words to the creation of new ones is a short step, since both are done with pen and ink. Stage copies of plays grew blotted and

34

stained and torn; or allusions became old-fashioned
and useless. Like old shoes, plays had to be patched
now and then. And so Ben the copyist became Ben
the botcher and earned another shilling or two by
adding a dozen lines here and a dozen there; stiff
and ungainly perhaps, but strong enough to stand
being blown about a theatre. Such anonymous
parcels were almost certainly Jonson's first contri-
bution to drama.

When he was so engaged *The Jew of Malta* was
being played at the Rose; that savage farce where
even Death becomes a clown and dark figures creep
out at night to poison wells; where nuns and sailors
go pell-mell to oblivion in a spate of irresistible
rhetoric, and Moloch obscures the sky.

At the Curtain a new moon came out to silver all
the fruit-tree tops; an old woman – sitting in the sun
under the dove-house wall – put wormwood on her
dug to wean young Juliet; Mercutio made play with
his fancies of Queen Mab and Italian fencing-masters
till his life leapt out through a sudden lych-gate
in his side; and Juliet and Romeo, rose-crowned,
followed him down to the brief darkness of a lover's
night.

Here, on either side, was achievement. On the
one hand Marlowe 'setting black streamers in the
firmament,' on the other Shakespeare already turning 'the meagre cloddy earth to glittering gold.'
And between them stood a gaunt angry boy with a
growing conviction in his head that he too could
write, make men after his own image and women the

Lord knew how, and put them on a stage to live awhile.

Inevitably he thought first of tragedy. That was the proper stuff for a stage. The turbulent splendour of Marlowe filled his ears. Death stalked everywhere. Ben himself had killed a man, fighting between two armies. In London ten thousand men and women had died of plague that year. Death was a good character. He could clear any stage. And beside the theatrical possibilities of death and tragic circumstance, comedy was only a humble figure allowed on the stage between acts to cut capers and propound riddles. True, Lyly and the new playwright Shakespeare had given comedy poetry to juggle with – fine court-like poetry – but that was only a humorous device like dressing a kitchenmaid in silk. And Ben, angry and very young and often hungry, had no time for the toys of comedy and no thought of buffoonery. Great drama surely meant tragic drama. Inevitably he made up his mind to write tragedy.

CHAPTER IV

GO BY, HIERONIMO!

His apprenticeship lasted half a dozen years, and at the end of that time Ben was counted one of the best tragic writers in England. He succeeded in his first ambition, and as soon as he had achieved success he threw it away and began to hunt another.

Of these 'prentice years we know something by actual record, and something by inference. It is safe to assume that they were full of strenuous work and that a tight belt was a commoner companion than feasting, especially as he got married, probably in 1594, to an honest girl with a temper nearly as hardy as his own. By that year, then, he had some acquaintance with hunger, love, and war; he continued to read widely in the classics; and he was beginning to observe his fellow-men. The materials of literature were in his pocket. But he was still far from recognizing the importance of his own observation. He was concerned with romantic tragical stuff in the high Elizabethan temper that, scorning the realities of earth, preferred to 'pluck bright honour from the pale-faced moon.' He used his imagination rather than his eyes, stories of the past in preference to modern instances. None of these early tragedies has survived, but there are extant certain additions which

Ben made to an old favourite of the stage, and these are alive with tense impatient poetry, with that leaping imagination which, touching the clouds, has also strength to pierce them and become a downward vision, a sun-shaft, to light with unexpected significance small daily things and cottage words. At the end of his six years he was heir-apparent to a romantic kingdom – and then he renounced his title and led a realists' rebellion.

For this role he found some preparation on the stage itself, for he became an actor of heroic and turgid parts and so got a closer knowledge of audiences than can be obtained from behind the scenes. He was not a good actor. He was not even competent, as Shakespeare was. But he had a loud voice and plenty of self-assurance, and these, after all, are the essential qualities of a player, more especially in the provinces. And Ben sometimes acted before rude enough and rural audiences.

Every now and then the players were driven out of London, either by official ban or a graver danger. For when the weather grew warm and the stink of unclean streets hung over the town, plague would come. It was never far away. There would be two or three hundred deaths a week. Then the death rate would mount to four hundred, five hundred a week, and the noise of the bells tolling, the creaking of the death-carts, were in every ear. One summer there were two hundred a day dying, and London was full of fear and a graveyard stench. So the playhouses stood empty and the players travelled from town to

town, walking all day with gravel in their shoes
behind an old horse loaded down with panniers that
held gay costumes for queens and princes. Then, in
the great yard of an inn, they laid broad planks on
barrel-heads and acted *The Pinner of Wakefield* to
gaping rustics who wondered when the clown was
going to appear.

One part that Ben played for the strollers was Old
Hieronimo in *The Spanish Tragedy*, that famous play
that age could not wither nor custom stale the variety
of its crimes. . . .

The inn-yard was full of the lesser people of the
little town, country-folk come in to market, a sailor
or two home from the Indies, a soldier from the Lowlands; and in the galleries that jutted from the second
story of the inn were the well-to-do merchants and
their wives, a lady or two, and some gentlemen who
took their pleasure rather in coverts than in courts.
Then, stalking down the unsteady stage that creaks
beneath them, come Revenge and the Ghost of
Andrea, the one in sheeted white, the other pale
and ominous and bloody about the hands; and these
declaim their swollen lines –

'Ere Sol had slept three nights in Thetis' lap,
And slak'd his smoking chariot in her flood' –

and talk familiarly of Hell, where in some parts
'lovers live, and bloody martialists,' and in others

'usurers are chok'd with melting gold,
And wantons are embrac'd with ugly snakes.'

39

So to the courts of Spain and Portugal, and three men tramping loudly across the barrel-heads to represent a victorious army, and the lovely Belimperia coyly letting fall her glove, that Horatio leaps to retrieve:

'HORATIO: Madame, your glove.
BELIMPERIA: Thanks, good Horatio; take it for thy pains.'

But the glove does no good to the poor brave lover, for very soon we see him overpowered by the villain-ous Lorenzo and the jealous Balthazar, a noose put round his neck, the rope thrown over a branch in his father's arbour – and there he hangs with all the audience to see if he twitches.

Now, carrying a taper whose flame can scarcely be seen in the sunlight, Hieronimo enters in his night-shirt and demands in Ben Jonson's voice:

'What outcries pluck me from my naked bed,
And chill my throbbing heart with trembling fear,
Which never danger yet could daunt before?

Alas, it is Horatio, my sweet son!
O no, but he that whilom was my son –
    Who hath slain my son,
What savage monster not of human kind?'

With murder once let in among the cast, no one is safe. Servants are killed – a dramatic *entremets*, as it were – and Hieronimo, brooding on revenge, shows signs of madness. He is restless, 'wearing the flints with these my wither'd feet.' A suppliant enters. He too had had an only son, and his son has been murdered. The world seems full of men weeping for their murdered sons. Old Isabel, Horatio's mother, lifts her wild hands to heaven:

> 'Ay, there sits my Horatio,
> Back'd with a troop of fiery cherubins,
> Dancing about his newly healèd wounds,
> Singing sweet hymns and chanting heav'nly notes.'

And, while the king sits with all his court about him, Hieronimo creeps on the outskirts, a halter in one hand and a dagger in the other, crying aloud for justice, justice, till the cold villain Lorenzo hustles him off the stage.

At last, by means of a play within the play, justice is done; Lorenzo and Balthazar are stabbed to death. For no good reason save sorrow Belimperia kills herself, and lest he should talk too much of this and that, Hieronimo bites out his tongue. The king, however, a bright though simple man, sees with the simple shrewdness of his kind that he still can write, and anxious to know the reason for so much turbulent behaviour offers him a quill. Hieronimo begs a knife to sharpen the pen, and receiving one from an unsuspecting bystander promptly stabs a duke, the innocent courtier, and then thrusts the red blade into his own fierce heart.

This, one might think, was the end of the play, for the cast by this time is reduced to a mere handful. But no. For there is a life after death compared with which life on earth is a curtain raiser only, and everyone is eager to know how the villains will fare beyond the grave. And so to their immense satisfaction Revenge comes forward, jutty-browed, with the assurance that

'This hand shall hale them down to deepest hell,
Where none but Furies, bugs and tortures dwell!'

Death indeed has put an end to them on earth, but across the slimy strand of Acheron they are about to begin an endless tragedy – a fruitful thought for the audience to take home to their suppers.

But there is more entertainment in the thought of Ben Jonson playing a part in this noisy play of blood that will not be staunched. Ben, whose learning and wit were to bring him the lordship of the Old Devil; who was to be English pope of the Comic Muse; the friend of Raleigh, Donne, Bacon, the Countess of Bedford, and the most learned king in Christendom; Ben, the scholar among dramatists, now in a patched and borrowed cloak opens his formidable mouth and roars his grief to bakers' wives:

'O eyes! no eyes, but fountains fraught with tears;
O life! no life, but lively form of death;
O world! no world, but mass of public wrongs,
Confus'd and fill'd with murder and misdeeds . . .'

42

And then when the plague grew less, back to London, and after this experience in the provinces a part to play in the shabby theatre of Paris Garden, which was more often a bear-pit than a theatre. There Ben acted the part of Zulziman in a play of which we know nothing except that it is now lost, and probably sank beneath its weight of corpses. And there too he continued to patch old plays or write tragedies of his own.

He was driven to work harder than ever by the new and strenuous argument he had added to his household. She had her points, this nameless girl. She was honest, and her spirit did not break under hardship. In spite of a hand-to-mouth existence for many years; in spite of her husband's erratic temper and the violence that constantly invaded his life; in spite of the death in infancy of their first child, she did not fall to weeping and seek comfort abroad from other men, but stood on her own feet, and when Ben's tongue grew unruly hers unleashed a pair of words for each one of his and taught him at least a measure of respect for the mother of his children. She may have dwelt only in the suburbs of his pleasure, but twenty years later, when he sat at Drummond's table with the wine between them – but rather to Ben's side of the board – and the gentle Scots poet listened hour after hour to the robust Englishman, then Ben spoke of her with that rough enjoyment and backward-looking affection that we keep for memories pleasanter than the facts they mirror.

'A shrew,' he said, and chuckled to think how often

43

she had bandied words with him. 'But honest!' he added, and smacked his great fist on the table so that Drummond started nervously and set back a glass that had come nearer to leaping from the edge. . . .

Jonson's employment at Paris Garden brought him into contact with Henslowe, who controlled that theatre and owned another and more important one called The Rose.

Some years earlier a gentleman named Woodward had lived in London. No one has any interest in Mr. Woodward except for this, that he had a servant whose name was Philip Henslowe, a cunning, greedy, ambitious man with one eye on his mistress and the better on his master's purse. Mr. Woodward died. His widow mourned him, sincerely it may be, but not long. For one morning the sun, rising briskly out of the North Sea, dallied a moment to glance through a chamber window and saw, as he had anticipated, Philip in his master's bed. With the fortune thus acquired Henslowe leased some land on the Bankside called The Little Rose. Once it had been a flower-garden. Now there were two houses on it, one of which Henslowe let to a grocer, the other to a bawd. On what land was left he built a theatre. He was an illiterate man, but illiteracy has never made people diffident about managing theatres, and Henslowe prospered rapidly. In 1592 Edward Alleyn married his stepdaughter Joan, and after that Henslowe's position became even stronger than money had made it, Alleyn being the most accomplished actor in London. His theatre flourished, and since he was ravenous as a shark and clever as a Jew the actors in his company had every opportunity to suffer for their art.

His dramatists, improvident poets, lived in a state of semi-bondage with a mortgage on their unwritten plays. Henslowe would advance ten shillings; the playwright would promise another act; sometimes he defaulted; but Henslowe had the first act safe in his own possession, and there were authors in plenty who could finish off anybody's play, no matter on what subject, for another twenty shillings or so. Whoever suffered, it was not Henslowe.

Till the end of the century Jonson did a good deal of literary hacking, some of it in collaboration with other dramatists-by-the-hour such as Chettle and Porter and Dekker, but he maintained his self-respect by vigorously prosecuting his classical studies. There were difficulties in his scholastic path that would have hindered most men – a sociable disposition, a young family, and poverty – but he contrived to overcome them. Even wine, on the rare occasions when he could afford to drink well, never quite banished the idea of books from his head, and though his gait grew unsteady his brain might still be considering theories of poetry. Household noises must, with less pleasure, have interrupted his reading, for his son Benjamin – 'Ben Jonson his best piece of poetry' – was born in 1596, following a girl who had lived for six months only, and preceding a brother who was to live without distinction and die inconse-

quently in early middle life. Till 1598 it is probable
that most of the money needed to keep these children
in wrappers and shortening clothes, the household
in food and firing, his wife in a new dress or two,
and to buy Ben himself an occasional pint of sherry
and a new book, came from Henslowe in small
instalments and grudging advances on work to be
done next week. In July, 1597, for example, Henslowe's
diary shows that he credited Ben with three shillings
and ninepence, and advanced him four pounds.
But as Ben's reputation grew his dependence on the
niggardly master of the Rose diminished, and he
began taking his wares to other markets. By 1597
he was known to be an excellent dramatic craftsman
– not as yet a great dramatist, but a skilful playwright
who could be depended on to turn out what was
wanted – and in the summer of that year a dangerous
opportunity came his way when Thomas Nashe
took fright at a comedy of his own invention, and
left it unfinished.

Nashe was a poet of some merit and a prolific
journalist. His pamphlets on current abuses tumbled
out one after another, full of a bawdy flavour and
Old Testament language; he wrote a novel or two
and helped to defend the Bishops against the attacks
of Martin Marprelate. Not a timid man, one would
think. But when he considered the first act of *The
Isle of Dogs*, the comedy he was writing for a company
of actors who, under the patronage of the Earl of
Pembroke, had leased the Swan theatre on the Bankside, his courage fled and he followed it as far as

Yarmouth, thinking that even the quarrelsome squires of Norfolk would be safer company than London after London had seen his play. The dynamic fragment, which in his hurry he had left behind, was far too good to waste, and Ben was called in to complete it. He finished it according to the original recipe, which was spiced with equal parts of lewdness, sedition and slander. And the play was produced.

With Assyrian promptitude the displeasure of the Privy Council descended on Pembroke's Men. The Queen herself was offended, and the Council ordered that no more plays were to be presented in London that summer, and condemned every playhouse to be demolished. But as the Privy Council invariably forbade the presentation of further plays, and habitually ordered the demolition of all theatres when its members were offended by wanton criticism from the stage, this injunction was tacitly ignored. Nor was the Council's order for the arrest of authors and actors of *The Isle of Dogs* fully carried out. Nashe hid himself successfully in Yarmouth, and most of the company escaped from London and reassembled a few weeks later to play in Bristol. But two actors and one author were caught and on July 28th imprisoned in the Marshalsea. These were Robert Shaw, Gabriel Spenser, and Ben Jonson; and they remained in gaol till the early part of October. Ben faced the more serious charge of authorship alone, for Nashe, though his lodgings were raided and his papers searched for other dangerous matter, was left in peace to write the praise of Yarmouth herring.

All through the hot months of summer, in the close and fetid air of the Marshalsea, the unfortunate three were left to regret their folly and to reproach each other with their several shares in it. In spite of its spirited effort in the provinces the company of Pembroke's Men was ruined, and news came in that one after another of the players, returning humbly to town, had engaged to play at the Rose in the hard service of Henslowe. One of them, Richard Jones, secured a contract for his friend Shaw, to become effective when the latter was released. Spenser had not even this meagre consolation, and constantly the thought recurred that Jonson was really to blame, by reason of his unruly pen, for their present discomfort and the bankruptcy of a promising company. Gabriel was not a sweet-tempered man. The previous year, a little before Christmas, he had gone to a barber's shop belonging to Richard Easte of St. Leonard's in Shoreditch, and found waiting to be shaved or shorn a man called James Feake. Gabriel sat down, and while waiting his turn passed the time of day with Feake. Their talk became an argument that presently failed – as an argument – for lack of syllogisms, but stiffened its expiring logic with insults. Spenser's tongue was sharper than Feake's, who found his supply of abuse run short even as his logic had. But a copper candlestick stood near him, a large one worth sixpence, and this he picked up very violently to throw at Gabriel. The actor was nimble, however. His sword in its scabbard lay on a table; he had laid it there, perhaps with a 'God send me no need of thee,'

48

when he entered the shop. Now he snatched it up, scabbard and all, and thrust strongly, piercing Feake through the right eye. Feake 'lived in languor' for three days, and died. Spenser escaped any serious consequences, perhaps by proving that he had acted in self-defence, more probably by simply pleading his clergy.

Now Ben's own temper was quick enough and he could not easily suffer reproaches, so that to Spenser's angry steel he must often, during that hot summer, have offered a ready flint, and the sparks of altercation would fall on the tinder of unlimited opportunity. The Elizabethans were as proud of their ability to quarrel as they were of new clothes. They 'fell out like giants and fell in like children.' And words came to their tongues, images to their brains, hard and keen and lively, full of coarse vigour, hot as ore in the smelter's fire and rich as miner's dirt that yields gold at sight. Their words were like pebbles washed ashore, all new and shining from a new-found shining sea, and they used them with a glorious contempt for economy, knowing the next tide would send thundering up the beach fresh lexicons, thesauruses flashing with undreamt-of mica, glittering with quartz and *argot* still bright with spray. . . .

There must have been fine quarrels in the Marshalsea that summer, and when at last the order came for their release it is unlikely that Gabriel dallied, that Ben felt any regret when he omitted to say good-bye.

CHAPTER V

FIN DE SIÈCLE

THERE is no reason why the last ten years of a hundred should be different in nature from the middle ten, but frequently they are. Queen Elizabeth did not choose to grow old in 1550, nor did Marston, Hall, Chapman, and Donne elect to grow up. They waited for the winter of their century, when leaves were falling to cover old bones, and frost made the air like crystal for young eyes to see through.

Leaves were falling in plenty, some of them before their time. Greene and Marlowe and Peele died. Sidney was dead, Grenville played his part to the end, Drake fell at Nombre Dios. Walsingham and Burleigh died, and Hooker. Hieronimo's cloak was growing threadbare, and the *Essays* of Francis Bacon came bright and new from the press – an epitaph with small sympathy for the ways of the dying century.

The wilder citizens of Bohemia were going, so that in the next century Bohemia could own a king. It must be remembered that Bohemian London in the last years of the sixteenth century was as different from Murger's Bohemia – which some still think an artist means when, wine-laden, he mutters to his cabman – as a caliph is from his eunuch. Jonson and Marlowe and Greene and Gabriel Spenser carried swords, which some used better than others. Murger's young men died of a consumption – and so did Greene's purse. But gout, pox, sack, stone, and steel were all livelier foes of the Elizabethans themselves. Within a year of each other Marlowe and Greene died, the one in a brawl about a tavern reckoning, the other in distressing squalor. And they were masters of the trade in which Ben was making his name.

Robert Greene, who had written sweetly of pastoral England, died penniless in a slum, feverishly repenting his grosser sins. He had sickened after a surfeit of Rhine wine and pickled herring. A slow poisoning set in which swelled his body from the belly upwards, threatening to strangle him when the distension reached his throat. Deserted by his friends; watched only by his drab (the sister of a thief called Cutting Ball) and their bastard son Fortunatus; his clothes in pawn and his puffy body in a borrowed shirt; sweating with fear when he thought of his drunken blasphemy, and turning pitifully to beg for a penny pot of malmsey – so a good poet miserably died, and it was left to the cobbler's wife with whom he lodged to bring bays to his dead body.

And Marlowe died in Deptford, struck through the eye by Ingram Friser's dagger, after a quarrel which grew senselessly out of the fumes of a day's drinking. Marlowe the atheist, it was whispered, killed in the heat of drunken anger . . . The Puritans in their prison cells praised their God for this manifestation of his power; poets who knew what Marlowe had done for their craft mourned bitterly the dead poet; and Philip Henslowe grew rich as every day crowds came over the river to his theatre, to see plays that had been written by so shameless and sinful a man. Strange stories were repeated. It was said that the Devil himself had interrupted a performance of *Dr. Faustus*, appearing on the stage to which he had been profanely summoned and causing the utmost consternation among both actors and audience. . . .

But London was growing self-conscious. The spacious vision that had occupied itself with countries so far away that their geography was a matter for individual fancy, now became aware of nearer things, and sacrificing spaciousness to intensity gradually discerned in its fellow-men a capacity to astonish equal to that of any fabled potentate or princess of myth. Its fellow-men, this new vision saw, were often fantastic and frequently ridiculous. The vision was delighted. Its relish for life was not going to be impaired by a change of diet, but rather to thrive as its meat grew more solid. But naturally it could not deal with this new human pabulum as it had with the courts of Portingal and the precincts of the Sophy. Satire must be the new medium, satire as vigorous as the old romance had been, and in the abundance of topical *humours* the satirists found good bones to pick.

A *humour* was then as fashionable as a complex is to-day, and, as the latter disability is popularly ascribed, nearly the same kind of thing – though more ostentatious. The origin of the word may be found

in medieval physiology, which declared the constituent materials of the human body to be the four
elements, fire, air, earth, and water, with which the
four major humours corresponded, and according
to the proportion in which they combined determined
the temperament of the individual. Strictly speaking,
then, the term had a limited application, and when
such purists as Jonson used it, they remembered that.
But ordinary people have never restricted their
language to the narrow cells grammarians prescribe
for it – freedom of speech, for the majority, condones
lèse pédantisme as well as *lèse majesté* – so *humour* was
popularly used to signify a fad, a freak of fancy, a
personal whim, and this misuse was, it may be,
palliated by the energy with which the citizens of
England then flaunted their crotchets, so that a
caprice was often really the burgee of an individual,
if not of individuality. In the procreant atmosphere
of that age folly ran wild and stupidity decked its
blunt horns with flowers.

It is a livelier and more inspiring occupation to
drive mavericks than to herd a placid field of dairy
cows, and so in response to the indiscipline of the times,
self-appointed censors appeared, as arrogant and wild
as their fellow-countrymen whom they proposed to
brand or drill, but differing from them by virtue of
their critical attitude. Ben Jonson was not the first of
these, though he became the most notable. He was
preceded by several clever and acrimonious young
men, one of them Joseph Hall, who at twenty-four
calmly asserted,

53

'I first adventure; follow me who list,
And be the *second* English satirist,'

and later became a bishop. All joyfully discovered
what a fine wounding weapon satire could be, and
some of them, not content with castigating the obvious
abuses of the time, turned to quarrelling among themselves, and tossed back and fore such epithets as
'Athens' ape' and 'filthy chimney-sweep of sin.'

Most of this was chamber satire, for a select
audience, but when Ben took up the theme he orches-
trated it fully, set his composition on the public
stage, gave it the bold inclusive title of *Every Man in
his Humour,* and made of it a masterly comedy in a
new kind.

Now on the day before this play was presented
Ben was known as an excellent craftsman in tragedy,
and that a tragic writer should become a comedian
overnight is at first sight surprising. But there were
two sound reasons for the metamorphosis. One was
the changing temper of the times, and the other was
the fact that Ben had a serious mind which discovered
in the course of time that Elizabethan tragedy, with
obvious exceptions, was not serious. It was romantic,
and to a serious, somewhat Puritanical intelligence
romance is either a cowardly or a childish escape from
reality – though to the romantic mind it is adventure
in its own medium. When Ben's serious mind grew
up – which it did in 1598, when his body was twenty-
six years old – he found it was difficult to be sufficiently
serious about life in a tragic play where death is the

normal solution. Because death, though a solution, is not necessarily an explanation. It may be wiping the figures off a slate to save working out the answer. Death is not a satisfactory criticism of Romeo's life. It is a dramatic escape from the trivial complications of his life. But comedy of the new kind was to be tight-bound to living. It was to have no escape. It had to criticise, it had to supply an answer, because the canons of its art forbade the convenient exit to a graveyard, and the convenient character who played maid-of-all-work with a scythe.

Comedy, as a criticism of life, is more serious than the tragedy which leads by way of reckless adventure to the omnibus of death. Mercutio, for instance, is a serious figure while he is alive, a commentator whose opinions are valuable. But death destroys his significance. Mercutio dead is only the salt in unavailing tears, stuff for girls. And Falstaff living is a glorious tun of a man who holds the balance down against a world of Hotspurs and mad Welshmen and two-faced princes and an illusion called incomprehensibly *honour;* but Falstaff dead floats into an unplaced heaven of his own under the halo poor Quickly gave him, while we weep for our loss and forget his wisdom in the measure of our sorrow. Death is nothing but a hindrance to knowledge. And so Ben, seeking knowledge and truculently bent on spreading knowledge, banished death from his *dramatis personae* and determined to write seriously about life in the only possible medium. Which was satiric comedy.

In the old morality plays Everyman had been face to face with death, and in such cold company whims and vagaries freeze and Everyman betrays the help-lessness of all men. But confronted with life, as Every Man is now shown, men behave with a whimsical variety and reveal their admirable repertory of cunning and fatuity, wisdom and humility, hypocrisy and valour and arrogance and love, filling the street with a many-tongued clamour that is the true stuff of comedy. Now Ben's own humour, when he first took humours for his subject, was serious indeed – he was convinced, that is, of the rightness of his method and the importance of his art – but so far genial. He treated the comic diversity of the world with high spirits and laughter free from that neighing scornful note that later (but not for long) was to dominate it. He chose his subjects to represent Youth and Age, Wit and Folly, and from the latent hostility between these groups the action of the play is born.

It was a magnificent achievement. Comedy, the Cinderella of the stage, was brought out of her kitchen and given language and attire of her own; with nothing behind it but tentative experiment, realism emerged whole and triumphant; superb advantage was taken of the new temper of criticism; stupidity and folly were castigated with dramatic skill and no anger; some excellent characters were added to the stage – the drooping pride of Bobadill, the irascible and hearty Clement, Cob the water-carrier – and, better than all his creations, the character of Ben himself, whose vital individuality was apparent in every scene.

One of the sequels to success, however, was another sight of prison. . . .

By 1598 the long friendship between Shakespeare and Ben had begun. It was never a close comradeship, but it survived a quarrel or two, and much vigorous jesting, and lasted for . more than eighteen years. Early in its course Shakespeare amiably agreed to stand godfather to Ben's second son, and enlivened the ceremony with a joke (good enough for a domestic occasion) at the expense of his classically-minded host. After the christening he stood (it is said) apart from the other guests, as if thinking deeply, and when Jonson, bringing what would cheer him, asked if he were melancholy, Shakespeare answered, 'No, faith, Ben, not I. But I have been considering a great while what should be the fittest gift for me to bestow upon my godchild, and I have resolved at last.' 'Prithee, what?' said Ben. 'I' faith, Ben, I'll e'en give him a dozen good lattin* spoons, and thou shalt translate them.'

Another tradition has it that Shakespeare took some part in bringing *Every Man* to the stage, and this is not improbable, for it was played at the Curtain Theatre by the Chamberlain's Men and not by the Admiral's Men with . whom Jonson had previously been associated at Henslowe's theatre. Now the Chamberlain's Men were a very distinguished company. Richard Burbage, Hemmings and Condell,

* Brass

57

Augustus Philips, Kemp, and Shakespeare were all
members of it: Burbage, who later acted Hamlet
and Lear, and won the reputation of living rather
than presenting a part, now played Brainworm, the
contriving servant; Hemmings, whose work with
Condell on the Shakespeare folio has given them a
kind of Siamese immortality, appeared as the merry
Justice Clement; Kemp, the clown who played
Dogberry and was a famous dancer of jigs, took Cob
the water-carrier's part; and Shakespeare was the
elder Knowell, in whose likeness he gave good advice
to a bumpkin squire:

> 'Let not your carriage and behaviour taste
> Of affectation, lest while you pretend
> To make a blaze of gentrie to the world,
> A little puff of scorn extinguish it' –

advice that somewhat suggests Polonius' admonition
to Laertes, though that is an aristocrat's wordly
wisdom, while this is bourgeois prudence.

This excellent play, then, was excellently acted, and
enjoyed a popular as well as a critical success. Money
flowed into the Curtain Theatre by Finsbury Fields;
and across the river, at Henslowe's Rose, there was
jealousy, ill-temper at the thought of profit unfairly
diverted from the Bankside, and many hard words
about Ben who had so coldly left his old associates for
a rival company. Only a month earlier he had been
working for the Admiral's Men, and Henslowe had
half a tragedy that Ben had agreed to write for him,
which now, likely enough, he would never bother to

finish. Greedy Henslowe was very angry indeed, and found a willing splenetic ally in Gabriel Spenser, who on his release from prison had joined the Admiral's company. To his jealous nature the thought of Ben's success was exquisitely exasperating – Ben, with whom he had shared bread, confinement, lice, and the hot squalor of the Marshalsea, was now become famous, and like other successful men had left his old friends for better company! They took pleasure in recalling his early poverty and the humble trade to which he had been apprenticed. 'A bricklayer!' said Henslowe, trying to efface the image of the successful author with a picture more pleasing to his malice. With the anger of a crafty man who has been out-generalled, of an avaricious man robbed of rich opportunity, of a wealthy illiterate mastered by his lettered servant – with the snarling anger of his kind, Henslowe maligned his lost playwright while Spenser rehearsed his own injuries, dwelt on the obvious injustice of Ben's triumph, exaggerated his desertion of the Admiral's Men, and found matter for a quarrel.

Henslowe sat in his empty theatre, snarling still, but Spenser took a boat across the river to the Old Swan stairs. He walked up St. Martin's Lane into Eastcheap, where perhaps he had a drink at The Boar's Head before turning into Gracechurch Street. Then he walked northwards to Bishopsgate Street and took another drink, it may be, at The Bull beside Gresham College, and went on past Fisher's Folly and the Artillery Yard to Hog Lane, where he turned left and presently found himself at the Curtain. Without waiting for his head to cool he sent a message in to Jonson, and when Ben came out he found the quarrel picked, for Gabriel promptly called him a traitor and a robber of honest men's pockets, and as Ben could neither stomach an insult nor leave a reproach unanswered, they very soon agreed to settle their difference in Shoreditch Fields.

Spenser had this advantage, that his sword, if it was the one which killed James Feake, was a better weapon than Ben's – it had cost five shillings, while Ben had paid only three for his – and certainly it was ten inches longer. First blood went to Spenser, who got home on his adversary's sword-arm. But Jonson came in upon the answer, controlled his point as Bobadill instructed, and made 'a full career at the body; the best practised gallants of the time name it the passado; a most desperate thrust, believe it.' – Mercutio's 'immortal passado,' and Gabriel's mortal one. It was a desperate thrust indeed, for it went six inches deep into the actor's side and when the poor provant rapier came reluctantly out from where it had so fiercely entered, Gabriel's life followed it, and jealous now only of freedom left his body to be dealt with by the worms and the Queen's justice.

This time Jonson was carried to Newgate, and while he waited trial he was visited by a priest, and persuaded to consider the state of his soul. He was in a mood for such consideration. His life had been a violent obscure battle towards a goal equally obscure, and then the clouds had parted, he had seen his destination clearly, and gripping the bright forelock of Time he had ridden to its very portals – and when the doors opened a dead man fell out. The quarrel had been forced upon him, but Ben's heart was hard only in the heat of conflict, and blood (however shed) has a pitiful hue and leaves a stain that looks like guilt. He had been proud, exalted in spirit, and he had killed a man who had once been something of a friend. He was, moreover, in prison when he should have been enjoying the plaudits and the company, the sack and sugar, of generous admirers. Heaven had offered him a cup brimful, and dashed it from his hands almost before his lips were wet. 'Look to your soul,' said the priest, and Ben in his wretchedness obeyed.

He scrutinized his immortal part as seriously as he had previously considered the state of poetry, and found it, like popular verse, 'half-starved for want of her peculiar food.' Having formed this uncompromising estimate of his spiritual state he characteristically reached an energetic decision to amend it, and turned Catholic. It was a dangerous thing to do, for in 1598 Catholics were regarded with as much suspicion as Bolsheviks in 1924. But the Jonsons were a stubborn people who made up their minds regardless of consequences. Ben's father had refused to acknowledge Rome when acknowledgment would have assured his safety, and Ben turned Papist when such a step would place his life, already on the threshold of jeopardy, by its fireside. The danger of Catholicism, however, may have been an argument in its favour, for bodily peril not infrequently provokes a sensation of spiritual security.

One cannot say whether sudden faith or the power of reason was responsible for Ben's conversion from what was perhaps no more than a nominal Protestantism; but as the time for dialectic was short, and as he believed in visions, it is probable that he became Christian and Catholic after special revelation. He saw, one supposes, the furnace in Christ's bosom:

> 'The fuel Justice layeth on,
>   And Mercy blows the coals,
> The metal in this furnace wrought
>   Are men's defilèd souls.'

Man's natural concern with the gods was then heightened by topical interest, for Protestants remembered the fires of Smithfield as keenly as Hindus to-day recall the punitive slaughter at Jallianwallabagh. And if Protestants kept their faith hot with Foxe's *Book of Martyrs*, Catholics had the example of a hundred and eighty recusants executed in the last thirty years of the century to sustain their creed. Religion had not yet become dull and apathetic, nor the pulpit accustomed to a yawn. And though it may seem curious that a man like Ben, so sceptical and hard-headed, so scornful of pretence, should suddenly believe

> 'Whole may His body be in smallest bread,
>   Whole in the whole, yea, whole in every crumb,'

there is no doubt that he did so believe, and was prepared to face considerable danger for his faith.

The Government learnt of his new-found Romanism and instantly set spies to watch him, to talk to him, to make him betray his complicity in some Catholic plot – for Rome was the suspect Moscow of those days, and every honest Protestant knew that every Catholic carried a plot about with him as faithfully as a donkey carries its tail. But Jonson's faith had not made him loquacious, and to all the cunning questions put to him he answered only 'Aye' and 'No.' Day after day Cecil's *agents provocateurs*, pretending to be simple prisoners too, plied him with clever words and leading questions meant to trip his heels and put a noose about his neck. And day after day Ben listened grimly, and answered 'Aye,' or 'No.' They got no change out of him.

There was a gaol delivery in October, and Jonson was arraigned in the Justice Hall of the Old Bailey. He was charged with attacking Gabriel Spenser when in God's peace and the Queen's, and 'with a certain sword of iron and steel called a Rapiour, wilfully beating, striking, and slaying Gabriel against the peace of their Lady the Queen.' He confessed the indictment and asked for the Book, to prove his right to benefit of clergy. (This was an amiable privilege according to which all who could read might claim, in certain offences, exemption of sentence on a first conviction.) The Book was given him, a black-letter Vulgate, and turning to the fifty-first Psalm Ben read his neck-verse in the powerful voice that had done duty for Zulziman and old Hieronimo: '*Miserere mei Deus, secundum magnam misericordiam tuam: et secun-*

dum multitudinem miserationum tuarum, dele iniquitatem meam.'

The empanelled jury listened respectfully to Hieronimo's voice and the scholarly accent. With curiosity touched with awe, perhaps with fear, or dislike, or downright admiration, they stared at the lean strongly-built man who killed a player as expertly as he wrote a play. They looked at his eyes, dark, nobly gleaming, full of energy and high purpose and strenuous poetry, but a little sinister because one was a thought larger than its fellow. They looked at his nose, a bold forceful nose with a jutting bridge and scornful nostrils. They looked at his dark curling hair and small thin beard, at his dark lean cheeks, at his plain shabby clothes and powerful hands. They looked at his mouth with its full generous lips that parted bravely for the Latin words that saved his neck, and one of the jury who had seen the new comedy at the Curtain thought of that passionate defence of poetry which Ben had thrust, with impetuous disregard for congruity, in the midst of his exposition of London humours:

'But view her in her glorious ornaments,
    Attired in the majesty of art,
    Set high in spirit with the precious taste
    Of sweet philosophy, and which is most,
    Crowned with the high traditions of a soul
    That hates to have her dignity profaned
    With any relish of an earthly thought;
    Oh then how proud a presence doth she bear!

Then is she like herself, fit to be seen
Of none but grave and consecrated eyes.'

But the poet had killed a man against the peace of
their Lady the Queen, and though according to statute
and the clerical privilege he might be restored to
freedom, his goods were forfeit and the displeasure of
the court made manifest in a Tyburn T burnt on the
brawn of his thumb. Neither worried him much,
however, for his chattels were few, and what does a
scar more or less matter to a man? He was free to
walk abroad again, free to write as he cared or could
afford, and his soul had found shelter under the great
walls of Rome.

Henslowe perhaps suffered as much as anyone –
except Gabriel – for his rage found no spilth in so
meagre a punishment as branding and forfeiture of
household goods, and all he could do to relieve the
pressure of his bile was to tap it now and then with
the word 'bricklayer.' The idea of Ben building walls
could still comfort him a little. It eased his anger to
refer to the poet of the humours as a labourer with
his hands. Even in letters he did it. There is one
extant, ill-spelt and ill-written, that reads: 'Since you
weare with me I have lost one of my company, which
hurteth me greatley, that is Gabrell, for he is slayen in
Hogesden fylldes by the hands of bergemen Jonson,
bricklayer.'

So Avarice wrote its verse on Envy's stone.

CHAPTER VI

PURITAN WITH A DIFFERENCE

BEFORE the felon's T on his thumb had healed, Jonson was at work refurbishing a year-old play called *The Case is Altered;* and because he was newly come into a state of grace, and because the air of freedom smelt sweet, and because the success of *Every Man* had made him bold, he boldly, briskly, and conscientiously set about chastising the enemies of true poetry. A poor man called Munday, a City poet employed in writing pageants and such, seemed to Ben to be cheapening the holy vehicle of verse by using it for shoddy wares, and as a convenient means of rebuke Ben added a caricature of Munday to the revision of his play.

There was nothing really personal in the attack, however. It was Munday's poetry, not Munday himself, that attracted punitive laughter, and all Ben's subsequent attacks on bad poets and stupid people were in a like manner to be occasioned by his hatred of their stupidity and their literary heresies, rather than by hatred of themselves. And if the poets and the fools failed to recognise this fine distinction, or would not be divorced from their frailties, that was their misfortune and not Ben's fault.

He came out of prison a Bohemian with a conscience; a mastiff conscience ever growling over some bone of artistic propriety; a conscience like the tail of an Irishman's coat, tender, flaunting, importunate to be trodden on; a conscience, however, different from a Puritan conscience in that its concern was with art rather than morals, that it busied itself with behaviour more ostensibly than with the soul, and that Puritans irritated it quite as often as poets. For in spite of his conscience he lived, when he could afford it, in fine Falstaffian freedom. His body had no high destiny, it was mortal stuff to be enjoyed while it lasted, and so Ben drank where the wine was good, and where the women were kind stopped long enough to encourage them in benevolence. But he did not waste his time making love songs and drinking songs. His body was a man, but his brain was a poet's, 'than which reverend name,' he says, 'nothing can more adorn humanity.' Arrogance grew at the thought. He walked fiercely. The sun behind him threw a huge and menacing shadow on the pavement, for his conception of a poet's duties was different from that which would have sweet singers dwell ever apart to contemplate the recondite significance of daffodils, grains of sand, and creaking light. Ben's ideal poet declares –

> 'But with an armed and resolved hand,
> I'll strip the ragged follies of the time
> Naked as at their birth;'

and before long courtier's satin, citizen's broadcloth, ladies' kirtles, and poets' paper were torn, with all the ruthlessness of that promise, between Jonson's brick-roughened hands. But not without retaliation. The way of the reformer is hard, and Ben found little peace in the next few years.

Before he could do much with his missionary task, however, he had to find a winter's fuel for his household, and to do this he accepted Henslowe's offer of employment. That astute man had swallowed his anger at Gabriel's loss – reflecting that though a dead dramatist or a dead horse may retain some value, a dead actor is worth nobody's time – and he persuaded Ben to collaborate with Dekker and others in a few good robust tragedies of the kind that went well at the Rose. So Ben kept the domestic pot boiling with expedient bloodshed and a popular pen while he worked with growing pride on another serious play. This was to be a continuation of the 'humours' theme. But where *Every Man in his Humour* had been a brave experiment, *Every Man out of his Humour* was audacious invention. The tone of the former had been genial. In the latter folly was harshly rebuked, vice condemned with indignation. The first play was a comedy, the second a moralistic revue.

There was no action in this new work, no scheme of fate or revenge like a keen hound unharbouring the stag of iniquity; no armies tramping across the stage to topple thrones in their stride; no cunning servant to tie old wits in a knot and cut it at last in the scissors of device. There was no plot or mystery, but scene followed scene with the set purpose of whipping ignorance and stripping the pretensions of folly. . . .

Ben worked at his play with a kind of cold and zealous fury. He knew exactly what he wanted to do, and his ambition was anatomical rather than dramatic. He had discovered the astonishing variety of human character, and with the eagerness of a medical student dissecting for the first time he wanted to expose and explain all that he had found. He took a dozen assorted types – a vainglorious knight, a scurrilous jester, a greedy farmer, a courtly fop, a doting citizen – and displayed their essential nerves by contriving situations that would induce in them only typical reactions. He arranged his scenes – they were scientific tests as much as scenes – with unfailing invention, and his explication of their significance shone with a sustained light that was short of brilliance by just so much as would let it illumine the matter rather than dazzle a spectator's eye.

He had no shame or modesty, for he put two characters on the stage that were like two halves of himself. One he declared to be 'of an ingenious and free spirit, eager, and constant in reproof, without fear controlling the world's abuses.' The other, wanting that reputation which he thought was his desert, fell into such envies that he could not bear the sight of others' happiness. Ben's taste was doubtful, but his courage indisputable. His face grew dark and pale as he worked night after night and far into the night. Sometimes he sat, hammering lines into rightness, shaping and reshaping, till he fell fainting on his table, knocking down his candle and spilling ink across laborious pages. His food was cheap and

scanty. He had no mercy for himself and none for
the creatures in his play. It grew longer than was
necessary, for by sheer weight of achievement he
meant to compel applause – he hungered to the
bowels for recognition – and desire to punish the fools
he had drawn was strong in him. He knew that
'Art hath an enemy called ignorance.' He failed
to consider that a dragon supported by so large a
majority and so many of one's own friends could make
things very uncomfortable for the critical St. George
who feutred his pen against it. . . .

Every Man out of his Humour was presented by the
Chamberlain's Men at the Globe, their new theatre
on the Bankside, north of Maiden Lane. The Globe
was the last word in theatrical architecture. It had
decorated columns – but the roof was thatch – and
outside stood a handsome Hercules with the world
on his shoulder and the motto *Totus Mundus agit
Histrionem.* All the regular members of the Chamberlain's Company except Shakespeare acted in the play,
and the audience contained a large proportion of
young men whose humour was to be more witty than
scholars, more scholarly than wits, and whose social
position lent to their culture a fashionable attire.
Many of these young men belonged to the Inns of
Court, where they lived in the discipline of a university
and cherished intellectual pursuits with the ardour
of a conscious minority. Ben recognised his affinity
with them and relied on their favour as an audience.
They, with youth's generous partiality for work
arrogant in its novelty, gave it whole-heartedly –

with one or two exceptions. The humour plays were to them what psychological novels are to us. But the ordinary people grumbled, and found nothing in satire to recompense them for the absence of drama. The ordinary people wanted to see things happen, not to watch character being dissected, muscle from muscle and nerve. They had no patience with these highbrow experiments, and left the Globe regretting their misspent shillings.

Every Man out of his Humour was a failure as popular entertainment then, and though the Inns of Court men praised it, even in that select part of the audience were one or two whom it violently displeased. Of these the most important was John Marston, a member of the Inner Temple.

Marston was three years younger than Jonson, but he had already written a play or two and made a considerable reputation as a reckless and bloodthirsty satirist. He too had a Puritan conscience, but he was tortured by wild lusts of the flesh. He wanted to be on the side of the sternest angels, and yet he had to smack his lips at lewdness, and he would write such stuff as this description of a witch:

> 'When she finds a corpse
> But newly graved, whose entrails are not turned
> To slimy filth, with greedy havoc then
> She makes fierce spoil, and swells with wicked
>   triumph
> To bury her lean knuckles in his eyes;
> Then doth she gnaw the pale and o'ergrown nails

From his dry hand; but if she finds some life
Yet lurking close, she bites his gelid lips,
And, sticking her black tongue in his dry throat,
She breathes dire murmurs. . . .'

He was a Shropshire man by his father's blood, but his mother was an Italian, and the different strains had not mixed well. He was conscious of the weakness bred by his disparate parentage and his dual nature, and he had been attracted to Ben as much by the latter's strength as by his wit. He had proffered his friendship eagerly, too eagerly, and Ben, recognising Marston's intelligence and not uninfluenced by his social position, had accepted it willingly at first, and then with some impatience. But the merest hint of displeasure had been enough to double the younger man's admiration, and he promptly decorated a play called *Histriomastix* with what was meant to be a flattering portrait of Jonson; a portrait that should notice both his scholarly attainments and his endeavours to reform an ungrateful world. This shadow of Jonson is called Chrisoganus, and on one occasion another character in the play addresses him as follows:

'How, you translating scholar, you can make
A stabbing satire or an epigram,
And think you carry just Rhamnusia's whip
To lash the patient; go, get you clothes!'

The depiction is a friendly one, certainly, but Jonson was annoyed by the public reference to holes in his breeches – how, between a little sherry, a few books to read, and a wife to provide for, could he find money to waste at a tailor's? – and Chrisoganus's imitation of his literary style was very clumsy. A little rebuff, thought Ben, might do some good to the importunate and maladroit young playwright. It would at least teach him not to essay portraiture in a public place if he found his own character glanced at on the stage. So into the mouth of a ridiculous creature called Clove, in *Every Man out of his Humour*, Ben put a number of pedantic and foolish expressions that Marston had proudly used in *Histriomastix* and some of his satires.

Now Marston went to the *première* at the Globe full of proleptic enthusiasm, all ready with appreciative laughter and excess of admiration for his friend's new play. And then Clove came on to the stage, lisping affectedly, to offer up to ridicule a batch of Marston's own fine phrases . . . The satirist's hot southern blood rushed to his face and ebbed again to leave it pale beneath his bright red hair. Tears came into his eyes, and the Italian in him was ready to weep in a passion of mortification at this insult, this bitter requital of his love, at Jonson's betrayal of their friendship. His friends, sitting about him, recognised the caricature as quickly as he, and did not conceal their enjoyment; for some of them also found a private application of Ben's wit, and some of them had suffered from Marston's clever ill-tempered pen . . . He, half-Italian, felt, as he had so often felt before, alone in this company of arrogant self-sufficient Englishmen, and his mother's blood compounded

73

with his sullen Shropshire clay to make that fierce hatred of the world which gave him the reputation of 'a querulous cur whom no horse can pass by without him barking at; yea, in the deep silence of night the very moonshine openeth his clamorous mouth.' His stool fell noisily to the floor as he stood up and ostentatiously left the theatre. And all the time he wanted to be on the side of the angels – or on Ben Jonson's side.

Once more, then, Ben found an angry man waiting for him, with a quarrel ready picked, when the play was over. But Marston was of a different temper to Gabriel Spenser. Marston trembled in the midst of his challenge, and carried a pistol instead of a sword. And Ben looked at him, at his spindly legs and narrow wrists, and laughed contemptuously, and took his pistol from him, and reached for a stick and beat him about the shoulders like a schoolboy, and so left him.

Marston went off to anoint his bruises and, unpopular as he was, he found a kind of sympathy from others who had suffered real or fancied hurts from Ben's castigation of the times. It was a proof of the efficacy of Ben's satire that, no matter how general might be its intention, there were never wanting self-nominated targets to complain that his arrows had found the white in their hearts. All his life he was to hear the complaints of these egotistical uneasy Sebastians who, whatever iniquity was impugned, saw its image in themselves and ran down the street shouting 'It's me he means, it's me!' And it must be admitted that hypersensitive vanity and touchy consciences had some excuse for their voluntary recurrent martyrdoms in Ben's insolent habit of putting himself on the stage. In *Every Man out of his Humour* he had done it, and in *Cynthia's Revels* and *The Poetaster*, his next two important plays, there were also likenesses flattering to the author and trumpets of denunciation to those whom he conceived his enemies and the enemies of his art. The Sebastians, therefore, argued that since one character in each of these plays was a signed portrait, the others had probably some representational intentions.

With their encouragement Marston began to write another play, which he called *Jack Drum's Entertainment*, and which contained a very insulting picture of Jonson; a picture of a bombastic man swollen with conceit of his own worth; a man who wore a perpetual exasperating grin and who, in the arrogance

'And glorious ostentation of his wit,
Thinks God infused all perfection
Into his soul alone, and made the rest
For him to laugh at.'

Now Ben at this time was really concerned with a larger ambition than schooling a fellow playwright. He had his eye on the Court. He professed lofty scorn for the supple flexure of a courtier's knee, but like other ambitious men had also a true Elizabethan reverence for the Throne. The Queen was the source of honour, the fountain of reward; and praise

75

of the Queen was more than a polite convention: it was prudent tribute to visible greatness. And Ben was ambitious in more ways than one. His artistic virtue was impregnable, his courage absolute, his pride burned with a white-hot flame – but he had no Quixotic notions about virtue paying its own dividends. He wanted recognition by scholars, by the young intellectuals of the Inns of Court, and by his Sovereign. Others might pleat his laurels for him, but to be really satisfactory his title to them must be confirmed by royal patent.

To recommend himself to the Queen Jonson had already formed the ingenuous plan of presenting her on the stage. Seventy years later Molière was to bring Louis XIV into his last act to restore sense and honesty to the world of Tartuffe, and in 1599 Jonson conceived an identical device for medicining to sweet sanity the distempered groups in his second Humours play. Official objections, however, were raised to the use of her Majesty by a playwright, even in the cause of art and ethics, and Ben had to find a less striking conclusion for his comedy.

He had felt the rebuff, but he was not the man to mistake a snub for a *coup de grâce,* and now he returned to a royal atmosphere in *Cynthia's Revels,* a play about Diana's court intended for Elizabeth's, and he took some pains to make it clear that he was on the Queen's side in opposition to the popular ill-feeling aroused by the recent arrest of the Earl of Essex.

Essex had been the Queen's Deputy in Dublin,

but driven to desperation by Irish weather and his mistress's neglect, he suddenly left his army to look after itself and posted with a few friends to London. Still in his muddy riding-clothes he had gone headlong to Elizabeth and found her among her maids, half-dressed. Her cheeks were unpainted, and instead of her splendid red-gold wig, a straggle of grey hair scantly concealed her head. Now in some earlier age Actaeon had seen Diana naked, and suffered grievously for his indiscretion. If Diana could visit presumption with severity, why should not Elizabeth? That was the point Ben added to his play to prick the Queen's attention with.

But in spite of his scholarship, in spite of his growing genius, Ben wanted tact; he was without that delicacy of intuition which may both embarrass a man and save him from embarrassment; at twenty-seven he lacked *savoir faire;* and the brusque naivety of this second attack on the royal indifference was coldly received. There was no command performance at Whitehall, and Ben was sadly disappointed. He had, however, no valid reason for surprise at its rejection. For his play to please a Court was largely concerned with the folly of courtiers. It was, moreover, tediously clever with the unrelenting cleverness of a young man proudly abstaining from the beaten path and rejecting, with self-conscious bravery, the reward of popular applause. It revealed with unerring strokes the unpleasantness and stupidity of a lot of unpleasant and stupid people; and gave its author the most exquisite delight.

Cynthia's Revels also offered Jonson a chance to reply to Marston's attack in *Jack Drum's Entertainment*. To bring a personal quarrel into a Court play was unusual, but by this time Jonson's estimate of his own significance was also unusual. He felt so sure of the importance of all his activities that he naturally assumed they were of general interest. It is difficult for a man with a mission to keep his balance, and Jonson's mission was the double task of reforming manners and setting poetry of a particular kind on a dominant throne. He was passionately assured of the rightness of his cause, and sincerely believed himself to be the champion of true art. Whoever tilted against him was *ipso facto* the enemy of all good poets – 'than which reverend name,' it will be remembered, 'nothing can more adorn humanity.' All in the cause of virtuous behaviour and proper poetry, then, he made for his new play a character called Crites, who was a very flattering portrait of himself and uttered Jonsonian sentiments with large freedom; and fashioned two of Cynthia's most unsavoury courtiers in the likeness of Marston and the well-known author, Thomas Dekker. For the quarrel had by this time grown, and the literary men of London, good angry fellows many of them, were busy taking sides. Munday had suffered his blow and lain quiet, but there were others who resented Ben's dictatorial attitude, and Dekker, his old mate in Henslowe's mill, was one of them. So Ben clapped him into his play as promptly as if it were the stocks, and made him twist and squirm at pleasure.

Nor was Ben's righteousness satisfied with two victims only. He wrote an elaborate induction to the play in which he coldly referred to contemporaries who bolstered their work with other men's jokes, stale apothegms, the gleanings of laundresses' and hackney-men's wit, and the leavings on their friends' trenchers; and then, lest the audience should sit too compla-cently and comfortably, he mentioned some of the more objectionable types of spectator: civet-wits who imagined a good suit of clothes entitled them to pose as critics; those with more beard than brains, who thought there had been no good play since *The Spanish Tragedy;* those who understood but a tenth of what they heard, and saved their credit by calling all the rest fustian; and lastly such dead souls as 'shake their bottle heads, and of their corky brains squeeze out a pitiful learned face, and are silent.'

These just and apposite aspersions on their char-acter came to the audience in the clear treble tones of youth, for *Cynthia's Revels* was acted by the Children of the Queen's Chapel, and the sweet schoolroom voices lent exquisite point to Ben's disquisition on human frailties. He made a number of new enemies before the play was over – and the battle had hardly begun.

CHAPTER VII

APOLOGY IN PARENTHESIS

To us the theatre is a sedative or a stimulant drug, an aphrodisiac, or – if the plot be criminal and strong enough – perhaps a diuretic. Quietly it fills a creditable place in society, quietly it does its therapeutic duty, and its activities, ruled by a decent regard for commercial success, are strictly impersonal. No longer does the stage – as the older one used to – thrust its way into the auditorium; nor are private citizens haled to justice on it, nor does dog eat playwright dog before the footlights. Even on the streets it is rare to find dramatists brawling lively enough to collect a crowd. For we are grown a quiet-loving people, conscious of policemen at every street corner and the law of libel hovering overhead. We are fastidious too, so that the incongruous upsets us more than the immoral, provided the latter be not loud nor pugnacious. Nowadays we should be offended by the sight of a circus-man walking his horse on the roof of St. Paul's. But in Jonson's time the ingenious showman Banks took a well-trained animal, called Morocco, up there, and all London clapped the obvious jollity of the proceedings.

The Elizabethans were braver stuff than we. They

ST. PAUL'S CATHEDRAL, WITH VIEW OF THE BANKSIDE

Section from Visscher's View of London

did not look Banks's horse in the mouth, but un-squeamishly applauded; they quarrelled in the middle of the street, and hunted their fleas in church. Why then should they hesitate to use Burbage and young Field, Alleyn and little Salathiel Pavy (actors whose daily fare was verse imperishable) to exploit their private differences? There are several reasons apparent to us, but their vision was rarely troubled by such hypercritical motes, and the poets continued their altercations on the public stage as innocent of impropriety as was Morocco on the roof of Paul's, and before audiences equally entertained.

London was still small enough for scandal to permeate, for gossip to spread across it. The playwrights, comparatively few in number, were almost as well known to theatre-goers as a village choir to village communicants, and their private affairs were comparably a matter of public interest. Jonson especially, in a century when modesty was the least of the virtues, had become notorious for his astounding arrogance. Only a cultured minority perceived the genius which substantiated his claims. To the many he was a tyrant in black rug, armed with a protean wit that now battered like a flail, now cut like a sword, and would bite anon like a nest of angry snakes. They saw his swarthy face, pin-pricked with large pores, and the wide mouth that spoke with such bitter eloquence. They heard his loud self-praise. They recognised the strength of his body, and passion in the dark brilliance of his eye. They saw danger, and were inclined to bait him as they loved to bait Harry

Hunks and Sacarson, the most dangerous brutes in the Bear Garden.

But Jonson's friends saw more than the multitude. They recognised the virtue in his belligerence, the valour of his arrogance. Behind that insolent front they knew a patient workman lived, a workman with a high and holy vision, and the enduring strength of dwarfs in Fafnir's hall. They knew his labours, and to their joy they knew that, prodigious though it was, his work did not exhaust him. His vigour responded to every contact, and his friends, strengthened first, were ultimately captured by the radiation of his enormous vitality. He loved good men as he hated thin souls, shoddy pretensions, hypocrisy, and meagre living. He loved his friends, and his love made of them valiant partisans, so that to oppose a battalion of enemies he had always at his side a patrol of stout comrades. And while he fought the war of the theatres, in a crusading spirit with neither doubt of its propriety nor hesitancy concerning the justice of his cause, he made new friends, a few here and there, to strengthen his little band against the growing army of the Philistines.

CHAPTER VIII

THE WAR OF THE THEATRES

THE harrying of Marston and Dekker had somewhat
relieved the inordinate length of *Cynthia's Revels*, and
in spite of its tediousness the play was not altogether
a failure. It gave London something to talk about,
for which a town is always grateful, and presently it
began to be whispered that the offended poets were
preparing a gigantic revenge. At booksellers' stalls,
in the taverns that affected a literary conversation,
and when playgoer met playgoer in the Middle Aisle
of Paul's, knowing gossip was retailed and foreboding
chuckles exchanged at the prospect of Ben getting a
bloody crown for playing King of the Castle on
Parnassus Hill, when Parnassus, as all men knew, was
common ground. Reports of this hostile activity and
expectation of his discomfiture soon reached Ben –
perhaps at the Mermaid, which he discovered five
years before Raleigh thought it would do for a poets'
club – and he made up his mind that his best defence
would be attack. He would have a play on the boards
before theirs was half done, and this time it would be
no comedy of the humours or Court motion, with a
few contemptuous sketches of the Philistines tacked
on to it, but a play deliberately intended to rout and

destroy his foes. He began work immediately and wrote with increasing gusto.

But Jonson was not a rapid composer. His literary conscience permitted no looseness of construction even in occasional satire, and if classical example were quoted then classical authority had to be consulted. Nothing slipshod, nothing slovenly or half-tied, would be permitted however great the hurry, and so Jonson, writing hard, took fifteen weeks to finish *The Poetaster*, while Marston had his new play ready long before that.

But Dekker was beaten in the race. Dekker was easy-going, assertive for the moment perhaps, a loud talker who ornamented his conversation with soldierly oaths, but not vindictive, not so retentive of anger that he could put aside all other work and write a whole play on the prudently edited impetus of revenge. He was a good poet, a man with a bawdy mind and a prolific pen. His bawdiness was not vicious. Rather it was an indication of his catholic appetite that relished alike poetry and great rolling phrases and the whimsical indignities to which nature has condemned our bodies. He was a journalist who wrote pamphlets that carried their cargo of news and opinion on a stream of rhetoric swift and dark. He wrote as if he were a minor prophet come to plague-stricken London; as if he were a son – got carelessly – of Theocritus; and again as if he were making jokes for Mother Bunch. He wrote plays of his own on anything and everything, and when other dramatists found their wits grow costive or spavin afflict their blown Pegasus, Dekker would sit down and scribble a scene or two, an act, or perhaps contrive a secondary plot for them. He was a good-humoured man, tireless, and a true erratic lover of poetry.

He was kept busy too, with his patching and tinkering of old plays and writing bits of new ones, and the money he earned never lasted long; for he had his pipes to fill, and wine to pay for, and petticoats to buy for his mistresses. Dekker was not the man to sustain a long battle, and so while Jonson prepared his elaborate riposte and Marston explosively concocted his second grenade, Dekker shrugged his shoulders and wrote another act for Henslowe, and bought a gown for his new sweetheart, and waited to see what would happen.

Marston called his new play *What You Will*, and caricatured Jonson under the name of Lampatho; a snarling scholar, a 'fusty cask, devote to mouldy custom,' 'a canker-eaten rusty cur.' Many of Lampatho's lines were a malicious parody of Crites' in *Cynthia's Revels*. This was fairly hard hitting, yet Jonson continued his work unperturbed, grimly assured that the Macedonian phalanx of his full attack would trample his enemies so flat they could never rise again. . . .

But unknown to him, unsuspected by Marston, a greater than either, impatient at this undignified brawling and, it may be, feeling some leanness in his pocket owing to a peculiar circumstance of the war, was already preparing an impartial offensive that was to silence both. Jonson's massed attack came first, however. . . .

The Poetaster was a better play than he had written since *Every Man in his Humour*, and he had Marston to thank for it, who drove him to explicit personalities. His comedies were threatening to become mere parcels of talk – admirable talk, but not essentially of the stage – and catalogues of character – vigorously invented, finely delineated character, but character described without much chance to prove itself. Now, when he was forced to fight in earnest, his characters took life and action reappeared on his stage.

The scene of the play was laid in the Rome of Augustus Caesar, and the story was concerned first with Ovid's unfortunate love for the Emperor's daughter, and secondly with a jealous attempt, equally unsuccessful, to disgrace the poet Horace. But Horace was Jonson, complete in his poverty, (shabbiness sat well enough on that broad back, as Ben knew) arrogantly professing his proud free soul, and amiably admitting his weakness for translating ancient authors; while Horace's enemies were Marston and Dekker, rechristened Crispinus and Demetrius; and so the second theme was developed at the expense of the first, to which indeed it was loosely attached. Crispinus, the poetaster, is described with an energetic particularity. He is mocked not only for his thin legs and red hair, but for pretensions to gentle birth, debts, bad poetry, eagerness to ingratiate himself with Horace, sweaty marks on his clothes, a meagre voice, and affected speech; he can protest he is enamoured of a Roman street because it is 'so polite and terse.' And when his conspiracy to discredit Horace has failed, and Horace himself is permitted to name his punishment, poor Crispinus is made to take certain pills to purge him of his literary affectations.

He swallows the medicine – and a basin is brought. Then, before Caesar and his poets and his courtiers, up comes the vomit: hard and indigestible words like *turgidous, glibbery, oblatrant,* and *furibund;* with a belch and a heave *prorumpt* is hawked up; Virgil, an interested spectator, bids a bystander hold Crispinus' head – up come *tropological, anagogical,* and *pinosity;* there is a lot of windy retching now, for the poetaster's stomach is almost empty; he still squirms though, and the Court watches eagerly; he slabbers, and with a final convulsion disgorges the great gobbety word *obstupefact.* And Marston's punishment is complete.

In contrast to this elaborate retribution, Dekker, as Demetrius, is dismissed with a simple contempt untroubled by any need for detail or explanation. Dekker is kicked out of doors by a scornful yet incurious boot, and that is all there is to say about it.

But after the play Marston and Dekker found themselves with a crowd of sympathisers, for half London had been offended by the miscellany of Jonson's incidental criticism. Lawyers were irate, players furious, and all the cast captains, old soldiers, veterans of the Lowlands and pretty fellows who had seen no service more desperate than drill on Finsbury Fields, swore tempestuously that arms had been insulted and Ben should suffer for it. For one of the most engaging characters in *The Poetaster* was Captain Tucca, a soldier who had fought (on lines of communication) in the wars against Mark Antony. And Captain Tucca amused some part of the audience with his bluff and vulgar geniality, his barking of strange tropes, with the lewd epithets he stuttered, and for a climax with the revelation of his gross cowardice; but other playgoers, who boasted their allegiance *tam Marti quam Mercurio*, saw in Tucca a mirror of their own allusive language learnt overseas, and of their own impudence in living on their friends' purses, and, worst of all, a reflexion on their professional courage.

Lawyers were angered by a suggestion that ignorance, insolence, and unscrupulousness were finger-posts to success in their calling; while actors not unnaturally resented an implication that they combined pimping with their other speaking parts.

Ben's critical pebbles had stirred a whole colony of hornets' nests, and he walked in a perpetual buzz and stridulation of threats. But so many were the libelled, as they conceived themselves, that they spent their energy in debating their dudgeon and shaking communal fists rather than in personally visiting displeasure on the author of contumely. Jonson outlived the storm, and was indeed only once in actual danger.

But his self-esteem suffered from the flank attack of one to whom he had given no deliberate offence, but who nevertheless had been offended by the tempest Jonson raised; as a man sitting safe at home may feel his anger rise against unruly wind and a batter of hail, though they come no nearer than to shake his windows. The new disputant was Shakespeare. With growing impatience he had watched Jonson waste his strength on windmills and parade his virtue for the laughter of fools; with increasing distaste he had listened to Marston's chattering abuse; and, as a shareholder in the Globe and a man of property, a man with a countryman's interest in his profits, he had seen with intensified concern that the income of his own company was severely cut by the success of the Children of the Queen's Chapel and of St. Paul's, who had produced Jonson's last two plays and those of Marston.

The Children were accomplished actors, and all this controversial matter had given them valuable advertisement. Their small voices produced a whimsical edge on Ben's massive cutting and thrusting, but the adult actors could hardly be expected to appreciate the joke when their own theatres stood half empty. Shakespeare then, as a business man and a poet, had some cause for displeasure when he saw poets wasting their gifts to the detriment of his purse. But he did not let his annoyance deform the play in which he expressed it. He found that Jonson and Marston could be introduced, without much distortion, into *Troilus and Cressida*. The one was sufficiently like Ajax, the other bore a striking resemblance to Thersites. Ajax was thought of not only as a champion, but as a somewhat mulish and obtuse champion; and Thersites notoriously would have quarrelled with his own shadow in lieu of better company. In still another guise then, the disputants appeared on still another stage, and we may with some interest compare Shakespeare's picture of Ben – taken in the stress of combat, be it remembered – with Ben's portraits of himself as a man of lofty spirit and judicious mind, a man in whom the humours and elements were peacefully met, and whom ill-fortune could not dismay. Here is Shakespeare's description of Ajax:

'This man, lady, hath robbed many beasts of their particular additions; he is as valiant as the lion, churlish as the bear, slow as the elephant: a man into whom nature hath so crowded humours that his valour is crushed into folly, his folly sauced with discretion: there is no man hath a virtue that he hath not a glimpse of, nor any man an attaint but he carries some stain of it: he is melancholy without cause, and merry against the hair: he hath the joints of everything, but everything so out of joint that he is a gouty Briareus, many hands and no use, or purblind Argus, all eyes and no sight.'

Jonson showed for once an admirable self-control, and when he wrote his commentary on the war of the theatres, though he defended himself against others like a pirate cornered on his poop – a very legally-minded pirate, for his defence was judicious as it was fierce – all he had to say of Shakespeare's criticism was:

'Only amongst them (the players), I am sorry for
Some better natures, by the rest so drawn,
To run in that vile line.'

A calm rejoinder for a hot-tempered man, especially
as Shakespeare's mockery had been deft, light-fingered
and crafty as a surgeon tapping a swollen belly
to make the patient cry 'Ah!' when he touches the
sorest place. The very butcher of a silk button was
Shakespeare in this affray, and compared with him Ben
seems indeed to move with something of elephantine
deliberation.

But if Ben said little, Marston must have wept
aloud; for Thersites is a cankered jester who matches
the world in terms of dirt; a deformity of wit who
takes his former protector's beatings like a cur; a
peeper round walls who finds lechery in every corner
and lewdly complains of his findings. Thersites is
made tolerable only by his admirable handling of
invective, for he can wind in one spool of commination
'the rotten diseases of the south, the guts-griping,
ruptures, catarrhs, loads o' gravel i' the back, lethar-
gies, cold palsies, raw eyes, dirt-rotten livers, wheezing
lungs, bladders full of imposthume, sciaticas, lime-
kilns i' the palm, incurable bone-ache, and the
rivelled fee-simple of the tetter;' and then turn to such
pretty conceits of disparagement as 'Thou idle
immaterial skein of sleave-silk, thou green sarcenet-
flap for a sore eye, thou tassel of a prodigal's purse!'
But it is doubtful whether even these compliments to
his invention soothed poor Marston's mutilated pride.

Troilus and Cressida might very well have concluded the war, but Jonson wrote an Apological Dialogue for *The Poetaster* which was so far from being an apology – tactlessly it proved his critics wrong and himself right – that it provoked more ill-temper than ever, and had to be suppressed after one performance. In its solitary exhibition, however, Ben affirmed with an ample gloomy tongue his determination to write no more comedy, but to leave the 'unclean birds,' his audience, to find their own entertainment while he retired to meditate matters

'high and aloof,
Safe from the wolf's black jaw and the dull ass's hoof.'

And then came the final action in the campaign, bloodless now, for the principal combatants had gone and only debris was left on the battlefield. Now, with a certain amiability, with a grin on his face, Dekker came out like a cynical good-humoured camp-follower to see what he could pick up among the remains.

He had at last yielded to Marston's persuasion; at last he had stirred himself to answer Ben's insults – for now it happened to suit his own convenience. He had on hand a partly-written play that threatened to be somewhat lean for a robust audience's taste. It might, however, be possible to graft on to it a new story about Horace and his enemies that would fatten it up.

Dekker's new play was based on an early incident

in the contiguous histories of William Rufus and Sir Walter Terrill. William Rufus was a king whom even an uncultured age called rude, and Terrill was the man who eventually relieved the embarrassment of the Court by killing him. The main plot of Dekker's unfinished work rested on William's endeavour to precede Terrill in the latter's bridal chamber. As William's courting consisted solely of tiresome jokes about the deciduous quality of maidenheads, the bride was unwilling to grant him so marked a favour as that which he sought. But Terrill was a simple youth, and her father an old man whose wits hung clumsily on many a stile, so that virtue seemed like a town without a wall and chastity an easy prize for any king. Tearfully the bride considered night, which, with the untoward speed of the theatre, came nearer and nearer. And then her father stopped wheezy jesting and proposed, with an icy disregard for sentiment, that she should poison herself. The bride, commendably clear-sighted, immediately re-cognised the advantages of this suggestion and drained the deadly bowl before Terrill could adequately protest. With fine dramatic economy the body is then used as the central figure in a masque designed to entertain the king, and the latter's remorse (having descended from his dais and unveiled the cold seated figure) is followed, after a few pregnant seconds, by his reconciliation with Terrill. This admission of the Divine right of repentance is promptly ratified by the revival of the corpse – the apparently poisoned Moselle had only contained a sleeping draught – and the bemused king takes the joke in good part and gives the happy couple his blessing.

On to this unpromising material Dekker cheerfully tacked his new canvas and introduced Ben – once more in the person of Horace – to the barbarous Court of William Rufus; an introduction with less regard for propriety than Alice showed when inviting herself to the Mad Hatter's tea-party. But what had Dekker to do with the tenuous elegance of congruity, he who wrote for people who might come to see his play in the interval between watching a recusant disembowelled and stealing a line from the *Amoretti* to sweeten a sonnet for a whore? He brought in Ben's creation of Captain Tucca too, and blew the gaff on him very prettily, for he had found the model Ben used for his soldier in a certain Captain Hannam, a decayed commander about the town. Under his new puppet-master Tucca's language becomes more hilariously allusive, larded more tropically than ever; and it is he who finally discomfits Horace, stripping his satirical suit, putting a wreath of nettles about his head, and administering the oath of amended manners. Tucca is the riotous agent of revenge, while Crispinus and Demetrius, whom Horace had far more seriously insulted, stand by and are most magnanimously reproachful. It is Tucca who taunts Ben with killing Gabriel Spenser, with his bricklaying, his delight in fashionable company, his coarse complexion, his itchy poetry that 'breaks out like Christmas, but once a year.' Tucca's the foining fighting man, while Crispinus and Demetrius consider the brawl with grave schoolmasterly eyes, and tincture their reproofs with kindness, and – most exasperating of all – affect an Olympian comprehension of poor Ben's weaknesses.

In time of conflict the temple of Janus stood wide open, and the two-faced god looked equally at front portal and back door. So now with Dekker, and one face was solemn. But the other was lop-sided by reason of the tongue that stuffed a protruding cheek with such happy impudence, and one eye was occluded by a lewd capacious wink.

When the grimace faded peace returned to the theatres. It was a peace of exhaustion, for though Dekker continued, unperturbed, to write as well as he could whatever was ordered, Jonson went into a kind of retirement – not monastic, however – and for three years Marston wrote nothing more for the stage. Authorship, indeed, occupied only little lurid intervals in his life, for though he returned to play-writing when the soreness of Jonson's pummelling and Shakespeare's wounds had healed, he took orders a few years later and buried himself in a Hampshire vicarage. There, perhaps, a truce was called between the hostile forces in his soul; or, it may be, the inter-necine war continued till Marston wondered, in a Shropshire agony:

> 'When shall I be dead and rid
> Of the wrong my father did?
> How long, how long, till spade and hearse
> Put to sleep my mother's curse?'

He lived for twenty-seven years in his country cure, and wakened many a night to hear the noise of London taverns, street singers, and a sword rattling on the table; many a time through his laced fingers as he prayed in church he saw the rocky face of Ben, Dekker's whimsical smile, some Mary Faugh perhaps – and clenched his hands the tighter, intoned the louder, to shut out song and old visions of the sinful world he had left. His epitaph, that he chose for himself, was *Oblivioni Sacrum*.

CHAPTER IX

FRIENDS AND MISFORTUNE

THOUGH his literary ambition was checked by a wall
of its own making, Ben's social aspirations had
meanwhile been gratified by several distinguished
friendships. The Inns of Court men, intellectually
alert and youthfully impatient with traditional art
forms, had been captured by the magnificent novelty
of his comedies, and association with them had been
both mentally stimulating and a valuable introduction
to the better society of the day. Not infrequently they
exercised their wit on trivial subjects – as when Mr.
Hugh Platt of Lincoln's Inn discovered, after several
experiments, that a draught of salad oil would prevent
drunkenness by floating on the wine and so suppress-
ing the fumes that otherwise rose to the brain – but the
excellence of their social connexions was indisputable,
and with disarming pride Ben had told the audience
of *The Poetaster* that he now kept better company than
actors.

Two years had made a lot of difference. Two years
before he had confided to another audience that a
dinner with the players was a rare and special
occasion for him, a festival that came not oftener than
once a fortnight, to which he went with a great
greedy appetite made fierce by a philosophical diet of

beans and buttermilk; and then, with his belly well ballasted, and his brain sailing stoutly on a flood-tide of Canary, then he would go home to work all night by the scholarly pale light of a farthing candle.

Two years before his only friend, outside the theatre, had been his old Westminster master Camden, but now he knew Selden and Christopher Brooke, the poetical Sir John Davies, Sir Robert Cotton the antiquary, probably Bacon, Sir Robert Townshend, and Donne. He could afford to be careless about some older friends.

Nor may his social eagerness be laughed at. Then, as now, genius might be born in a butcher's shop or a cobbler's room, but then, incomparably more than now, genius had to climb away from its original environment to find company of its own feather. Scholarship and wit are the ultimate luxuries, and though Elizabeth's England spent its new riches with a prodigal hand, yet most of the Spanish gold bought nothing more imaginative than silks and velvets, sack and new furniture. Only improvident Bohemia and the aristocracy could afford to buy books, and acquire learning, and be witty; and even in Bohemia there was not always that regard for solid classical culture that Jonson entertained. He had to climb, then, to find the associates he was in need of, and who can blame him if, mounting steadily, he thought with satisfaction that every step took him farther from those detestable memories of bricklaying?

There is no surer evidence of Jonson's magnetic personality than his friendship with John Donne.

Even the congregation of young men about his bed, in the decline of his life, scarcely proves the substantial spell of his presence so thoroughly as this intimacy with Donne, whose passionate nature, whose solitary and arrogant spirit, were matched by an intellect so muscular that, like a strong man tearing a pack of cards, it tore conventional moods into marvellous fragments, and twisted the very currency of thought into shapes unsuspected of the beholder.

Of Spenser and the writers who modelled themselves upon him, Donne thought nothing. For Elizabethan drama he showed no enthusiasm. Of English scholarship he had opinions qualified by an education based as much on Continental schools. He had the self-sufficiency of a satirist who had scourged his world and could die with his best work written at twenty-five. He had been with Essex on the Islands voyage, and brought back the only booty taken: two poems called *The Storm* and *The Calm*. He knew that he could eclipse the morning sun with a wink, and love all women so they were not true. He thought in an atmosphere too rare to support common illusion or his contemporaries, and he suffered Ben to tell him he deserved hanging for not keeping a regular accent in his verses. But this was the only adverse criticism Jonson offered, for his admiration of Donne was as generous and enthusiastic as his scorn for poetasters:

'Donne, the delight of Phoebus and each Muse,
Who, to thy one, all other brains refuse,

Whose every work, of thy most early wit,
Came forth example, and remains so yet.'

So he wrote, and in spite of his fierce lofty self-regard
submitted his poems to Donne's criticism:

'Read all I send, and, if I find but one
Mark'd by thy hand, and with the better stone,
My title's sealed.'

But when the fury aroused by Ben's truculent
apology for *The Poetaster* culminated in a threat of
prosecution before the Star Chamber, Donne was
no longer in a position to help him. He had been for
some years chief secretary to the Lord Keeper, and
just before Christmas, 1601, he secretly married Anne
More, a young relative of Sir Thomas who lived with
the family (as Donne did) at York House in the
Strand. When the secret was broken Donne's secretaryship promptly came to an end and he found himself in prison for conspiring to break both Common
and Canon Law. The other conspirators, who lay
with him in the Fleet, were Christopher Brooke, who
had assisted at the marriage ceremony, and Christopher's young brother Samuel, who had celebrated
his newly-taken orders by performing it. So Donne
was powerless to succour anyone, even himself; even
his wit lay on a pauper's death-bed and spent its last
breath on a pun: 'John Donne – Anne Donne –
Undone,' he wrote to his wife, who at that moment
was trembling before her father's anger.

But Jonson fortunately had still an acquaintance

or two at liberty, and Richard Martin, a lawyer and for long a friend of King James, intervened with the Chief Justice and succeeded in preventing the threatened proceedings in the Star Chamber.

Delivered from the consequence of offending audiences, Ben also found himself, about this time, freed from the necessity of entertaining them; for Sir Robert Townshend, a wealthy patron of letters, had offered him the hospitality of his house. He read Horace's *Art of Poetry* and considered the baseness of the age in congenial surroundings. His environment, for the first time, was apparently ideal. He had books, cultured society, and pleasures of the table. One would imagine him to be perfectly satisfied with this eclectic entertainment, and think that a few epigrams, a footnote or two, would satisfy a creative need mollified by such comfort. But as a matter of fact he presently put away his Horace and began to write some new scenes for that vulgar old play *The Spanish Tragedy*.

No one knew better than Henslowe what profit there still was in the story of Hieronimo's misfortunes, and Henslowe astutely realized that occasional additions, some fresh paint, a new cloak for the Marshal, made its performance still more attractive to his simple audiences. Jonson, he now thought, could refurnish it very prettily if he cared to. He had no great liking for Ben's new comedies, but he remembered with regret for its passing the headlong manner of his romantic plays: no strait-laced art-forms there, but tragic flashes and the fruits of blood, wild thoughts that took you by the throat, and phrases like a palace gate flung open. Ben, he thought, could do what was wanted very well, and because letter-writing, with its obstacles of spelling and grammar, was a weary exercise, he sent his son-in-law Alleyn to discuss the matter. There had also been, at his last meeting with Ben, some talk of a chronicle play about Richard III. Alleyn, he said, might see if the bricklayer was yet in a mind to write it.

Henslowe chose a good agent, for Alleyn was not only a good business man, but an actor of so supreme a skill that Jonson, who had small opinion of the ruck of players, did not hesitate to rank him with Roscius and Æsop. 'Others speak, but only thou dost act,' he said once – an injustice to Burbage and such clever children as Field and Salathiel Pavy; and yet the bearded nobility of Alleyn lent a presence to his parts that others might not convey. He had given such life to so much poetry that a poet must confess his gratitude. When he spoke of *The Spanish Tragedy* he woke in Ben's mind a score of intimate, ineffaceable, humorous, half-sentimental memories of that rowdy tragedy, and Ben agreed to accept yet another of Henslowe's commissions. At a price, however. He was independent now, and Henslowe would have to pay more handsomely than he had paid in the past. But for ten pounds he would write new scenes for Kyd's ageing play, and promise to start the history of Richard III.

Henslowe complained bitterly, but agreed at last to pay Ben's price. And then he looked doubtfully at

Alleyn. Ten pounds was a large sum to trust one man with, even when that man was his daughter's husband. It would be safer, more business-like, if its delivery were witnessed. It happened that Byrd, the composer, was in his house at the time, with some madrigals to sell. Perhaps Byrd would go with the actor? Henslowe did not doubt Alleyn's honesty, of course. But ten pounds was a good round sum. . . .

Alleyn's name and Byrd's were both entered in Henslowe's book as having received the money, and Ben put aside his Roman authors and blew upon the embers of romantic invention. An angry gust or two from more recent memories helped him, and the coals flared redly. He wrote a couple of scenes that showed Hieronimo mad indeed, after the Elizabethan convention of madness that set a lunatic fancy prowling in the dark forests of imagination to find at last, in that tropic growth, something homely and simple: quails for supper, a dog in office, or the assumption that a painter could draw comfort. Hieronimo raved with the percipient tongue of poetry, and that was good stuff for Henslowe's public, stuff to pluck their blood-stiffened nerves with magical cold fingers, and make the comfortable light of day seem dark as Hieronimo's taper supposed it.

These few scenes show the quality of Ben's romantic power, and the quality of his renunciation when, at the command of a Puritanical artistic conscience, he abandoned romantic tragedy for satiric comedy and classical models. The romantic power is remarkable, but the power to suppress it and redirect its energy in alien channels is yet more astonishing. Ben's genius never had a chance to ride him to ruin or the heights, for he rode it – bestrode it, indeed, like a Colossus; and though sometimes it faltered in its gait, it went the road he ordered. When this excursion was done, Ben, still sitting in Townshend's house, returned to his study of Horace. He had translated *The Art of Poetry*, and he was writing a preface to it in the form of a dialogue between himself and Donne. – By this time Donne was also living on charity. His young wife and he, after his release from prison, had been in sore straits, but soon a kindly friend invited them to his house at Pyrford in Surrey, where they lived in tolerable comfort for a couple of years. A Maecenas in the seventeenth century was quite as useful as a large circulation in the twentieth.

After some months of Townshend's hospitality Jonson went to live with Lord d'Aubigny, a younger brother of the Duke of Lennox. This association was so mutually agreeable that Ben found no occasion to sleep in his own home for the next five years; though he maintained extra-mural relations with his family. D'Aubigny's hospitality was of a spacious kind that permitted his guest to pay country visits when he pleased, and return in the agreeable certainty of an ever-renewed welcome.

In 1603, while the plague was making London disagreeable – thirty thousand died of it that year – Ben went visiting to Sir Robert Cotton's, at Connington in Huntingdonshire. Cotton, who was a year older than Ben, had also been at Westminster, and carrying

the inspiration of Camden's teaching into practice
became justly famous for his researches in English
history. He gathered a magnificent library in his
London house, and entertained among his books the
members of the Antiquarian Society. There, it is
probable, Jonson met among other celebrities the
essayist and politician, Francis Bacon.

But in 1603 Cotton was more interested in his
country house, which he had recently been recon-
structing, and into which he had built a new room
with ghastly but alluring associations. It was a room
from Fotheringay Castle, bought by Cotton, its
panelling stript, its joists and floor-boards and ceiling
taken piecemeal into Huntingdonshire, and there
reassembled for his pleasure. Its walls had seen a
Queen come in, clothed all in black at one moment,
and the next, pulling off her gown, clad terribly in
scarlet. Then she had knelt – on that floor – and that
ceiling had looked down upon a white neck laid in a
still bravery on the block . . . It was the room in
which Mary Queen of Scots had been executed, and
Sir Robert had thought his friend Jonson and their
old master Camden might care to see it.

One night after a long discussion on the antiquity
of English castles, of which Cotton knew more than
other men; after some talk of Roman remains and
scandal in the Heralds' College; after gossip of the
Queen and a Roman traitor called Sejanus; after
debate on the advantage of rhyme in poetry, and
rumours of the plague in London, Ben was wakened
from sleep by a vision of his elder son, a boy of seven

years whom he had left with his mother. The child's forehead bore a bloody cross that looked as if it had been cut with a sword, and he seemed taller, of a more manly build, than when his father had last seen him. But the features, despite that red incision, were unmistakable, and the apparition filled Ben with a fearful wonder that set him praying hard. His prayers to some extent were successful, for the image of his son faded, but it was long before he fell asleep again. In the morning, still worried, he went to Camden's room before his old master was out of bed, and told him of the vision. Camden was not so impressed by the story as Jonson had expected; he was a little testy, perhaps, at that hour in the morning, and a schoolmaster rarely believes all that his scholars tell him; at any rate, 'It was but an apprehension of your fantasy,' he said, and then in a more kindly voice, for Ben's face was troubled, added, 'Be not disjected,' and patting his former pupil on the shoulder, lay down to doze a little longer.

But not long after a letter came from London with news that the boy had died of plague, and Ben's spirit failed. It was a pretty piece of irony that he, who had recently given Hieronimo such mounting terms of sorrow to mourn his dead son, should now have grief of his own to express, and expresss it in words so simple:

'Farewell, thou child of my right hand, and joy . . .
Rest in soft peace and, ask'd, say here doth lie
Ben Jonson his best piece of poetry.'

He returned to London and continued to work slowly, in collaboration with Chapman, on his new play, a Roman tragedy called *Sejanus*, which he had begun some months before. Chapman was a scholarly man, twelve years older than Jonson, who had taken to dramatic writing because drama was the surest means of gaining a livelihood that literature then offered. He had preceded Ben with an experimental comedy of humours, and already published part of his translation of the *Iliad*. Jonson had the highest regard for him, both as classicist and innovator, and because *Sejanus* was intended to be a model play, classically designed, impeccable in historical accuracy, he persuaded Chapman to advise and assist him. But they had not been working long before they were interrupted by an event which engaged the attention of all England.

CHAPTER X

SCOTCH SOLOMON

AFTER literally standing up to death for a preposterous time, the Queen had died in the early morning of March 25th, 1603 . . . Almost beating her last breath, Sir Robert Carey leapt to his horse and rode northwards. He rode with hot spurs, for such good news suffered no delay. At Norham, however, his eagerness nearly undid him. He took a toss and his horse kicked him on the head. But Sir Robert remounted and rode on. He reached Edinburgh on the third day after leaving Richmond, and found that James had gone to bed. Sir Robert thought it was no time for sleep, and without formality entered the royal apartment.

James, who was no stranger to conspiracy, woke with a fright to see at his bedside a man in mud-stained riding-clothes with a bloody clout round his head. The horseman knelt, and hailed him 'England, Scotland, France, and Ireland!' They talked for a little, and then James cautiously asked what letters Carey had from the Council.

'None,' said Carey, who had not waited for the Council to write letters which they would not have entrusted to him; but he showed a sapphire ring that James had sent to Lady Scroope – Carey's sister –

which was to be returned when Elizabeth died. It was a welcome sight, that small blue stone, and almost persuaded James that Carey's tale was true; an old woman had to die some time; and yet– three years before he had almost lost his life by swallowing a story about a pot of gold; perhaps it would be wiser to do nothing till official messengers came; and so with admirable prudence the secret was kept a secret, and for two whole days no one outside Holyrood knew that James VI of Scotland had become James I of England.

But though their tongues were silenced, hearts beat cheerfully as the Scots courtiers thought of London's ample prospects. Carey, the opportunist and the son of an *arriviste* family, sunned himself in their presence and felt that his fortune was made. Queen Anne was frankly relieved to see the end of her constant indebtedness to George Heriot, the Edinburgh jeweller, and hoped that in England opinion might regard with more lenience the occasional extravagance of a Sovereign. And the King moved nervously to and fro, fingering his clothes or stooping to fondle his hounds and terriers, and thought 'At last, at last!' At last he could live free from fear of conspiracy and assassins and traitors who used witchcraft to further their schemes. There would be no second Gowrie dealing in magic and commanding devils, nor Bothwell with warlocks at his bidding – Bothwell had got three covens of witches into North Berwick church to wreck the bride-ship that carried James and Anne from Denmark. In England there was no such open trafficking with the Devil. There would be small fear of witchcraft now. Nor in Whitehall would he be so likely to wake and find his enemies armed within the palace, as he had been wakened both in Falkland and in Holyrood. There were no warring earls in England, who broke peace like monarchs and made treaties like conquerors. Nor would there be stern solemn churchmen ever ready to rebuke him for swearing – publicly in St. Giles he had been rebuked – and bid him repent of his sins, and tell the Queen to go to bed earlier, and come oftener to church; churchmen who complained that he talked during their sermons, and called him to his face 'God's silly vassal,' and suspected him of dealing with Rome, the mother of vice and 'hoorishe synagog of devils!' He was rid of them now, contentious clergy and turbulent nobles, and instead there would be wits and ripe scholars to whom his own wit and scholarship would surely recommend him, and who would agree that it was a kingly ambition to wish himself the best clerk in his country. He sipped the strong Frontenac wine that he was fond of. There would be men with whom he could discuss, sure of their interest, his plans for translating in verse the Psalms of David; and other men, who kept horses and hounds, to go hunting with. There were deer-parks in England that always offered sport, and hounds with fine noses; packs so cunningly chosen, with such skilfully graded voices, that their music alone was a long day's enjoyment; and the horses were the best in Europe, and men knew how to ride them – England was 'a paradise for women and hell for horses.' He was not very interested in women, but it was good to be going to a country where men rode hard for love of riding. . . .

With such musing the first day of waiting passed quickly, but the second dragged, and James read a little in the *Basilikon Doron*, the book of kingcraft he had written for the instruction of Prince Henry. It was full of wisdom:

'Laws are ordained as rules of virtuous and social living, and not to be snares to trap your good subjects. . . .
'Learn also wisely to discern betwixt Justice and Equity; and for pity of the poor rob not the rich. . . .
'Where ye find a notable injury, spare not to give course to the torrents of your wrath. . . .
'But above all vertues, study to know well your own craft, which is to rule your people. . . .'

Could there be better counsel for a prince? And in England, so much larger and more powerful than Scotland, there would be correspondingly greater opportunities for a monarch to show his abilities. To keep peace within his own marches would be easy, thought James – had he not cozened Scots faction into quietude? – and he might use England's strength, not in the profitless carnage of war as former sovereigns had, but to establish and maintain peace in all Europe. It was not the least part of his wisdom that he could see the profits of peace overtopping the dubious increment of war. He would be James the Peacemaker. . . .

On the second day after Carey's arrival, Sir Charles Percy and Thomas Somerset came with official letters from the Privy Council, and a week later James left Edinburgh for London with an eager retinue in attendance. At Berwick he was received with hospitable pomp, and he flattered the garrison artillery by expertly firing a cannon for them. Then he mounted a fine horse and rode thirty-seven long Scots miles in something less than four hours, leaving his attendants panting behind him. His retinue grew as he went south, for there were time-servers on both sides of the border. At York a conduit from the gate to the Minster ran white and claret wine, and at Durham the Bishop waited on him with a hundred gentlemen in tawny liveries. His Majesty charmed everyone with his geniality, and was always ready to delay his progress if there was a deer to be hunted. Once he fell heavily and dangerously bruised his arm, but he said it was nothing, and remounted. The next day, however, he was too stiff to ride. At Hinchinbrook Priory he was magnificently entertained by Oliver Cromwell, uncle of the future Protector. Sir Oliver (so he was before the King left) presented James with a gold cup, horses, hounds, and hawks of excellent wing; and an acute observer noted there that the new sovereign regarded all who approached him with a straight and seeing eye.

BEATI PACIFICI

Crownes haue their compasse, length of dayes their date,
Triumphes their tombes, felicitie their fate:
Of more then earth, can earth make none partaker,
But knowledge makes the KING most like his maker.

Simon Pass... fecit Lond... Ioh: Bull excudit

JAMES I OF ENGLAND
(Simon van de Passe, 1616)

It was at Theobalds, Sir Robert Cecil's house in Hertfordshire, that the King's journey really ended, for London was too full of plague to offer a healthy greeting. And where, after all, could James have more comfortably or more naturally come to the end of his travels? For Cecil and the Howards (Lord Henry and Lord Thomas) were there to welcome him, and give him all the advice he needed, and tell him with circumstance of detail whom he should trust at court and who were his secret enemies. They promised him the security of their wealth, their wisdom, their scholarship, their knowledge of affairs, and their family connexions. Cecil and Lord Henry had for some years written so often to him – by a secret post through Dublin – and he had written so often to them, that they were old friends already. It was pleasant to meet them in the flesh, and find Sir Robert so gently grave, Lord Henry (who once had courted the Queen of Scots) so agreeable and smooth. . . . But there was anxiety in his eyes. An old man with a plausible prolix tongue and a secret fear – of what? Of inability to please his new master, thought James profoundly, and was inclined to like Lord Henry the more; though he had been often bored by his letters, which were 'Asiatic and endless volumes.' There was no anxiety on Sir Robert's face, however. It was a calm and lovely countenance, oddly dissimilar from his twisted meagre body, and in his voice James recognised dulcet authority.

At the gate of Theobalds a multitude of loyal

subjects tumultuously cheered the wisest king in Christendom. Gloriana was dead, and the night after she died bonfires had been lighted to honour her successor, who, despite a Scotch accent, had the wit of Solomon and the healthy instincts of Nimrod. He considered the mob (roaring their fickle loyalty) with a doubtful eye, for he was getting tired of crowds. Still, it comforted the heart, if not the brain, to find such enthusiasm after the dour faces of Edinburgh; and having talked for a while to Cecil, James stood for half an hour at a chamber window while his people applauded and generously threw their caps in the air. Gloriana was dead, and her successor too honest to wear black for her; though she had gone into strictest mourning after executing his mother.

In May the Queen came south, and every hedgerow bloomed extravagantly for the gaily laughing, high-spirited Danish lady whose careless way with money had so pained the Scottish Court, and whose love of dancing had provoked the pious ill-temper of the General Assembly. She had found Scotland dull after the hearty ways of Denmark, and because she enjoyed herself despite its dullness scandal had whistled her name up the High Street and then – a miracle indeed – sung it aloud in pure loveliness. For she had looked with less prudence than pleasure on the bonny Earl of Murray, and the Earl had died thus: he was summoned to Court to discuss a feudal quarrel with his neighbour and enemy the Earl of Huntly, and when Murray failed to appear Huntly was sent to bring him in. But Murray defended himself in his house of Dunnisbrisell till its gate was fired, and then the defendants made a sally through the flames. Murray's long essenced hair took fire, and by its dancing light he was followed down to the shore, where between the weedy rocks and the black sea he fell under twenty swords. The first was John Gordon's of Buckie, who held up the dying earl and cried for his master to come and kill him. Huntly stabbed him in the cheek, and Murray laughed as well as he could, and said 'Ye hae spoiled a better face than your ain, my lord,' and so died. Then the ballad was made, and in farm-town and ale-house, in closes of the High Street and on market-days, the people heard his requiem:

'He was a braw gallant
And he play'd at the gluve;
And the bonny Earl of Murray,
O he was the Queen's luve!

'O lang will his lady
Look owre the Castle Downe,
Ere she see the Earl of Murray
Come sounding through the town!'

It is not every Queen whose indiscretions are remembered in such honest beauty, but Anne, with her flaxen hair and high colour, her mirth and extravagance and lordly way with life, was such a one as ballad-makers choose to celebrate.

It was her arrival that interrupted Jonson in his work on *Sejanus*, for when Lord Spencer of Wormleighton was honoured with the duty of entertaining the Queen at Althorp, during her southward progress, he summoned Ben to help him with a masque or some such matter; and Ben wrote a pretty thing about Mab and her fairies, made lively with morris-men and a lurking satyr, and apt for the occasion with a loyal address of welcome. It was a curious translation from the grim nobility of his Roman play to this sprightly dancing matter, apparently so foreign to his nature. Yet *Sejanus* was destined to failure, and this new well he had tapped of courtly and romantic fancy would flow for many years with unabating vigour. And now, after his failures to impress the old Queen, Ben succeeded in recommending himself to the new one – for who could fail to hear with pleasure the flyting of Mab and the satyr?

MAB: 'Satyr, we must have a spell
            For your tongue, it runs too fleet.'

SATYR: 'Not so nimbly as your feet,
            When about the cream-bowls sweet
            You and all your elves do meet.
            This is Mab, the Mistress Fairy
            That doth nightly rob the dairy . . .
            She that pinches country wenches
            If they rub not clean their benches,
            And with sharper nails remembers
            When they rake not up their embers.'

And how charming to learn that the cause of the quarrel was spite because she

> 'Would not yesternight
> Kiss him in the cock-shot light!'

Anne's good favour, won here and strengthened after some delay by the King's more learned approval, was to bring Ben to Court, to give him, for his pleasure and theirs, a witty and elegant, a charming and worthless audience, when the worthless and far from elegant audiences of the Bankside rejected him. It gave him a medium frail as a soap-bubble's hide to spend his poetry and learning on. It led him to honour and allowed him to waste himself on ephemeral decorations. It took him, too long and too often, from the theatre, and bade him create the butterfly art of the masque.

CHAPTER XI

CONSPIRACY AND MASQUES

EARLY in 1603, that busy plague-stricken year, Sir
Walter Raleigh established a poet's club that met
in the Mermaid Tavern in Bread Street on the first
Friday of each month; and in the summer of the same
year the club lost its founder when the new King
had Raleigh taken to the Tower.

His arrest was partly due to his foolishness in
associating with Lord Cobham, who was altogether
a fool; it was partly due to his old rivalry with Essex;
and it was very largely due to the malevolence of Lord
Henry Howard. James had relied on Essex's friendship, and Lord Henry had been of the Essex party.
After the Earl's downfall Cecil and Lord Henry had
done their best to infect the Scottish King with their
own fear and hatred of Raleigh. Raleigh was his
enemy as well as the Earl's, and would oppose the
Stuart succession: so Lord Henry wrote to James,
and padded his story with redundance and Asiatic
profusion of periphrases. All James knew for certain
was that his friend Essex was ruined, and in his
stead had triumphed that figure of arrogance and
splendour and ever-growing power, the Devon sailor,
the courtier in his silver armour, the poet and empire-
maker who could so dangerously win men to follow

him. Howard's story was too plausible to be discredited, and Raleigh too great a personage to ignore. He must be either a friend or an enemy, and it was James's fate to believe him the latter.

There was a silly plot (silly in its origin, stupidly mismanaged) to put Arabella Stuart on the throne. As though to advertise its general ineptitude, Lord Cobham was one of the conspirators. He was suspected, arrested, and questioned. He squirmed in terror and declared that Raleigh was the instigator. Raleigh's enemies, knowing he had endured Cobham's company on several occasions, gleefully accepted this ridiculous evidence – no one knew better than Lord Henry how unsubstantial it was – and Raleigh was arrested. His trial was a caricature of justice – Lord Henry was on the specially commissioned bench – but Cecil and the King and all the Howards felt safer when Sir Walter was lodged in the Tower, where certain African lions were also imprisoned for life: the penalty of too regal a bearing and their power to inspire fear.

With graver matters to think of, he may have forgotten his poet's club. He had, in any case, no cause to think lonelily that while he dreamt of El Dorado, others built of their wit an airy Manoa in the Mermaid. In the summer of 1603 the Mermaid was deserted, for the plague had returned to London with uncommon virulence, and all who could afford it fled to the country, carrying with them contagion and fear. Huge quantities of mithridatum and dragon-water were drunk for prophylactics, and to keep off infection frightened citizens went abroad with rue stuffed in their ears and wormwood in their nostrils, so that, in Dekker's words, they looked like 'boars' heads stuck with branches of rosemary, to be served in for brawn at Christmas.' Lazarus lay groaning at every door, he says, but there was no Dives to relieve him, for Dives had hurried to the provinces, where the very sight of his London clothes was enough to make a market-town give up the ghost. There were no dogs even to lick poor Lazarus's sores, for dogs too died of plague, and those that did not die were killed lest they carry infection.

Shops stood empty, and the need for grave-clothes had robbed every bed of its sheets. But gardeners grew fat, for gardeners saw rosemary, a great bundle of which brought twelve-pence in normal times, selling now at six shillings a handful. And the servants of the Church prospered, for there were such thousands to bury, such funeral sermons to preach, and always bells to be rung, that clergymen, clerks, and sextons thought their fortunes would be made. The three bald sextons of St. Giles's, St. Olave's, and St. Sepulchre's ruled the roast in London, it was said, more absolutely than Triumvirs in Rome.

Men prayed for winter, and when cold weather came the town refilled as if for holiday. . . .

It was with the exuberance of a holiday crowd that the groundlings hissed *Sejanus*. The new play was built on a plan too classical for their liking. The actors spoke of violence, but omitted to heap the stage with their victims. The bloodshed was remote and literary, and the groundlings shouted their disapproval. Only the small intellectual minority applauded. But Jonson could find comfort for the masses' abuse in contempt for the masses' mentality; and had popular disapproval been the only sequel to *Sejanus*, he would have suffered nothing more serious than disappointment and a fit of reasonable spleen. But a graver codicil was added when he was accused before the Privy Council of propagating seditious ideas. It appears unlikely to us, and it must have astonished Jonson, that evidence for such a charge could really be found in this model play, so lofty in every mood, so disciplined in its crises, and as impeccable a transcript from history as hourly reference to Tacitus could make it. But Sejanus, its hero, was a traitor, and Jonson, its author, a Papist.

There was the pretext for an accusation against him. And the cause of its lodgment? The cause was the enmity – once again – of Lord Henry Howard. The reason for his enmity was a thrashing Ben had given to one of his servants. Why the fellow got a beating we do not know, but for his master's sake we may hope that his ribs were left tender, his bruises unsightly and painful, and his wounds loth to heal.

For Lord Henry had not spent his anger when his man was disgraced, but kept it till he might use it profitably – his venom, being cold, did not lose strength – and now he saw such an opportunity in *Sejanus*. Lord Henry, like Jonson, was a Catholic; but he kept his religion hidden by a screen of anti-Catholic activities, and saved his private faith by persecuting those who practised it openly. It would nicely cloak his real sympathy to discover some Roman treason in a stage play; and how exquisitely the sight of Ben beheaded, or even Ben in prison, would mollify his fretted pride. When he thought of that mannerless poet in his rough black jerkin, Lord Henry felt his mind contracting with malice, as though the blood were drawn from it to feed some hateful tumour. The huge wen that, in like manner, had starved his shrivelled thigh, itched in sympathy. He re-read *Sejanus* – he had procured a manuscript copy – and marked another passage. *There* was treason, *there* incentive to riot, *there* popery. He read false meanings everywhere and sedition between the lines, and with currish exultation brought Jonson before the Council.

The prosecution, however, failed to establish its case, and Ben, after only a brief twilight of suspicion, escaped official displeasure. But the twilight, transient as it was, lasted long enough to obscure his claim to make a New Year masque for the Queen. After his success at Althorp he would almost certainly have been chosen had not Lord Henry intervened. But now instead of him the poet Daniel was honoured, and Daniel was a mere rhymer, a man with a mellifluous and serviceable tongue perhaps, but without learning and certainly without those theories of his art which Jonson professed. With a kind of candour he had actually defended his ignorance by attacking the classicists. Oh, an honest man, Ben admitted, but no poet and not much use to his wife. It was mortifying to see him honoured with so notable a commission. . . .

Some weeks before Christmas, Anne with her ladies began to cut up the enormous wardrobe of her predecessor to make costumes for the masque. Elizabeth had left two thousand gowns 'with all things else answerable,' and the new Queen found in this gorgeous heritage everything she wanted for *The Vision of the Twelve Goddesses*. . . . With little gasps of delight and constant exclamations of excitement, the ladies plundered the inexhaustible store, holding for each other's admiration shimmering treasures of silk, the heavy softness of velvet and brocade sewn stiffly with uncounted jewels.

Here were thick satins, and cambric night-gowns embroidered with black silk, and gowns of figured velvet. Here were the farthingales, canvas domes sparred with cane or whalebone, that had held out the Queen's skirts for Leicester's admiration – some were as old as that – and here the doublets, rigid with steel, into which she had forced her body for Monsieur to wonder at. Here was a fan of red and white plumes, its gold handle bright with diamonds, that Drake had given her. Now someone found a kirtle with Venetian gold lace and seven buttons like the birds of Arabia, that Lord Audley had offered his mistress one Christmas-time; and lying under that was a petticoat of white satin whose broad edges were fairly embroidered with snakes and fruit: this had been a present from Francis Bacon, and in return he got a piece of gold plate weighing thirty-three ounces. There, all piled together, were the silk purses in which her lords and ladies had given her £10 in dimy sovereigns or £15 in angels; and here was a hat of tiffany with twenty-eight gold buttons and eight of other metals, stitched round the band and up the feather. Perhaps it was a petticoat of yellow satin, fringed with silver, silk-lined with tawny sarsnet, that now caught the Queen's eye; perhaps it was that velvet suit powdered with pearls that Lady Mary Howard had once worn – but once only, because of Elizabeth's jealousy – and then, to expiate vanity, given to her envious mistress; perhaps Margaret Ratcliffe's embroidered satin, cut upon cloth of silver, that cost £180, had found its way into that omnivorous wardrobe; poor Margaret –

'Rare as wonder was her wit,
And like nectar ever flowing' –

and long before her wit grew tired, or her gown faded, or she old, her brother was killed in the Irish wars and she, a tender soul, grew pale at the news, and before long died of the wound her love had taken. And now, perhaps, scissors ripped open the seams of her famous dress, and the cloth of silver was reshaped for Iris's wear, or Juno's, in *The Vision of the Twelve Goddesses*.

Daniel's masque was to have been presented at Hampton Court on Twelfth Night, but an unfortunate *contretemps* arose when the French Ambassador intimated his intention of being present. For the

Queen had already invited Señor Juan de Tassis, the representative of Spain, and to have both ambassadors and their followers at the same masque was to endanger the festivities with bloodshed. James was in a predicament from which he happily emerged by offering the Frenchman inferior entertainment – dinner and an exhibition of Scotch sword-dancing – on the important date, and postponing the major entertainment and his Spanish guest to a night of no particular significance. An air of diplomatic triumph, then, pervaded the Great Hall as the masque entered – but Jonson, who was among the guests, had his ears open for solecism or absurdity in Daniel's verse, and beside him stood his friend Sir John Roe, a soldier, a duellist, a good fellow, something of a poet too, and ready now to back Ben's opinion against the whole court.

At the far end of the Hall a stage mountain had been built, and at the other one could recognise Somnus sleeping in a cave. The action began when Night, in a dark star-set gown, entered from a hidden door and roused her son. He, waving a white wand, caused a curtain to be drawn that uncovered a temple with a Sibyl attending the sacrifices within. (Daniel had felt some qualms at the dramatic impropriety of showing Sleep awake, and compromised with his conscience by dressing him in black and white to admit confusion of thought.) Now running down the mountain comes Iris, the messenger of Heaven, to say the goddesses are coming, and to give the Sibyl a perspective-glass through which she may descry their features and report upon them to the audience. But when the Sibyl opens her mouth she seems more like a simpleton than the interpreter of oracles. 'What have I seen?' she asks, putting the glass to her eye. 'Where am I? or do I see at all? or am I anywhere?'

Lord Suffolk, the Lord Chamberlain, looked round with displeasure at the courtly crowd. From somewhere in the press of spectators, so gorgeously clad in satins of every hue and velvets most tropically dyed, a loud and scornful laugh had sounded. Heads turned towards it, twisting in their ruffs, and following the direction of their eyes the Chamberlain saw two men, bold and dark of countenance, one dressed at variance with the mob in common black, the other in the very extravagance of fashion. They were laughing still. He recognized them as Sir John Roe, a soldier lately home from the Netherlands or Russia; and the poet Ben Jonson, recently a subject of the Privy Council's attention. He frowned, and pondered, and divided his attention between them and Her Majesty, presently descending from the mountain.

The Queen had chosen to represent Pallas, and appeared helmeted, clad in a blue mantle short enough to disclose a presentable leg, and embroidered in silver with weapons of war. She carried a spear and shield. It was a truculent disguise for the consort of a peace-loving King, and James, sipping his wine, considered her with a dismal eye. While satyrs on the hill sounded a march her ladies followed, and the tedious Sibyl described them in dull quatrains. In spite of the Queen's spirited demeanour the masque proceeded somewhat heavily to its culmination in a dance – but before that there had been another interruption. Jonson and Roe had laughed again; perhaps at Daniel's commodity verses; perhaps because Venus wore a Girdle of Amity instead of her cestus – room for a timely jest there; perhaps Diana was not so chaste as the Sibyl said she was; perhaps the mountain shook. Who knows? But whatever its cause laughter so halely issuing from such robust throats was a destructive thing, and the Lord Chamberlain, pushing through the crowd, spoke sternly to the unruly poet and the noisy soldier, and finding them unrepentant ordered them to leave the Hall. It was Suffolk's brother who had brought Jonson before the Council, but Suffolk was a bolder man and a more dignified man than Lord Henry. He was capable of direct action. When the poet and the soldier still protested their right, their bodily obligation indeed, to laugh at what was laughable, he argued no more but beckoned assistance and promptly had them thrown out.

They were not unmanned by the insult. They were, on the contrary, rather pleased with themselves. They felt exhilarated by a tussle with authority, and they knew that everybody had heard them laughing at Daniel's rhymes. They laughed again, listening to the faint music of lutes and viols, and hearing the murmur of the dance. The night was fine, and the starlit convexity of the sky, so disciplined and so remote, induced in Roe a fine philosophical attitude to the oppression of superiors. It was a cosmic law, a commonplace in nature – and who cared? All suffered alike. 'God threatens kings, kings lords, as lords do us,' he said, and the cheerful noise of a galliard fortified his words.

CHAPTER XII

THE FRIENDLY KING

In March, 1604, Raleigh and his fellow-prisoners were removed from the Tower and lodged temporarily in the Marshalsea and other prisons, in order that their apartments might be occupied by members of the Royal household. Soon every walk and corridor filled with courtiers and the King's domestics. There was no room for prisoners. Only the lions were left undisturbed, and the destruction of their peace was imminent. . . . Presently from the Lion Tower issued sounds of jungle fury, and a mighty baying of dogs. There came a roar so terrible that it seemed to shake the earth, and the courtiers looked round with curiosity not wholly unperturbed. Their calm was restored, however, when they learnt that His Majesty was amusing himself by matching with the lions some mastiffs from the Bear Garden.

The King and Queen, with Prince Henry, had taken up residence in the Tower prior to their triumphal progress through the City and the completion of some coronation ceremonies that the terrifying epidemic of the previous year had made it necessary to postpone. On the day after his arrival the King created Lord Henry Howard Earl of Northampton, and discovered the presence of the lions, in which he showed great interest. Someone told him that English mastiffs equalled in courage any lion ever cubbed. The royal eye grew bright, the royal nose smelt sport immediately, and the royal Scotch voice bade Alleyn the actor, who was also Master of the Bear Garden, fetch speedily but in secret three fell dogs. A glorious battle followed, that James directed in person. The dogs were hideously mauled, but the two lions were bitten so about the face, and so shrewdly in the belly, that their roaring made the ground quiver and finally they fled to the safety of their dens. Then two of the mastiffs, wounded and bloody but still pugnacious, turned on each other and fought anew. These two ultimately died, but the third, who had conducted himself with a happy combination of skill and ferocity, recovered from all his hurts, and by the Prince's command lived peacefully the rest of his life in Alleyn's particular care.

After this diversion the King submitted to the welcome of his loyal city with great patience and good humour; though he had little of that love for popular acclaim and the contiguity of the multitude which his predecessor had so fortunately possessed. In the hunting-field the presence of enthusiastic spectators particularly annoyed him, but for such an occasion as this the plaudits of the mob were not wholly unwelcome, and he endured them graciously.

The royal procession was marshalled with pomp and the elaborate ritual of precedence. Gentlemen and esquires, sewers, chaplains having dignities, aldermen, secretaries of the Latin and French tongues, carvers and cupbearers, the Lord Chief Justice, the Master of the Jewel House, Knights of the Garter, Barons of the Parliament, the younger sons of a marquess and the firstborn of Earls – these and dignitaries of fifty other degrees, in a scale of ascending greatness, preceded the King, who, mounted on a white jennet, rode under a canopy carried by the Barons of the Cinque Ports, with pensioners and Equerries of the Stable on either hand, the Earl Marshal in front of him, and the Master of the Horse, leading a spare horse, behind. Then came the Queen, with more pensioners, gentlemen ushers, footmen, ladies according to their rank, and the Maids of Honour; the Captain of the Guard (less splendid than Raleigh in his silver armour would have been), the Guard itself, and lastly a cheerful ever-changing mob of devoted sight-seers, following the progress like a turbulent excited wake.

Between the Tower and Whitehall there were seven triumphal arches to pass under, and a great variety of pageants to witness. Loyal speeches and leal songs must be heard, and when the royal ears were idle or listening only to the crowd's applause, the royal eyes, if they did their duty, were unriddling a score of allegorical devices.

Jonson and Dekker were both employed by the City to contrive literary ornaments for the ocasion, not orations and ditties only, but pageants of recondite significance such as would flatter a bookish king by their knowing bookish appeal. Here, by happy chance for a learned poet, was a king who would

recognise a quotation from Martial or Claudian, and
the pageants in Fenchurch Street and the Strand,
both of which Ben designed, were riddles whose clues
lay deep in classical authors. There was a figure of
Thamesis, the river, in a skin-coat that resembled
blue naked flesh. His mantle was water-colour, thin,
borne out like a sail; about his wrists were bracelets
of sedge and willow, and on his head, loosely circling
his long hair, he wore a crown of reeds and water-
lilies. Did James apprehend the allusion to Virgil's
description of Tiber in the Eighth Book of the Aeneid?
Perhaps not. But when he read Jonson's pamphlet
(a kind of guide-book that Ben published for the
occasion) he would find the description of Thamesis
neatly buttressed by the appropriate quotation, and
would doubtless appreciate the interesting parallel.

Beyond question he was gratified by a speech of
Genius Urbis, who declared he had brought

'Sweet Peace to sit in that bright state she ought,
Unbloody or untroubled; had forced hence
All tumults, fears, or other dark portents
That might invade weak minds; had made men see
Once more the face of welcome Liberty!'

James was entirely sincere in his ambition to be a
peacemaker, and to maintain so stoutly as this that
his succession had already borne pacific fruit, could
not fail to please.

When, however, the progress at last reached the
Strand, the King and those with him were so weary of

praise and spectacles and the shouting citizens, that they hurried on without listening to the prophecy spoken there. It was, perhaps, more prayer than prophecy, for though Ben hardily used the indicative, it was only the indicative of exalted hope. 'This shall be,' he says boldly; 'Would that it might!' he means.

> 'The dam of other evils, Avarice,
> Shall here* lock down her jaws, and that rude vice
> Of ignorant and pitied greatness, Pride,
> Decline with shame; Ambition now shall hide
> Her face in dust, as dedicate to Sleep,
> That in great portals wont her watch to keep.
> All ills shall fly thy light; thy court be free
> No less from Envy than from Flattery. . . .'

James rode on without hearing. He was thirsty. His plumed hat, a size too small for his massive head, was growing heavier and heavier, and his ears were tired of the unceasing noise. He rode on, with Avarice and Pride, Envy and Ambition pacing before and behind him, and flatterers meditating, while their eyes looked blankly at the shouting spectators, new compliments for the pleasure of their master. The prophecy, nobly conceived, was stillborn and born unnoticed.

Jonson believed, almost as firmly as James himself, in the divine right of kings, and he was equally convinced they should rule in such a manner as constantly would bear witness to their authority. He

*In James's Court.

flattered James, but his flattery had often the warning
note of a priest addressing an untried god, for Jonson
knew that God, in His infinite wisdom, had made
many bad kings, and in His equally infinite mercy
suffered His common people to dethrone them. The
divine right did not exclude a compensatory right of
criticism; and who more fittingly than a poet should
voice that criticism? In his panegyric on James's
first opening of Parliament, which took place four
days after the triumphal progress, Ben pays his
sovereign compliments enough for any king; but
they are compliments spoken outright, not with a
crooked knee or courtier's tongue, but in the sturdy
voice of an honest well-wisher, who feels that good
advice will not spoil the flavour of his praise. He
bids James think that the actual possessions of a king
are no more than those of a private citizen: only
his responsibility is greater. He cautions him not to
rejoice too much in popular acclaim, and reminds
him of the fierce curiosity that surrounds a throne.
He remembers (with some misgiving for divine right)
the pride and independence of Englishmen, and
warningly suggests:

> 'that those who would with love command
> Must with a tender, yet a stedfast hand,
> Sustain the reins, and in the check forbear
> To offer cause of injury or fear;
> That kings by their example more do sway
> Than by their power, and men do more obey
> When they are led, than when they are compelled.'

Flattery so salted is Jonsonian flattery, far removed from adulation; and when he writes his last line:

'Solus Rex et Poeta non quotannis nascitur,'

it is the frank courtesy of a poet secure in the generosity of his own genius that prompts this salute to a royal versifier.

It was flattery, moreover, that would surely recommend its author to the King, for James was by no means the fool that reputation calls him – though he had his weaknesses. He was inclined to prefer unconvincing flattery to no flattery. He had scarcely the bluff heterosexuality of the Tudors. He believed in peace, and very stubbornly worked to promote and maintain peace, though both his countries had a costly genius for war. And in England the peace-maker is naturally suspected of folly or fear. But James rode his horses to a standstill; and sound behaviour in the hunting-field will quit any man, in England, of the suspicion of cowardice; so a legend of his folly began to grow. It is true that he had a bawdy Scotch humour, and loved to laugh. It is true that he had ideas about translating the Psalms in metre. It is true he was extravagant with the nation's money, and wasted on sport time that might have been spent better in council. And it is true that he trusted the word of a Spanish ambassador. . . . Perhaps, after all, he was a fool? And yet if all are to be labelled fools who laugh at bawdry, who waste time and money, who nurse quaint literary ambitions, and are misled by foreign diplomacy, England must be rechristened Gotham, and the rest of the world Bœotia.

But though his judgment of men was not always reliable, James had an eye for literary merit – an eye that Ben further opened with his epigram *To the Ghost of Martial:*

> 'Martial, thou gav'st far nobler epigrams
> To thy Domitian, than I can my James;
> But in my royal subject I pass thee,
> Thou flatter'dst thine, mine cannot flattered be.'

The dexterity of this quatrain can scarcely have eluded the King's discernment, and as he was a genial man it is unlikely that he concealed his appreciation of it. His dignity was a loose gown, easy to throw off, and Jonson, when he was presented, found him ready to talk, to bandy quotations, to establish his position as a scholar rather than parade the eminence of his majesty. He may have asked Ben (as he asked Sir John Harington, the old Queen's godson) 'Should not a king be the best clerk in his own country? and does not England entertain good opinion of my learning and good wisdom?' He may have quizzed him on Aristotle – as he quizzed Sir John, to Sir John's dismay – and gravely discussed the uses of philosophy. They may have talked about witchcraft. James, by reason of personal danger from them, was interested in witches, and he frequently pondered why the Devil so often used old women for his agents. Ben recalled Lucan's Erichtho and Horace's Canidia. They agreed that woman's propensity for evil was no new thing, and discovered, from classical to modern times, how conservative was magic in its use of black lamb's blood, the fat of slaughtered infants, and the spurging of a dead man's eye. Ben had a favourite passage in Lucan, that described Medea's rites. It began *Nec cessant a caede manus.* James was interested in the picture of a ghoul at work . . . .

And then he spoke of the detestable weed tobacco that, six or seven years ago, was grown for a rarity (with potatoes to rival its strangeness) in Lord Burghley's garden in the Strand; and now made the whole town stink, and filled its users with such wicked vanity they might spend three or four hundred pounds a year on their pipes, and sometimes smoked themselves to death. Jonson agreed with the King in condemning tobacconists and all their ways. Smoking, he found, impaired his palate, and the flavour of Mermaid sack was not to be bartered for any Indian weed. The foppery of smokers, too, their fads and affectations, seemed contemptible to him: they boasted of filling their lungs in London and venting smoke at Uxbridge, and called such madness the Cuban ebolition, the euripus, or whiff! 'I can well remember who brought in the stinking habit,' said James, and Ben, thinking of Raleigh in the Tower, was silent. 'Englishmen,' said the King, 'have ever disdained to imitate France or Spain. Will they now imitate these beastly Indians, slaves to the Spaniards, refuse to the world? Then why do we not also imitate them in walking naked?' He laughed loudly at this droll *impasse*. He had a Scotsman's love for destructive argument. . . .

Ben, he found, disapproved of corporal punishment, and the King, remembering his old tutor Buchanan, who had beaten in Latin with a tawse, once more agreed with his poet. He felt his heart warming to Ben, and considered showing him some verses (the translation of another psalm) that kingship still gave him time to write. And then he remembered the proud poet Philoxenus, whom the Tyrant Dionysius of Syracuse had sent to work in the quarries because he would not praise his master's indifferent odes. Dionysius gave him a second chance; summoned him from the rock; showed him a new batch of poems. Philoxenus glanced at them. '*Reduc me in latomias*,' he said. 'Take me back to the quarry.' And Jonson looked as proud as Philoxenus. 'Send me back to bricklaying,' he might say. So James conquered his impulse and sensibly made another joke. Their talk grew jocular. There was a story Ben used to tell about a painter who could paint nothing but roses, and when besought by innkeepers to make a new inn-sign, would tell them: 'A horse was a good one, and so was a hare, but a rose was above them all.' James also knew some humorous anecdotes. . . .

In a little masque presented some six weeks later Ben's tone is pleasantly familiar, as though he knew what liberties he could take.

The masque, called *The Penates*, was presented by

Sir William Cornwallis at Highgate on the first of May. Sir William was a man of some wealth and rather less principle. He had a fancy for entertaining royalty, and his house was sufficient for the purpose; both in the amenities of his garden, which provided a suitable stage for the first part of the masque, and in the richness of his table, that providently warmed the air for the more intimate humour of the second.

It was May Day, and Ben's voice, that on occasion was loud and harsh as winter, may seem unapt for such an occasion. But his sweeter strain had once or twice been heard already, and it would be heard again, often enough, before at last it was strangled by jealous Inigo. It is strange that a satirist of such massive power could turn at will to lyric measures, and sing in easy numbers. Perhaps Ben found it strange himself, for constantly he excuses his lyricism by producing a Greek precedent for it, as though pretti-ness should be pardoned him because the ancients too sang pretty songs. Now at Highgate he welcomed the King and Queen in verses charmingly consonant with a spring morning, and yet took care to show that vernal jollity, like all else of worth, had a classical pedigree. Even when dinner was over and Pan let loose to make more boisterous fun, Mercury, as *compère*, had to acknowledge with a perfunctory blush that this scapegoat deity was his son. No unfathered child of a romantic mind, be it noted, but the authentic offspring of the god, begot in a hairy frolic upon the fair Spartan Penelope. Nor till it was shown thus that he had been duly entered in the studbook of classical mythology was Pan allowed to mingle with the official guests, but then the licence proper to an accredited lord of license was permitted him.

He brought wine to the King, to the Queen, to their lords and ladies. He rallied the King and chaffed the Queen and made ribald allusion to the connubial felicity of a countess. A Queen who, being born in Denmark was born to drink well, and a King who preferred hunting to love! Pan laughed, and turned to mock a poor lady whose husband was too old for her, and another for drinking with the miminy lips of a citizen's wife. He knew Court gossip, and he was not afraid to use it for his rhymes, so completely at his ease was Ben. He was more sure of his courtly audience than he had ever been of a common one. It was the audience he had wanted when he had tried, in vain, to storm the walls of Elizabeth's household. It was an audience of noble birth, whose master had a taste and a talent for literature, and whose untidy geniality gave to his Court a looser fabric than Elizabeth's: a fabric of so ample a weave that not only slim adventurers, but even so broad-shouldered a poet as Ben, might enter without straining it.

By the end of the year he had made his position very secure with the first of his Christmas masques. The Queen had a fancy to blacken her face, and she called Ben to her to see what Ethiopian fable he might contrive. Taxing his memory a little, he recalled that such authorities as Pliny, Solinus, and Leo the African, had written of the river Niger, and declared the people of its banks to be the blackest nation on earth. On this base, built so firmly by classical authority, he raised a fable of his own invention, according to which the daughters of Niger, growing tired of their dark complexions, sought through the world a way to lighten their swarthy beauty, and found it at last under the tempered sunlight of Britain – a name which the Union had newly re-established. The Queen was satisfied with this amiable fiction, and preparations for the masque proceeded.

It was a busy winter at Court, for there were disputes about the Union (then being arranged) so grave that the King's hunting was interrupted, and while domestic policy was being argued the ambassadors of France and Spain, with ceaseless distrust of each other, conducted their own sometimes elementary manœuvres. The Frenchman gave six fine horses, saddled and bridled, to the King, a golden helmet and a fencing-master to Prince Henry. The Spaniard had thriftily brought a supply of Spanish gloves with him, which he distributed among the Queen's ladies; and he bought a new town house for the Earl of Northampton. Then there were solemn ordinances promulgated to curtail the extravagance of the royal kitchens; and having made this economical gesture, the King spent a great deal of money with an easy conscience. The Queen was pregnant, there had been an apparition of war at Berwick, and to keep tongues busier yet the nuptials of Sir Philip Herbert and Lady Susan Vere were fast approaching. This important marriage was celebrated at Whitehall with a riotous combination of royal ceremony and such homely diversion as sewing people into sheets and pulling off the bride's stockings.

Meanwhile the Banqueting Hall was being transformed, under the direction of Inigo Jones, into an ocean-bordering landscape of wandering beauty. A great shell, like mother-of-pearl, rocked upon the waves, and far off, in a heaven of blue silk, a throne of silver for the moon was built. Sewing-maids worked busily on costumes of Inigo's designing for sea-nymphs and mermen, negroes and the daughters of Niger; while the Queen and her ladies rehearsed their dances, and two or three professional actors conned the stately verse that Ben had written.

Twelfth Night came, and Ben saw his masque presented with all possible splendour. Here and there some captious onlooker was affronted by the blackamoor faces of the Queen and her ladies, and found their airy costume immodest for such great ones; but the majority were well pleased with the strangeness and grandeur of the scene. The Spanish Ambassador sat with the King (his colleague of France stayed sulkily at home) and when he was taken out to dance, danced lustily in spite of his years, and showed no fear that kissing the Queen's hand might blacken his lips. The Ambassador's gallantry, however, was soon forgotten in the hilarious gaiety that succeeded the formal entertainment. Indeed, a certain extravagance of spirits became apparent as the evening wore on, and when supper-time arrived such a charge was made on the Great Chamber, where a banquet was spread, that all the tables were upset and the dishes broken before a pie could be broached.

This masque cost the Exchequer £3,000.

CHAPTER XIII

GUNPOWDER PLOT

HERO-WORSHIP has never been a characteristic of the English. Always a native selfishness, humour, or sense of proportion, or perhaps the national constipation, keeps enthusiasm well to this side of any fanatical regard. The more popular idols may establish a cult, but even they cannot start a crusade; merit may find an audience, but it will not recruit an army; and loudest applause may only mean that the mob is in holiday spirits.

The English had greeted their new king with demonstrations of fervent loyalty, but when the excitement of his southward progress was forgotten and the coronation pageants were faded, his subjects began to find pleasure in laughing at the royal accent and ridiculing the manners of northern courtiers. The admirable industry of the Scottish people, that has sent them pilgrimwise over all the earth in search of profitable Meccas, seemed to the English a humorous characteristic; but as more and more Scots arrived in London, English laughter acquired an angry note. Then the knighthoods that James conferred, with a cynical estimate of titular honour, for thirty pounds apiece, awoke derision, and by and by loyal vociferations gave way to a jest, and the honest red face of welcome wore an irreverent grin. The King's foibles and the peculiarities of his Scots lords were even represented on the stage, and mockery so daring naturally pleased many of those who saw it.

With little wisdom Jonson collaborated in such a play, though his part in its making was very small. The real authors were Chapman and Marston, and it was the latter, unruly as ever, who wrote the offensive lines that brought all three of them into danger. *Eastward Ho!* was a play of London life, a pleasant comedy in which Virtue acquired an alderman's daughter for reward, and a wicked apprentice trod the downward parallel to ruin. The collaboration of Chapman, Marston, and Jonson to such an end is curious, but Jonson's own realism had taught people to be interested in themselves. The eyes of wonder, opened by the Renascence and exercised by the romantic-geographic writers to see infinite oceans and courts beyond the sun, had grown so sharp they could now see marvellous riches in their own lives, and a rank world of humour in their neighbours'. Domestic comedy grew fashionable, and both the translator of Homer and the author of *The Scourge of Villainy* must have found that middle-class drama paid better than *Iliads* and satires; while Ben, to whom financial considerations were for the moment unimportant, may have been persuaded to assist by his regard for Chapman, and by way of acknowledging Marston's once-more proffered friendship. Crispinus had dedicated his last play to Ben. But Marston was a dangerous companion, and into their blameless comedy he wrote, with a snigger for one and a snarl for the other, two passages that angered a tell-tale knight, and through him the King.

There was first some discussion of the colonists in Virginia: 'Only a few industrious Scots perhaps, who indeed are dispersed over the face of the whole earth.' Harmless comment so far, but a couple of stings lay on its tail: 'There are no greater friends to Englishmen and England, *when they are out on't*, in the world than they are.' And as if that were not enough, there came the odious optative: 'I would a hundred thousand of them were there (in Virginia), for we should find ten times more comfort of them there than we do here.' Scots in the audience, thin-skinned and quarrelsome, felt their hackles rise, and glared umbrageous at their laughing neighbours. Followed a scrap of dialogue between two gentlemen. Said one, imitating James's accent: 'I ken the man weel, he's ane of my thirty pound knights.' 'No, no,' replied the other, 'this is he that stole his knighthood o' the grand day for four pound, giving to a page all the money in's purse, I wot well.' In the audience a knight grew red. Marston may have heard gossip, or innocently have been capping fools in space; this cap seemed to fit the hot forehead of a man called Murray, not long sir'd. The previous reference to his countrymen had made him peevish; now he buzzed like a wasp and presently ran to the King with his tale of insult to Scots and Scotland.

James gratified him by showing anger, but the

146

situation was complicated by the fact that one of the authors named was busy writing the Queen's masque. It was impossible to arrest Jonson without ruining the main item in the approaching Christmas festivities. And perhaps the King realised, in his wisdom, that the damage was done, the words had gone forth to many ears, and all the king's horses and all the king's men could do nothing about it. At any rate, ruffled as he was, he did nothing, and the playwrights might have kept their liberty had they not, in the following year, sent their play to be printed. When he heard this (Murray most likely brought the news again) James remembered his displeasure and, as print was graver than flying speech, ordered the imprisonment of the authors. Chapman and Marston were at once lodged in gaol, but for some reason Jonson's arrest was delayed.

He took characteristic advantage of the respite by voluntarily yielding to the authorities. His pride may have suggested – without foundation – that the King was showing him special lenience, and lenience may have looked no better than a bribe. True, it was not he who had criticised James's accent, but as a free man, as a somewhat contentiously free man, the right of criticism was his, and that right was not to be sold for any favour. His pride demanded that this should be made clear, and the passionate generosity of his nature insisted that friends should not suffer without him for misconduct in which he had a part: though to condone their indiscretion was all his part. He knocked at the prison door. With unexpected alacrity it opened, and without the formality of a trial closed behind him.

Such immediate acquiescence in his protestation of guilt astonished Ben, for though he had been eager to support his colleagues in their defence, and willing to suffer with them if necessary, he had not anticipated sharing with them a silent invisible martyrdom. Gaol had not even the attraction of novelty for him, and the weather was growing warm. Another circumstance more seriously provoked his anger, for by some obscure means Marston had vanished. Influential friends may have procured his release; or perhaps a warrant had been made out for two prisoners only, and when Jonson appeared the gaoler let Marston go. It is a curious story, not without humour, and though the precise explanation is elusive, the main facts are plain: the middle-aged respectable Chapman, and Ben as innocent as he, shared a gloomy confinement after the real culprit had regained his freedom. Nor was their lot made happier by a rumour that their punishment was to be mutilation, and they would likely leave prison without ears or noses.

Written under these conditions the letters in which Ben sought release, through the intermediacy of eminent friends, are restrained and dignified in tone. To Suffolk, the Lord Chancellor, he wrote as follows:

'Most honorable Lord:

'Although I cannot but know yor Lo: to be busied wth far greater and higher affaires, then to haue leysure to discend sodainlye on an estate so lowe, and remou'd as mine; yet, since the cause is in vs wholie mistaken (at least misconstrued) and y^t eurie noble and iust man is bound to defend the Innocent, I doubt not but to finde yor Lordshipp full of y^t woonted vertue, & fauoure; wherwith you haue euer abounded toward the truth. And though the Imprisonment itselfe can not but grieue mee (in respect of his Maiesties high displeasure, from whence it proceedes) yet the Manner of it afflicts me more, being commytted hether, vnexamyned, nay vnheard (a Rite not commonlie denyed to the greatest Offenders) and I made a guiltie man, longe before I am one, or euer thought to bee: God, I call to testimonye what my thoughts are, and euer heve bene of his Maiestie; & so may I thryve when he comes to be my Iudge and my Kinges, as they are most sincere:

'And I appeal to posteritie that will hearafter read and Iudge my writings (though now neglected) whether it be possible, I should speake of his Maiestie as I haue done, without the affection of a most zealous and good subiect. . . .'

He appealed to the Earl of Salisbury, to Lord d'Aubigny, to the Earls of Pembroke and Montgomery – those great twin brethren of the Shakespeare folio – and to some gentlemen of lesser name. He wrote to that spendthrift lady, a poet herself and the true friend of poets, Lucy, Countess of Bedford:

'Excellentest of Ladies.

'And most honor'd of the Graces, Muses, and mee; if it be not a sinne to prophane yor free hand with prison polluted Paper, I wolde intreate some little of your Ayde, to the defence of my Innocence, wch is

as cleare as this leafe was (before I staind it) of any
thinge halfe-worthye this violent infliction; I am
commytted and wth mee, a worthy Friend, one Mr.
Chapman, a man, I can not say how knowne to yor
Ladishipp, but I am sure knowne to mee to honor
you; And our offence a Play, so mistaken, so misconstrued, so misapplied, as I do wonder whether their
Ignorance, or Impudence be most, who are our
aduersaries. It is now not disputable, for we stand
on vneuen bases, and our cause so vnequally carried
as we are without examyninge, without hearinge, or
without any proofe, but malicious *Rumor* hurried to
bondage and fetters; The cause we vnderstand to be
the Kinges indignation, for which we are hartelye
sorie, and the more, by how much the less we haue
deseru'd it. What our sute is, the worthy employde
soliciter, and equall Adorer of youre vertues, can best
enforme you . . .'

And still there came no order for release. The
days passed. The prisoners sighed, and scratched
themselves. They listened to the muted crying
of London beyond the walls, and the mutter of prison
noises beside them. They fingered their noses that
might not long be left to finger. But as the white
monotony of light is broken by a prism, so this dull
idleness by genius was broken, and in the hot summer-
stinking gaol was conceived that superlative comedy,
The Fox.

It came in hot brilliant colour, vivid with jewels of
the Renascence, a play that danced with the muscular
vivacity of Harlequin, glittering still, and turned at

last Iniquity bottom-up for the smacking hand of a robust comic Destiny. It invaded like a peacock the grey squalor of prison. It laughed uproariously at human folly, and terribly at human greed. It was salt on the tongue, and spiced wine in the throat. Ben forgot discomfort and confining walls, forgot too the solemn good man who shared his captivity, and thought of Mosca gulling with such riotous invention the rapacious suitors for Volpone's wealth; thought of Volpone doctoring his lust in vain with gold and amber, the milk of unicorns and panthers' breath, and Cretan wines; thought of that splendid fool Sir Politick, the traveller agape for news and swallowing rumour as young starlings gobble worms – Sir Politick who agreed

'That your baboons were spies, and that they were
A kind of subtle nation near to China' –

nodded wisely indeed to confirm so knowing a suggestion, and amplified it with information of his own:

'Faith, they had
Their hand in a French plot or two; but they
Were so extremely given to women, as
They made discovery of all. . . .'

The order of release came at last. Suffolk or Salisbury, d'Aubigny or Lady Bedford, had spoken to the King, and the King had been mollified. Chapman and Ben walked out of prison with features unmarred, and to celebrate their escape Ben gave a dinner to his friends. Camden was there, and, it is likely, Richard Martin; perhaps d'Aubigny, perhaps young Francis Beaumont. Sir John Roe was fighting in the Low Countries, so he could not be present. But Donne may have been, for he was dividing his time between a small house at Mitcham, that grew uncomfortably full of children, and a lodging in the Strand more placidly filled with books. Cotton and Sir John Davies may have been invited – Selden was there – and Mr. Leech, who was Pembroke's secretary, and Mr. Bond, the Lord Chancellor's.

The most prominent figure at the banquet, however, was none of these, but an oldish woman with bright indomitable eyes and a heart as tough and sinewed with pride as Ben's own. Camden knew her. He had met her first at a cottage in Hartshorne Lane, and been gladdened by her staunch belief in learning. And her belief had been justified. She had lived to see Ben come into his own world of achievement. They had been right, she and her son, to scorn a common life. They had been right to waste their money on candle-light and Greek; to pinch and spend and quarrel with that blind mouth (honest grumbling man) the bricklayer: there was taller building and braver heights than brick could reach to. A thousand times they had been right, and her good womb was glad.

But she would not declare it in tears and softness, nor could if she had wished to. Her voice was harsh, and her pride flew out in a cackle of laughter when she stood up and drank to her son, and showed the table a screw of paper that, she told them, was full of a lusty strong poison. If noses and ears had been cropped, as the rumoured sentence threatened, she would have gone to prison and mixed that poison in Ben's drink. 'Ay,' she said, 'and for that I am no churl, I had minded first to have drunk of it myself!'

Her dark eyes shone, and her leathery old mouth shut tight as she looked up and down the board with humorous grim assertion. She was enjoying herself. She seldom had so good an audience as this, and, as her son did, she liked an audience. She was as true as truth's simplicity – but not too simple to be ignorant that truth sounded all the better when a score of ears were listening to it. She cut a brave figure, vaunting her true untender breast. In like manner had Spartan mothers loved, and pampered honour at the expense of their children. Had the King's clemency been withheld there would have been no more masques for Queen Anne, no *Fox* or *Alchemist* or *Bartholmew Fair*. But the King had been wise in time, and so the poison could be put by for rats. It was a Spartan comedy they played, not a Spartan tragedy.

Meanwhile, not far away, a melodrama was being planned in which Ben, all unknowing, was cast for a minor part. The principal actors were some Catholic gentlemen angered by the renewed enforcement of the penal laws against their Church. James, despite his love of peace, had spent too many years in pious dispute with the General Assembly to be tolerant in religious matters. And the offended Catholics had acquired for their stage a cellar beneath the House of Lords, into which they presently conveyed thirty-six barrels of gunpowder. The barrels were hidden beneath some coal and a few loads of faggots. In the cellar, ostensibly as a caretaker, sat Guy Fawkes, lately a mercenary in the Spanish service. About three o'clock in the afternoon of November 4, he was visited there by Suffolk, the Lord Chamberlain, and Lord Monteagle, who had lately received an anonymous warning letter. And the plot was discovered.

The news of this horrible conspiracy filled London with savage excitement. The Jesuits were immediately suspected of instigating it, and rumour went round that the whole body of Catholics had been consulted, and given their assent in return for a promise of general absolution from the Pope. The Jesuit Fathers Garnet and Greenway were arrested, and most of the active conspirators were run to earth in Warwickshire. They were said to bear an evil mark on their foreheads, and it was agreed that in company with such wretches Nero and Caligula were fly-killers. James was curious to see the prisoners, but he felt so appalled at the prospect of confronting them that he wisely forbore. Uneasily the Government began to probe for ramifications of the plot, and Ben Jonson did service to his country as a special investigator.

He was Catholic and patriotic. He was also under some obligation to the King – or to the King's counsellors – for the safety of his nose. The judicious Salisbury may have remembered this providentially rescued feature when the need arose for an agent with Romish connexions, impeccable loyalty, and some address. He may have summoned Ben and suggested the mission to him. Or Ben, stirred with all good Londoners to generous indignation, may have volunteered his services.

Whichever was the way of it, he received from the Privy Council a warrant and an offer of safe conduct, to and from the Lords, for a certain priest who was supposed to have valuable information. The priest was unnamed, and his lodging unknown. It was Jonson's task to find him and persuade him to speak. He went first to the Venetian Ambassador's chaplain, who, through the peculiar channels of diplomatic privilege, or by virtue of representing a Catholic power, might have heard more than other men. The chaplain was friendly, and gave his encouraging opinion that 'no Man of Conscience or any Indifferent Love to his Country' would refuse to do what Jonson wanted. He promised, moreover (and the witness whom Ben had sagaciously taken with him testified to this) to find a reliable man who would get into touch with the hidden priest. The Venetian Embassy, it seemed, was efficient as well as friendly. The chaplain found his man, but the priest had gone to earth and would not budge for all Ben's promises of safe-conduct. He stayed where he was and told nothing. So that line of enquiry was blocked. And wherever he went Ben found a like state of affairs. People with second-hand information talked readily, though vaguely, while the few with personal knowledge had fled and could not be found. But what Ben learnt was enough to convince him of the magnitude of the plot, and in his report to Salisbury he stated: 'I think they are All so enweaved in it, as will make 500 gentlemen less of the Religion within this week, if they carry their understanding about them. For myself,' he added, 'if I had been a priest, I would have put on wings on such an occasion, and have thought it no adventure where I might have done, besides His Majesty and my country, all Christianity so good service.'

There was, however, no such catastrophic conclusion as Ben predicted. Guy Fawkes and the Warwickshire men were condemned and died with the usual indecencies attendant on public execution. Father Garnet followed them to the scaffold, and his dead face pressing against the bloody straw left his likeness there – so it was said – as clear as that on Veronica's handkerchief. Over the other conspirators (if there were others) settled a cautious obscurity that lingers still.

Though Ben failed to unravel the mystery of the Gunpowder Plot, his endeavour to do so was remembered in his favour when he and his wife, a few months later, were summoned to appear before the Consistory Court of London on a charge of habitual absence from the Communion Table of their parish church. From the time of the Plot, in spite of his Popery, Ben had gone to church with some regularity. This was admitted by the informers. He went to show his hatred of Guy Fawkes and the brewers of Catholic treason. His engaging view that the religious life of England was a province of national sentiment rather than of God has had so many distinguished adherents that one need not trouble to apologise for his use of the altar to express loyalty rather than piety. He was an Englishman first and a Catholic second. And yet he was a Catholic, and so remained for six years more. Patriotism led him to the altar, but it could not make him drink. The Communion cup passed him by, and stoutly he maintained his intention to ignore it till his doubts of Anglican pretension should be dispelled. He was not bigoted. He was ready to be convinced if his parish minister or anybody else could show him proper reasons. 'As for my wife,' he said, 'for anything I know she hath gone to church and used always to receive Communion; and she is appointed to receive it to-morrow.'

He was also more gravely charged with being 'by fame a seducer of youths to the popish religion.' This he doubly denied. He had never sought to make converts for Rome, nor was this scandal current about him. He had given no cause for such a report, and hotly he demanded how the churchwardens or any other body could accuse him of it. He had in mind, perhaps, the previous machinations of Northampton, and Northampton indeed, whose enmity had never been appeased, may well have inspired this dangerous charge. There is a smell of his hand about it. The judge was puzzled, and ordered the churchwardens and the other witnesses who had presented Ben to appear in court on the first court day of the following term to particularise their accusation. Jonson was warned to be present, and in the meantime champions of the English Church were appointed to converse and argue with his stubborn soul. The Dean of St. Paul's was one, and the Archbishop of Canterbury's chaplain another. We do not know how often they met and debated upon doctrine, sacraments, and government, or what reasons Ben gave for his continued obstinacy. He may have been voluble in defence of his faith, or like Sir Andrew Aguecheek confessed, 'I have no exquisite reasons for't, but I have reason good enough.' The Dean of St. Paul's made no convert of him.

He was again presented on the charge of proselytising, and the case was again remanded, presumably for lack of evidence. On June 2 he was warned to await further proceedings, and asked to certify that he and his wife had been going to church with diligent regularity. The court was curious to know what progress he had made in his theological studies with the appointed champions. And after this there is no reference to Jonson in the records of the Consistory Court. The case was apparently withdrawn – perhaps on the authority of Salisbury – and the problem of the Bread and the Wine was left to Ben's own conscience. One may suppose that the Dean and the Archbishop's chaplain did not oppose this tactful evasion of the task they had been set.

CHAPTER XIV

FIGS AND THISTLES

ABOUT this time two visitors of very different natures arrived in London. One was a mild and rather melancholy young Scot named William Drummond, who some twelve years later was to be Jonson's host for a memorable fortnight in his house at Hawthornden. The other was Queen Anne's brother of Denmark. Drummond, who had newly left Edinburgh University to continue his studies on the Continent, came too late to see the enthusiastic reception of *The Fox*, but in good time to observe the extravagant arrangements for the King of Denmark's visit. He saw with interest the preparations for a court pageant at Greenwich in which the Earls of Lennox, Arundel, Pembroke, and Montgomery challenged the world in high, astounding, but not quite serious terms, to deny the four Indisputable Propositions:

'That in service of Ladies no Knight hath free will.
'That it is Beauty maintaineth the world in valour.
'That no fair Lady was ever false.
'That none can be perfectly wise but Lovers.'

Because the age of chivalry was over, an answer soon came that flatly denied these superb amenities and promised the sceptics would do battle for their lack of faith. King James was delighted, and everyone looked forward to an amusing combat. The King of Denmark, however, was late in arriving, and the tilting had to be postponed. He reached the Thames in July. Drummond thought him a man of goodly person and very like his sister. He rode with distinction in the tournament, wearing blue armour touched with gold, and the spectators applauded him generously. Ben's share in his welcome was some Latin verses, lonely in their austerity.

His month in England was thirty days of hard drinking, heavy feasting, untidy revels, and constant discharge of cannon. Up and down the Thames went the two kings, drinking each other's health while peals of ordnance, proclaiming their emptied glasses, startled the swans and drowned the lusty 'Westward ho!' of the watermen. At Greenwich, in the City, and at Theobalds, banquets were spread and amity, national and domestic, pledged in tipsy kindness. Men who were life-long abstainers till that time forsook sobriety and drank with Danish throats. At Theobalds after a great feast there was a pageant of Solomon's Temple and Sheba bearing gifts. But Sheba forgot the steps that led to the kings' dais and fell headlong into Christian's lap, spilling her caskets about the throne. He, laughing, got up and would have danced with her, but fell at her feet and once down could not rise again. So he was carried to an inner room and laid upon a bed of state, all smeared with cream and jelly and wine, the cates of Sheba's offering. A little later Faith, Hope, and Charity appeared to gratulate King James. But Hope was speechless and Faith reeled in her gait. Only Charity bore her gifts in safety, and to some extent covered the multitude of her sisters' sins. Victory and Peace followed these three, but Victory was tearful and Peace so angry that, when the crowd would not part quickly enough, she laid about her with a stout olive branch.

And still the cannon pealed, trumpeters blew for empty bottles, and drums beat to every toast. Cheerful Londoners crowded about the Court, and when the kings went hunting followed in noisy droves to fling their caps in the air. But graver minds condemned the royal folly. Even some who were no Puritans looked angrily at such heavy-headed revel, and frowned when new clamour told:

'The king doth wake to-night and takes his rouse,
  Keeps wassail and the swaggering up-spring reels;
  And, as he drains his draughts of Rhenish down,
  The kettle-drum and trumpet thus bray out
  The triumph of his pledge. . . .'

Drummond continued his journey into France, spent his time in picture galleries instead of study, and wrote home: 'Man is always a fool, except in misery, which is the whetstone of judgment.' In August King Christian sailed from the Thames, and the Queen wept to see him go. . . .

The Danish visit gave head to some unfortunate tendencies already apparent in the English Court. A kind of loose brilliance had begun to invade it.

Favourites acquired large estates, and intrigue flourished. Scots courtiers quarrelled with English, and the English lampooned the Scots. Vast sums were spent on jewels and weddings and wedding gifts, and foreign visitors were received with prodigal display: grandees of Spain, the Princes of Moldavia, Vaudemont, Hesse, and Anhalt, nobles of Portugal and the Rhine, were entertained in wanton generosity. £500 a year was spent on velvet coats for the palace guard, and £1300 for the royal shirts and sheets. The King's Embroiderer bought twenty ounces of small pearls for the King's saddle, and three hundred and twenty fair round pearls for his Majesty's hose. And the King went hunting at Royston and Newmarket, leaving Salisbury at home to find the money – his little beagle, whose shrivelled body was always full of pain – and while he hunted a thought would sometimes strike him that the Queen was unfaithful, and glum suspicion would elbow out all his good humour. The last-born princess had lived for a day only, and her two-year-old sister died a year later. But Anne controlled her sorrow, comforted herself with masking, and accumulated new debts.

Nor were Londoners, though they grumbled at the King's extravagance, more careful of their own money. The Puritans might rail and prophesy tribulation, but London was too rich to care. It bought feather-beds and Venetian silk curtains and pearl necklaces. Coaches grew as common, some said, as those who rode in them. Cooks flavoured their dishes with ambergris. Foreigners of many nations

came to sell their alien products and share in the
City's wealth, so that London bawds, twirling their
death's-head rings under the blind Cupids on their
doors, could count upon French, Dutch, Spanish, and
Italian customers to keep away impoverished captains
from Ireland and 'two-shilling Inns of Court men;'
and yet the best clients were honest English flat-caps,
who paid for their pleasure more liberally than any
foreigner. What was the use of saving? When the
weather grew warm again the sickness would come, and
the sickness took miser and spendthrift with equal hands.

Wealth multiplied, and Court and city flaunted
their luxury like ensigns against the June solstice of
recurrent plague. In this air, now perfumed and now
stinking of death, *Othello* was acted, the monstrous
passion of *Timon*, and the huger agony of *King Lear*.
For part of the year London might live fearfully
under the threat of plague, but for the other months,
such lust and life were in them, the golden shade of
Priapus, like a canopy, might have stretched from
Finsbury Fields to Southwark. Lurid history, roaring
comedy, bawdy interlude, and incessant poetry
flowed from Dekker and Middleton, Webster and
Drayton; Bacon's lean-fleshed essays swelled roundly,
and *The Advancement of Learning* was born (like Gargantua) with provisions for future growth; Burton
was gutting libraries for *The Anatomy of Melancholy;*
the springs of enormous invention were feeling for
issue in Beaumont and Fletcher. Mild-seeming Shakespeare, in whose bald head volcanic fancy threw up its
fertile continents, sucked for their procreant air the

163

heat and cold of London's crowded streets, and side by side with Shakespeare was Jonson, turning now with brilliant strength the antique machinery of tragedy to comic use. Their plays would never have been written in the doldrums of time, or a land with peace in its heart. Othello and Volpone came to life because intrigue, jealousy, and violence were at home in London, and London was glutted with gold and too proud for prose.

So also the Court and King redeemed their looseness and luxury by feeding art and literature, and while the King brittled his deer, scholars by his command worked diligently in Oxford and Cambridge and Westminster to make one true and lasting Bible out of the chaos of existing texts. The President of Corpus Christi College had first suggested such a work, and James, quick on a true scent as his good hound Jewel, instantly professed his dissatisfaction with every extant version of the Scriptures, and outlined a scheme for a uniform translation to be done by the best learned of both universities, reviewed by the bishops, submitted to the Privy Council, and ratified by his own royal hand. Let special pains be taken, he said, and wisely bade the translators refrain from adding such comments of their own as marred the Geneva Bible. So now, in the universities and elsewhere, nearly fifty chosen scholars, High Church and Low Church and laity working together, 'sought the truth rather than their own praise,' and often conferring together did not disdain 'to bring back to the anvil that which they had hammered.'

From so enduring a labour to the ephemeral art of the masque is a long step, and yet the masque, like dragon-flies, had a beauty more than sufficient for its brief existence; and that costly beauty was fostered only by the Court; and only a Court so given to prodigality, learning, and poetry could have employed such artists as Inigo Jones, Ferrabosco, and Ben Jonson for a short night's pleasure. To see the Palladian splendour of his scenery forgotten after an hour must have galled Jones sorely. Ferrabosco may have been more philosophical about his music. But Jonson, with characteristic fortitude, determined that the soul of the masque (which was his verse) should not perish in the quick oblivion that awaited its material parts, and spent his genius and learning on this frail vehicle as generously as on his largest tragedy.

Perhaps he was wasting his time. His masques have indeed survived their scenery, but rather, in the untouched privacy of libraries, like jewels in a Pharaoh's tomb. All unseen they retain the brightness of their humour, the polish of their wit, their lyrical felicity, and the deftness of their craftsmanship; but once unearthed and the first question is, for whom were they made? Plays that were written for common people live by their own virtue, but the *Masque of Queens*, *Oberon*, and the *Hymenaei* were made for courtiers; and posterity, when it bothers with them at all, is infected with a kind of cannibalism more interested in the dancers than the verse. But posterity is not so wise as the Lord, who delighteth in no man's legs. Even Ben was sometimes embarrassed to remember for whom his masques had been written.

With generous lines and gracious invention he celebrated the wedding of the Earl of Essex and Lady Frances Howard, the Lord Chamberlain's daughter: 'beautiful little Fanny Howard, of the beautifullest face and figure you would find in all these islands.' She was thirteen years old. Under a great golden crop of curly hair she looked with sidelong gaze at the extravagant splendour of her wedding. Her face was a demure and lovely oval. Her eyes, wide-open under arching brows, were darkly beautiful, but her eyelashes, of a scanty growth, were so fair as to be almost invisible. This gave her an expression of childish surprise and innocence that might be deceptive.

Ben played a small part in the masque himself, but it is unlikely that he thought much about the bride. It was no concern of his whether crooked or candid thoughts lurked behind the frank sweetness of her face. His attitude to women was very simple, and he preferred grown ones to girls. More interesting to him than Fanny Howard were his lines rising and falling to Ferrabosco's music, the splendour of Inigo's scenery, and even the gorgeous apparel of the masquers, in whose hair were such jewels, and on whose shoulders such ropes of pearl, that beside the plainest of them the Spanish Ambassador (old jovial reveller) seemed poorly clad indeed. But Jonson was wrong, for little Fanny Howard had a more eventful history than his verses, and when the dust lay thick on Jones's scenery, and the pearls had been re-strung for other necks, she wakened intrigue and passion and horror. Eight years later, when rumour was already itching, Ben wrote for her a new epithalamium, and of her second wedding was born a revelation of monstrous crime. But Ben was no crystal-gazer.

CHAPTER XV

THE MERMAID TAVERN

'A GOOD sherris-sack,' said Falstaff, 'ascends me into
the brain; dries me there all the foolish and dull and
crudy vapours which environ it; makes it apprehen-
sive, quick, forgetive, full of nimble, fiery, and delectable shapes; which, delivered o'er to the voice, the
tongue, which is the birth, becomes excellent wit.'

Drummond, after Ben had been his guest, considered
his depleted cellar and wrote moodily, 'Drink is
one of the elements in which he liveth.' To a temperate age that looks like disparagement, and for
disparagement Drummond (counting the cost of
hospitality) certainly meant it. But why should one
deprecate the enemy of vapours and the propulsive
fountain of wit? Does anyone blame Magellan for
adventuring in dangerous seas because a Cockney
clerk, ignorant of tides, upsets his boat on a Saturday
afternoon excursion? Strong drink, like the sea,
will drown a weakling, but the natural sailor may without wrecking navigate an Atlantic of wine. Ben was
such a happy one. And what coasts, unknown to
sober sight, must have made glad his eyes! What
kindness, wisdom, and pride inhabited his brain as he
snuffed the off-shore wind of alicant and muscadine,
claret, canary, and charneco! Sometimes he voyaged
in time, and one night, having weathered a great

storm, fetched to an anchor in bed and saw that his big toe had become the battlefield of Zama, on whose hot surface plunged Hannibal's elephants, Numidian horsemen charged, and against the stern wall of a Roman legion the Punic infantry broke in vain.

But drinking at the Mermaid, when the poets met there, was improbably so hearty as on that Carthaginian occasion. At the Mermaid 'nimble, fiery and delectable shapes' were fitter ornaments than the more extravagant vestments of Dionysian piety. Scholars drank with the wits at the Mermaid, and thus ballasted, the monthly voyage to Lanternland and the Oracle of the Bottle kept, it is likely, a fairly even keel.

Raleigh, who founded the club, was still in the Tower. He busied himself with his *History of the World;* or with a ship model for Prince Henry; or in his laboratory, condensing fresh water from salt, or compounding his Great Elixir; he talked to his fellow-prisoner the Earl of Northumberland, who was an amateur of astrology, alchemy, and other obscure sciences, and a passionate lover of tobacco. Men of learning visited them, and alchemists came to discuss their preposterous art in terms as strange. They spoke of *lac virginis* and oil of luna, of Hermes' seal and furnaces and reverberations in Athanor. Raleigh listened, and was interested; but no privileges could reconcile him to prison, and Northumberland's pipe smelt too strongly of Virginia for him to forget the western sea.

Perhaps the club lasted longer with him in prison

than it would have done had he been able to attend it, for he had an arrogant demeanour that might not have commended itself to Donne, for instance, or to the touchy assertive Inigo Jones. It is unlikely, indeed, that there was always an hilarious atmosphere when a session opened at the Mermaid; for Jones was splenetic, Shakespeare (in 1608) at the nadir of his pessimism, and Donne, poor and thwarted on every hand, had lately been on the brink of suicide. Men so concerned with the undigestible misery of life would not have been attracted by Raleigh's imperial bearing, at any rate before the sack had dried up their crudy vapours. Donne had made a little money by theological pamphleteering, but his brain was empty of poetry, and now he had been refused a secretaryship in Ireland because the King remembered with displeasure his elopement with Ann More seven years earlier; and Ann had just borne another child in poverty exacerbated by contiguous wealth, for Lady Bedford ('God's masterpiece' Donne called her) stood godmother to it. And Shakespeare was afflicted with a larger bitterness, for he who had loved the sweetness of life hated now mankind's profanation of it. He saw corruption in high places and a bestial stupidity in low. He looked at the Court and anger took him that 'men should wear a sword who wear no honesty;' he looked at the common people and found that he who trusted them trusted hares and geese. Shakespeare was sick of men's lying hearts, sick of their stupid flesh; and poor Inigo was troubled with a melancholy nausea that expressed itself in recurrent vomiting.

There was need, then, of good sack at the Mermaid, and when it had circled once or twice Shakespeare would remember the strawberries growing under the nettle, Inigo feel the warmth of it coming to his heart, and Donne recapture the brave mood in which he could write: 'When I must shipwreck, I would do it in a sea where mine impotency might have some excuse; not in a sullen weedy lake, where I could not have so much as exercise for my swimming.' And Ben's voice by then would be richer and more round, and his great spirit show itself not in his own wit merely, but in the revived and answering wit of others.

It is Shakespeare, Jonson, and young Francis Beaumont whom we first remember when we think of the Mermaid. We know so much about them, and yet how vain the attempt to reconstruct their familiar talk! It would be easier to carve a new head for the Victory of Samothrace; it would scarcely be more idle to bait with a fine young elephant a trap for unicorns; hardly more foolish to build a nest of hot and odoriferous twigs and wait for the phoenix to fly thither. And yet – for we know them so well – we may think about the quality of their talk. We may think of the language they used: not the awful sounds that affright us when their thunder strikes Parnassus' peak, nor the enormities of their most magnanimous imagination, nor the silken flexures of their courtly vein; not their loudest or their loveliest voices, but the middle notes they used to give Shallow words, or Mistress Merrythought, or to make 'a little winter love in a dark corner.' And when we consider small phrases and contemplate their littler words, we feel to some extent reassured and easy in our minds, for this is the language that men still use.

When Shakespeare writes:

'The hearts
That spaniel'd me at heels, to whom I gave
Their wishes, do discandy, melt their sweets
On blossoming Caesar; and this pine is bark'd,
That overtopp'd them all. Betray'd I am:
O this false soul of Egypt! this grave charm –
Whose eye beck'd forth my wars, and call'd them home;
Whose bosom was my crownet, my chief end –
Like a right gipsy, hath, at fast and loose,
Beguiled me to the very heart of loss,'

we admire, but we do not feel any particular consanguinity of thought with him. When Evadne, in *The Maid's Tragedy*, threatens the King:

'I am as foul as thou art, and can number
As many such hells here. I was once fair,
Once I was lovely; not a blowing rose
More chastely sweet, till thou, thou, thou, foul canker,
(Stir not) didst poison me,'

we respond with a special sensitivity that the play has awakened in us, but we find nothing comfortingly

172

familiar in Beaumont's thought. And in a similar
fashion when we read in *The Fox:*

> 'See, a carbuncle,
> May put out both the eyes of our St. Mark;
> A diamond would have bought Lollia Paulina,
> When she came in like star-light, hid with jewels
> That were the spoils of provinces. Take these
> And wear and lose them; yet remains an earring
> To purchase them again, and this whole state.
> A gem but worth a private patrimony
> Is nothing; we will eat such at a meal.
> The heads of parrots, tongues of nightingales,
> The brains of peacocks, and of estriches,
> Shall be our food, and, could we get the phoenix,
> Though nature lost her kind, she were our dish,'

we marvel at such heroic concupiscence, yet hardly
feel ourselves capable of sharing it.

We should let such passages colour our imagination,
but not expect them directly to promote a taste of
the Mermaid talk, for it is unlikely, when the wine
was before them and they were comfortably untrussed,
that Shakespeare cut his full harvest of metaphors,
or Ben voiced the huge voracity of poetic appetite,
or Beaumont spoke in hot envenomed beauty. To
get the flavour of their talk we should rather think
of Shallow's man Davy saying, 'I grant your worship
that he is a knave, sir; but yet, God forbid, sir, but
a knave should have some countenance at his friend's
request'; we should recall the dialogue between
Merrythought and Mistress Merrythought:

173

MISTRESS M: 'But how wilt thou do, Charles? Thou art an old man, and canst not work, and thou hast not forty shillings left, and thou eatest good meat, and drinkest good drink, and laughest.'

MERRYTHOUGHT: 'And will do.'

MISTRESS M: 'But how wilt thou come by it, Charles?'

MERRYTHOUGHT: 'How? Why, how have I done hitherto these forty years? I never came into my dining-room, but at eleven and six o'clock I found excellent meat and drink on the table, my clothes were never worn out but next morning a tailor brought me a new suit; and without question it will be so ever! Use makes perfectness;'

and we might remember stout Ursula in the heat of *Bartholomew Fair*, shouting for 'my morning's draught quickly, a bottle of ale to quench me, rascal! I am all fire and fat, Nightingale, I shall e'en melt away to the first woman, a rib again, I do water the ground in knots as I go, like a great garden-pot; you may follow me by the SS I make.'

This is no vintage stuff, but plain water; yet the

glasses are stained by the great wines they previously held, and while we drink we cannot close our eyes to the colour. The masters' tongues, it is true, wag cottage-talk as easily as the castle kind, and reading it we feel a great affection for the language – theirs and ours – that is so nimble, and sweet, and strong with honest easy strength. But they did not, and we may not, forget the idiom of the castle while taking our ease with the tenants. And they, the masters, had this advantage: that English in their day still had the flush of spring while it was ripening with the yield of autumn. It was like an orange-tree, that bears blossom and fruit together, and matching the seasons the masters were there to make garlands of the flowers and with the golden harvest of the other fill their wagons in the sun. Of a truth, no words but English words would have done for the Mermaid, to rumble with laughter in its oaken corners, and fly so cleanly in the lamplight, and share (not steal) the warmth of a sea-coal fire, and mingle in the ventricles of the brain with the subtle fumes of Castalian wine, and even to match, by excess of virtue, rude ale-blots on the table and comprehend the green humility of rushes underfoot.

The language they used, then, was a good easy one, stiffened by familiarity with a better, and the wit their words bodied forth had kinships that we can trace in their plays. There is so much that we know. But Shakespeare, Jonson, and Beaumont were only three in a round company, and we may not forget their friends: the amiable lawyer, Sir Richard Martin;

Selden and Cotton, learned men whose learning was
not of that jealous kind which would divorce them
from laughter and a good table, but in the overplus
of its zeal rather wed them (at least on certain Fridays)
to friendly bottles and the bliss of talk; and Christopher Brooke, who built no barns for his genius, but
spent it all on conversation, where it looked the gayer
for associating only with flyaway words that, like
wantons, had no wish for a home. Camden too would
be there. His scholar's ear was open harbour to all
knowledge, and he might listen, though none else
paid attention, to Inigo's enthusiasm for Italian art,
and accept his loud assertion of Palladio's supremacy;
or lean towards Donne to rebuke his heretic suggestion
that the worst voluptuousness was 'an hydropic
immoderate desire of human learning and language.'
But Donne, though he talked for company's sake,
was thinking of the £800 – his wife's *dot* – that his
father-in-law still owed him.

And there must have been others: Chapman, with
the *Iliad* changing in his head to swinging lines of
English; Michael Drayton, who was Shakespeare's
good fellow-countryman, and loved his patron's
daughter with such sweet sobriety; Sir John Roe,
perhaps, Ben's soldier friend, who spent his money
with royal profusion, a man whose wit had coarsened
with rude exercise in camps and yet retained a
lightness graceful enough to sing:

'Dear love, continue nice and chaste,
For if you yield you do me wrong;

Let duller wits to love's end haste,
I have enough to woo thee long;'

and Bacon – did Bacon ever go to the Mermaid? Did his lapidary brilliance sometimes glitter there more warmly than its wont? Did he ever sit in Raleigh's chair?

But there is no profit in adding puzzles of our own to that already baffling room, the room so loud with voices that we know and words that we cannot hear. If only Boswell had lived in time to attend the elder Jonson, what a book there would be in the world to-day! But there was no professional Ear at the Mermaid, no Pepys or Chamberlain, no gossip to spread its drolleries abroad. Of so many jests that were made, none has survived except a frail story that, when the poets amused themselves by composing each other's epitaphs, Shakespeare suggested:

'Here lies Benjamin
With little hair upon his chin,
Who while he lived was a slow thing,
And now he is buried is no-thing.'

So starlings fly off when a house is burnt. But nothing of worth escapes the door that echoed such richness beyond a tradition of wit-combats (livelier than this) between Shakespeare and Ben, in which the one, for his nimble use of every breeze, seemed like an English ship, trimly built, handled most sailorly; and the other, by his massive bulk and his fair huge sails of learning, looked like a Spanish galleon wafted on its way by favouring gales. It is a pretty comparison and in some ways it is likely a just one; though Shakespeare carried heavy metal for so small a craft, and Ben from his galleon did not disdain occasional popguns: his epigram, for instance, *On Cashiered Captain Surly* –

'Surly's old whore in her new silks doth swim.
He cast, yet keeps her well? No, she keeps him.'

But the comparison will serve. It makes a definite picture and we would welcome more such, for Beaumont's verses do not assuage but aggravate our wonder:

'What things have we seen
Done at the Mermaid! heard words that have
    been
So nimble, and so full of subtle flame,
As if that every one from whence they came
Had meant to put his whole wit in a jest,
And had resolved to live a fool the rest
Of his dull life.'

CHAPTER XVI

THE PASSIONATE SCHOLAR

DUELLING, imprisonment, violent controversy, and war make Jonson's early life more exciting than that of most poets, but under the pacific influence of success even Jonson lived for some years in physical uneventfulness. The period between his pursuit of treason after the sensational discovery of the Gunpowder Plot, and his scandalous visit to France with young Raleigh in 1613, shows nothing turbulent, and this calm did much to soften his truculence and something to increase his weight. They were not unimportant years, for in them his great comedies were written; but because his extra-literary activities were now social, instead of antisocial, the history of this time is not dramatic.

There is in Jonson's life none of the sentimental or pathological problems which have made other poets, from Shakespeare to Baudelaire, such attractive quarry for psychologists. You may hunt him from Hartshorne Lane to Whitehall, from Bartholomew Fair to Scotland, and your keenest hounds will get no scent of Œdipus, Ganymede, or the pale spirochaete. His genius lacked the *haut goût* of perversion or disease. He escaped the lurid stain of moral tragedy. His conflict with life was external rather than internal:

he fought stupidity, vice and folly and Gabriel
Spenser, but he had not to struggle with chimeras
of lost love or dragonish inhibition. Such inner conflict as he knew was intellectual, and intellectual
campaigns are unattended by the persistent odour of
a moral defeat – or victory. He had affairs with
women, some of which were curious, but his attach-
ments were so transient and so purely physical that
they left him uncankered and happy as a sailor in
his divagating love.

Not all his amours had the simplicity of perfect
success or that irresponsibility which depends upon
absence of contiguous and tangential relationships.
He was sometimes embarrassed and sometimes exasperated, but neither embarrassment nor exasperation
led to suspect malice in God's providence. Rather
he found entertainment in the diversity of God's
creatures. Once only did his anger at a woman,
for a womanly sin, cry deep enough and bitter enough
to need a voice on paper.

There was a Lady of the Queen's Bedchamber
called Cecily Boulstred, and known without kindness
as the Court Pucelle. Having no beauty she gave
much thought to her wardrobe and exerted herself
to be witty. Twice she had contracted to marry,
and twice decided not to. She grew hysterical, made
bawdy jokes in a mild little voice, and then gave up
loose company for priests, or rode to church with much
ostentation of new velvet and spangled petticoats.
Donne was her friend and thought her virtuous.
Sir John Roe was her friend, and had no such illusion.

He wrote verse to her of a kind men do not write to innocent women, but finishing a poem with 'Keep thou my lines as secret as my love,' balanced the implication of looseness by a compliment to her discretion. Ben, for some reason, she heartily disliked.

Now Cecily was a cousin of the Countess of Bedford, and to the Countess Ben paid poetic court as did also Donne, Drayton, and Daniel; for she was a lovely, spendthrift, witty, and magnificent lady, a friend to poets, an amateur of painting (she bought Holbeins at extravagant prices), and a hostess of princely generosity. Donne wooed her with passionate flattery and a reverent prolixity of compliment; Ben, with simpler art, celebrated equally her sweetness and starry beneficence. She, it is possible, was the Charis in that rare series of poems in which he tells, so gaily and so tenderly, of a love that kept its freshness for fifteen years. She, it is likely, played Venus in Ben's masque *The Hue and Cry after Cupid*, where in a scene obscure and cloudy 'on a sudden, with a solemn music, a bright sky breaking forth, there were discovered first two doves, then two swans with silver gears, drawing forth a triumphant chariot: in which Venus sat, crowned with her star.' And, if so, it was she of whom he wrote so exquisitely:

'Have you seen but a bright lily grow
    Before rude hands have touch'd it?
Have you mark'd but the fall of the snow
    Before the soil hath smutch'd it?

Have you felt the wool of beaver,
  Or swan's down ever?
Or have smelt o' the bud o' the brier,
  Or the nard in the fire?
Or have tasted the bag of the bee?
O so white, O so soft, O so sweet is she!'

And the Countess's cousin Cecily was neither rich
nor lovely. A soft voice, a little wit, and some fine
clothes were all her capital. And poverty makes one
critical, while jealously will sometimes, in a greenish
light, perceive most opportune absurdity. To see
Ben at Charis's feet, to hear a man so outwardly
rough moved to such delicate passion, may with
malice have sharpened her wit to an unwonted point.
At any rate (whether or not this was the occasion
for it) she criticised him, libelled and lampooned him,
in such stinging terms that he was stung to retaliate
– for her pasquinade was naturally reported to him
without delay.

His revenge was unworthy of him and without
dignity: yet a wasp, creeping below his armour,
would sting Bayard himself to unlovely antics. And
still Ben's anger was regrettable. He wrote an epigram
of some coarseness and no little brutality on the
unfortunate Cecily, and then very foolishly got drunk.
He had rid himself of irritation and he wanted to
forget it. But unhappily, while he was snoring away
the excess of sack, a false friend to whom he had shown
his verses took the opportunity of removing them
from his insensitive pocket, and carried them straight

to Mistress Boulstred herself. This mishap, as Ben gloomily remembered long after, 'brought him great displeasure.'

A year or two later Cecily Boulstred fell sick of a fever so extreme that her stomach (as Donne with melancholy exactitude wrote to his friend Sir Henry Goodere) would not keep down even a preserved barberry. She died in her cousin's house at Twickenham Park. Donne wrote for her an elegy of sombre and imaginative power. The Countess wrote another. And when Ben heard of her death he remembered his epigram and his conscience smote him, so that, while the letter-bringer waited at his door, he composed an epitaph whose handsome praise would have dried all Cecily's tears had they not been more safely stopped. She might, he said, 'have taught Pallas language, Cynthia modesty.' She might; but his discovery was too late to be of much use.

Both his repentance and his brutality, however, reveal something of his character. Drummond, ten years later, observed that he was 'passionately kind and angry,' and all three words are true. From the swelling vindication of poetry in *Every Man in his Humour* to the vibrant yearning for woodland beauty in *The Sad Shepherd*, there is passion in most of his work. The very thickness of scholarship which sometimes obscures it is due to his headlong love of books. And it is because his nature was so vehement, so whole-heartedly one thing or the other, that his characteristics so often stand opposed. Anger is contradicted by kindness, revenge by repentance.

Consider the imaginative ugly brutality of this passage from *The Fox:* Corvino, a legacy-hunter, believes himself to be the rich Volpone's heir. When Corvino comes to see what prospect there is of Volpone's death, Volpone feigns mortal sickness, while for his sophisticated amusement his inventive servant Mosca aids the deception by telling Corvino that Volpone is very near his end. His hearing has gone, and at last it is safe to say what they think of him. Mosca begins to abuse the horrible figure that lies so still, and encourages Corvino to follow suit:

> MOSCA:　Would you once close
> 　　　　　Those filthy eyes of yours, that flow
> 　　　　　　with slime
> 　　　　　Like two frog-pits; and those same
> 　　　　　　hanging cheeks,
> 　　　　　Covered with hide instead of skin –
> 　　　　　Nay, help, sir –
> 　　　　　That look like frozen dish-clouts set
> 　　　　　　on end!
> CORVINO: Or like an old smoked wall, on
> 　　　　　　which the rain
> 　　　　　Ran down in streaks!
> MOSCA:　Excellent, sir! speak out:
> 　　　　　You may be louder yet; a culverin
> 　　　　　Discharged in his ear would hardly
> 　　　　　　bore it.

Consider that, and contrast it with the tenderness of this epitaph on Salathiel Pavy, one of the Children

184

of the Chapel who had acted in *Cynthia's Revels* and
The Poetaster:

'Weep with me, all you that read
    This little story:
And know, for whom a tear you shed
    Death's self is sorry.
'Twas a child that so did thrive
    In grace and feature,
As Heaven and Nature seemed to strive
    Which owned the creature.
Years he numbered scarce thirteen
    When Fates turned cruel,
Yet three filled zodiacs had he been
    The stage's jewel;
And did act, what now we moan,
    Old men so duly,
As, sooth, the Parcae thought him one,
    He played so truly.'

He was 'passionately kind and angry.' There is
obviously not much room for pity in his plays, but
anger, though it no longer interrupts the action
with a personal voice, is deep in the humus of his
master comedies, nourishing their roots and supporting
their great structure. For this difference is apparent
between Shakespeare's comedy and Jonson's: that
Shakespeare's comic scheme is the restoration of
injured innocence to its proper happiness, but
Jonson's the discomfiture of foolish or vicious pre-
tenders. They are both magnificently on the side

of the angels, but while Shakespeare (in his comedies) plays the comforter, Jonson is retributive destiny. For *The Fox*, *The Silent Woman*, and *The Alchemist*, he borrowed the machinery of Greek tragedy, and his rascal heroes move to their catastrophe with the end-impelled pace of King Œdipus. Iniquity hoists its lurid colours – for the glamour of strong iniquity attracted the romantic part of Jonson's mind – only to be bleached by the noonday sun; and by night its flag has been struck. Even in *The Silent Woman*, (that Dryden called 'the pattern of a perfect play) where Ben's laughter is free and joyous, his mirth is still moral, and the wretched misanthropy of Morose is blown away on a gust of jubilant retribution.

His romantic inclination and the classical discipline he imposed on himself make another contrast. On the one hand are order, restraint, and measured form, *Sejanus* pressed between two volumes of Tacitus and Suetonius, and *Catiline*, that Ciceronian narration; and on the other hand is romanticism that finds in the masques a score of happy tongues to tell of nymphs and witches, satyrs and mermen. Even in the comedies this conflict of instinct and intention is visible, for while their structure conforms to the classical unities, the *dramatis personae* are rogues, heroic in stature, but romantic in conception. They are explorers in a world whose streets are lit only by the lightning of individual invention. They live – till a virtuous destiny puts them in bilboes – with the freedom of amorality, and that glamorous liberty is a romantic poet's thought.

186

PENTHESILEA

Design by Inigo Jones for Jonson's
Masque of Queens (Devonshire Collection)

And poetry was the major influence in Jonson's life. He drank as lustily as Silenus, made love as loosely as Lothario, and quarrelled with the readiness of Cyrano de Bergerac. But he drank, fought, and wooed out of the superfluity of his strength, and despite his vigorous pursuit of all three diversions he was always dominated by devotion to his art and the learning so inextricably woven into it. When the two universities showed their appreciation of *The Fox*, he composed for them a dedication that reaffirmed with noble vigour his faith in the divine nature of poetry; and when that paragon of royal youth, the Prince of Wales, asked where Ben had acquired the curious knowledge embodied in one of his masques, Ben set about retrieving his authorities with loving zeal.

The masque was *The Masque of Queens*, presented by Queen Anne and her ladies at Whitehall on the night of February 2, 1609. The main part of it was notable chiefly for Inigo Jones's scenery and dress-designing, but in an anti-masque of witches Ben had opportunity for poetry, and it was this that aroused Prince Henry's curiosity. For the technique of witchcraft was explained in some detail.

For his benefit Jonson made a fair copy of the masque and added to it pertinent extracts from his sources. The manuscript is still in existence. It is written with singular delicacy and great exactness in a small cursive hand. Surrounding the text are copious notes, columnar citation of authority, and invading wedges of transcription from Hesiod, Remigius, and

Lucan. Before the witches recite a charm their Dame commands them to bare their feet and knees. Ben quotes Ovid, Horace, and Seneca for this small rite. Perhaps Prince Henry might wonder if a troop of witches was really ruled by an elder witch or Dame? – Ben cited Delrio and Apuleius. Then the witches dance, and authority for such a habit is taken, with exquisite tact, from the King's own book on daemonology.

When the witches in *Macbeth* concoct their brew of Turks' noses, babies' fingers, and bats' wool, we feel – though none could deny the sufficient horror of the soup – that its recipe was the author's own invention. But when Jonson's witches put in the pot adders' ears, mad dogs' foam, the spurging of a dead man's eye, the sinew of a murderer, hemlock, henbane, deadly nightshade, moonwort and mandrakes, we know that this is the proper composition of witch-broth on the authority of Pliny, Lucan, Ovid, Porphyrie, Psellus, and others whose names are like the shadow of a Renascence library. One reference is seldom regarded as sufficient. When Pliny tells how to dig up mandrakes, that mysterious anthropomorphic vegetable, Ben notes that later experimenters found the operation so dangerous – for to hear the groan of a plucked mandrake is generally fatal – that they used dogs to uproot it; and this tip, he suggests, they got from Josephus when he paused in his history of Jewish campaigns to botanize upon the root *Bæœras*.

So much for mandrakes. The witch-custom of

killing children is too well known to need many
authorities: Paracelsus and Porta are enough to
guarantee that infant fat, boiled down, is a constituent
of the ointment witches use. But if you doubt, as you
may, their power to plant stars in the noonday sky,
to turn back rivers and make forests walk, to poison
the moon, bring fog, and without wind create tempests
on the sea, then Homer, Theocritus, Virgil, Tibullus,
and Horace are all massed in evidence against you. But
do not suppose Ben was credulous of any marvel.
Far from it. When one of the hags declares:

'We all must home i' the egg-shell sail;
The mast is made of a great pin,
The tackle of cobweb, the sail as thin,'

he adds for the Prince's information that such things
are merely an illusion of their fantasy.

An even better example of the glee with which
Jonson delved in obscure fantastic shires of learning
is offered by *The Alchemist*, the best of his plays.
Its appeal to the present day is unhappily impaired
by the comparative scarcity of alchemists in modern
society. There are a few, but not enough to make
an audience familiar with their methods. In 1610,
however, all London knew Simon Forman, who had
a lucrative practice in magic and sought the Philosopher's Stone, while many could remember Kelly
the alchemist, and Dr. John Dee, with whom Queen
Elizabeth had dealt, and whose house the mob had
burnt because his chemistry smelt of hell-fire. Sir

Giles Mompessom was soon to be granted a patent to manufacture gold and silver lace in 'a new alchymistical way,' and people *au fait* with Continental gossip were aware that the Emperor Rudolph II was already an amateur of the art. Alchemy, obscure in origin, mystical in theory, had grown strong in medieval darkness and still flourished in Jacobean London. Its practice, moreover, had long been part of the equipment of roguery. It was this circumstance – that says so much for the basic opportunism of man – which combined with its abstruse terminology to recommend it to Jonson.

Chaucer had written, in bitter detail, of an alchemist's trickery. Methods of producing the Philosopher's Stone are related, quite incomprehensibly, in Gower's *Confessio Amantis*, Ripley's *Twelve Gates of Alchemy*, Lydgate's *Secrees of Old Philosoffres*, Bloomefield's *Blossomes*, and possibly other works even more obscure. Their talk of calcination and fermentation, congolation 'of soft white things,' of exaltation and projection, of the Red Man and the White Woman and the Fiery Dragon, are the very lunacy of bewildered science. Yet Jonson dredged this mystical nonsense, with all its false analogy and meaningless vocabulary, and so digested what he found that he could handle his material with a kind of lavish dexterity, and even state a speciously convincing case for alchemistic theory. Then, taking Chaucer's way, he made his practitioners rogues, and rogues so consummate that in the thieves' kitchen of literature they must have their chairs at the table-top.

They blind their victims with the dazzle of imminent wealth; fill their ears with promise of the Elixir; noose them in whirling talk of calx, and Hermes, and oil of luna; overwhelm them with a recitation of sulphur, aludels, philosopher's vinegar, the peacock's tail, the red ferment, the magisterium itself; and bleed them white. As their dupes grow in importance so their knavery mounts to meet them, and their talents ultimately find expression in rooking Sir Epicure Mammon, that figure of inspired Marlovian gluttony. Only Ben could draw such rascals, and only Ben provide them with a victim whose stupendous appetite so clothed itself in poetry. 'My meat,' Sir Epicure declares –

'shall all come in, in Indian shells,
Dishes of agate set in gold, and studded
With emeralds, sapphires, hyacinths, and rubies.
The tongues of carps, dormice, and camels' heels,
Boiled in the spirit of sol, and dissolved pearl,
Apicius' diet, 'gainst the epilepsy:
And I will eat these broths with spoons of amber,
Headed with diamond and carbuncle.
My foot-boy shall eat pheasants, calvered salmons,
Knots, godwits, lampreys; I myself will have
The beards of barbel served, instead of salads;
Oiled mushrooms; and the swelling unctuous paps
Of a fat pregnant sow, newly cut off,
Drest with an exquisite and poignant sauce;
For which I'll say unto my cook, *There's gold,
Go forth, and be a knight.*'

191

The Alchemist was presented by the King's Servants in the autumn of 1610, another plague year that had seen London half deserted through the hot summer. There were those who disliked it – it satirized Puritans and laughed at simpletons – but in spite of a few hisses its performance was a triumphal occasion. Its superb craftsmanship, its wit and brilliant poetry, its incisive characterization, were alike indisputable, and all Ben's arrogance was justified.

Two hundred years later Coleridge coupled it with *Œdipus Tyrannus* as having one of the three best plots in literature. It is a pity that Ben could not have heard this handsome judgment, but it is pleasant to think he may, unaided, have come to a similar conclusion.

CHAPTER XVII

A MALIGNANT MOON

ON some hospitable occasion at Theobalds, Jonson found that his place at table was below the salt. It was indeed at the very foot of the board beside Inigo Jones. His displeasure at this slight may have been audibly expressed. It was, at any rate, sufficiently apparent in his demeanour for Salisbury, at the top of the table, to observe it and enquire why he was not happy. 'My lord,' said Jonson, measuring with his eye the distance between himself and his host, 'you promised I should dine with you, but I do not.'

Though in the fashion of the time Ben wrote much complimentary verse, and though he associated with the men and women who decorated (some more worthily than others) King James's court, he kept intact his fearless independence and audacity of speech. The accidents of wealth or birth – except in the case of his Majesty – excited little respect in him, and merit he judged by exacting standards. He attached himself to no court favourite. Even the great ladies whom he flattered, and who deserved to be flattered, were sometimes reminded that their fame in posterity's opinion would gain considerably from his celebration of it. He never coveted wealth, for he recognised the freedom which indifference to it gave him, and years later, when age and sickness made him poor indeed, he still treated money with cavalier or Bohemian irreverence.

But in the happy meridian of his life there was little thought of poverty. The Exchequer paid well for masques, the Countess of Bedford sent him venison, the Earl of Pembroke entertained him at Penshurst and gave him a yearly gift of £20 to buy new books, he visited Sir Robert Wroth and Sir Henry Goodere, he was a guest of Lady Rutland, and though d'Aubigny's marriage had suggested that Ben should live in a house of his own – which he found in Blackfriars – he retained the interest of his former host.

He was on terms of scarcely qualified intimacy with Lady Wroth and Lady Rutland, whose friendship he valued the more because one was a niece, the other the daughter, of Sir Philip Sidney. Lady Wroth was herself a poet of some skill and considerable fluency, and her pastoral romance called *Urania* was considered a rather daring production. Ben copied in his beautiful hand her verses for her; addressed to her several pleasant poems; and honoured her with the dedication of *The Alchemist*. With the virtuous and gifted Lady Rutland his association, perhaps, was still closer. It exasperated the Earl; but as the Earl, because of an unfortunate physical disability, was peculiarly liable to jealousy, that may signify little. It also appeared to that witty and headstrong knight, Sir Thomas Overbury, a likely foundation for his own advancement with the Countess. For Ben was a friend of his, and Ben, he hoped, would say a word in his favour.

Overbury had established a position at court by favour of Carr, the rising favourite. He composed epigrammatic character sketches that achieved some reputation, and entertained the King with his remark that 'Marriage frees a man from care, for then his wife takes all upon her.' 'Taverns,' he added, 'are more requisite in a country than academies, for it is better that the multitude were loving than learned.' The King, who loved a joke, also appreciated his answer to the riddle, 'Why is it better to marry a widow than a maid?' '*Causa patet*,' said Overbury.

But his best-known work is the poem called *A Wife*, a somewhat prosaic and sententious disquisition on marriage which he dedicated to Lady Rutland. Now Ben had a good voice and was held to be an excellent speaker of verse, so it seemed to Overbury that his poem had its best chance of pleasing the Countess if Ben were to read it to her. Ben made no objection, and his recitation of the blameless lines was doubtless very agreeable. They averred it was better for a wife to be good than beautiful, and that chaste behaviour was a surer guard of reputation than mere protestation of chastity. A stanza amplifying the latter contention remained in Lady Rutland's memory, and she was sometimes heard to quote it:

'Women's Behaviour is a surer bar
Than is their No: That fairly doth deny
Without denying, thereby kept they are
Safe ev'n from Hope; in part to blame is she
    Which hath without consent been only tried;
He comes too near that comes to be denied.'

On the following morning, however, Overbury made a suggestion that Ben declined to comply with. Having begun his siege of a married woman's heart with a poem in praise of chastity, the author of *A Wife* now made his second mistake in asking Ben to persuade the Countess of his merit, not as a poet, but as a lover. Ben refused in words disagreeable enough to precipitate a quarrel, and after that Overbury became his bitter foe. Overbury had an unfortunate knack of alienating his friends, but so long as he retained the affection of Carr he did not mind. Before long, however, Carr's friendship was to become a fatal enmity.

Carr had grown a figure of large importance at court. Although the King was fond of discoursing with scholars and arguing with divines, he was much affected by outward appearance, and even good tailoring might recommend a gentleman otherwise insignificant. He liked a parti-coloured doublet, not too short; a falling collar; and a good stiff bushy ruff. He was pleased if his visitors praised the roan jennet that he usually rode, and gratified if they noticed his gilt stirrups. Carr, a good-looking and athletic young man who wore his clothes well, was expert in such amiable flattery, and though he was deficient in learning the King undertook to remedy that by teaching him Latin. Carr daily advanced in favour, and was presently created Viscount Rochester.

His influence might have been discounted by Salisbury, or the growing authority of the Prince of Wales; but Salisbury was dead, and in August, 1612, the Prince, to England's grief, fell sick of a strange malady. He grew pale and sad, and in a languor strange for him who had been so active, took melancholy pleasure in walking by the river at night, considering the moonlight that slipped in silver ease on dark water, and listening to the far sound of trumpets. Lethargy alternated with feverish animation. He played tennis and looked 'wondrous ill' and shivered with a dreadful ague. On October 29th a sign appeared in the heavens, a lunar rainbow that for two fatal hours hung over St. James's Palace, and though cocks, split open, were applied to the Prince's feet, and new-killed pigeons to his shaven head, his corrupt and putrid fever could not be drawn out. The doctors argued and would not agree. The Great Elixir that Raleigh made was given him, and brought a little sweat, but did no more than that. It was too late for medicines. The Prince, the true grandson of James IV of Scotland, who would have built great ships and befriended poets, could not be saved; and when he died the King leant more heavily on Rochester. . . .

During the autumn of the Prince's illness Jonson

went to France in the unlikely capacity of a tutor. His charge was the son of Sir Walter Raleigh, a youth of nineteen, who had taken his degree at Oxford some two years before in spite of a marked addiction, while at the university, to strange company and violent exercises rather than to his studies. Jonson's acquaintance with Sir Walter, that dated from the early days of the Mermaid club, had been strengthened during the latter's imprisonment by some collaborative work on *The History of the World*. He contributed an account of the revolt of the Carthaginian mercenaries, a dramatic episode that he may have been considering for his own purposes. It was possibly this that persuaded Raleigh of Ben's ability to look after young Walter and keep his mind occupied, in Paris, with classical subjects; or Camden may have recommended the scholarly and didactic qualities of his old pupil. At any rate Ben left England with the wild young man in his care, and found a tutor's life more trying than he had anticipated. There is reason to believe that young Raleigh had in uncommon measure all those youthful afflictions of an excessive interest in life, an uncontrollable appetite for novelty, and the enthusiastic inclination to make swans of geese. We have cause to suspect that he could not be trusted too near a fruit-barrow; that the sight of a parrot or a monkey would keep him happy for hours; that he would cheerfully take part in other men's disputes, and get his pockets picked while protesting his ability to look after himself. And his head was full of tunes and catches that he learnt from casual acquaintances and sang, to Ben's annoyance, at supper or even in sermon-time.

Paris at that moment was much concerned with theological controversy. The Edict of Nantes had given the Huguenots freedom to worship as they willed, and also – which they possibly enjoyed as much – freedom of speech. But instead of uniting against French papistry, which (as Donne remarked, who was also in Paris that year) was 'like French velvet, a pretty slack religion that would soon wear out,' they quarrelled among themselves and con-voked a synod to discuss whether their salvation should be attributed solely to the passive, or also to the active merit of Christ. Into this atmosphere of pious dialectics came Jonson and young Raleigh.

Jonson's interest in religion was robust – not long before he had re-entered the Church of England, and to show the completeness of his reconciliation, drained the full Communion cup – and he accepted an invita-tion to what was a very dull debate on the doctrine of the Real Presence. One of the disputants was Daniel Featley, a Protestant minister then resident in Paris, whom Raleigh knew well, as Featley had been his tutor at Oxford. The excitement of this encounter, and the length of the argument, may have been responsible for what followed.

Ben, with one of his occasional submissions to wine – as a salmon swimming ever against the stream reaches at last the peaceful shoal beyond which there is no going, so man may drink deeper and deeper into the bottle till he comes to the keel, and finds the air there sleepy – Ben got very drunk. He lay inert, and the sight of his passive form suggested a joke to young Raleigh, on whom such quantities of theological discussion had had their effect. He found a hand-cart, and hired a loafer or two to lift Ben on to it, whose dull limbs he disposed in a certain shape. Then he ordered his loafers to pull their burden through the streets, while he walked beside, and at every corner he stopped, and pointing to the author of *The Alchemist* and the Queen's masques, bade the curious passers-by see there a likelier image of the crucifix than any they kept in Paris.

The power to humiliate, that small men fear so, is truly part of the general benevolence of wine; for humiliation means humility, and humility is a Christian virtue. It was in some such mood as that in which he awoke after this exhibition of his maculate humanity that Jonson wrote the hymn:

> 'Hear me, O God!
>   A broken heart
>   Is my best part:
> Use still Thy rod,
>   That I may prove
>   Therein Thy love.
>
> 'If Thou hadst not
>   Been stern to me,
>   But left me free,
> I had forgot
>   Myself and Thee.

'For sin's so sweet,
  As minds ill bent
  Rarely repent,
Until they meet
  Their punishment.'

Yet humility is only one side of the Christian
attitude, for Christ came bearing a sword, which undoubtedly he left behind him, though it has rusted
a lot since his followers first discovered how much
lighter and easier to wield was an olive-branch.
And when Jonson had recreated his virtue in
repentance, he reached again for his accustomed
weapon.

He met Cardinal Duperron. The Cardinal was a
most eminent man, a scholar of large reputation, and
a brilliant politician. He had contrived the election
of two French popes, he had persuaded Henry IV
into Catholicism, he had defended his Church against
the Calvinists, and yet found time to translate Virgil
and Horace, and to invent *mots* whose brightness
much repetition failed to dull. His translation of
part of the *Æneid* had roused the warm admiration
of King James, and when Jonson visited him he
produced this work for his guest's inspection, antici-
pating with natural complacency a reiteration of the
compliments with which he had grown familiar. But
Jonson read, and read, and made no sound of pleasure.
This was not the Virgil he knew. The Cardinal's
translation was *une traduction libre*, and Ben, revering
the classics, was indignant at so impertinent a hand-

ling. The Cardinal saw his visitor's expression and grew anxious. 'What do you think of it?' he asked. 'Naught,' said Ben, 'naught, my lord!' and smacked the manuscript with a denouncing hand.

CHAPTER XVIII

CAUSE CÉLÈBRE

ON a sunny afternoon in June, 1613, *Henry VIII* was being played with unusual magnificence at the Globe theatre on the Bankside. The supers who impersonated the Cardinal's guards had new embroidered coats, and so many walking noblemen wore property Georges and Garters that one of the audience thought such a display would make 'greatness very familiar, if not ridiculous.' But before the first act was over, when Wolsey had newly remarked 'A good digestion to you all,' two cannon were fired to salute the entrance of King Henry, and some wadding, blown on to the thatched roof, set it on fire. For a little while no one saw anything amiss, but then the flames began to roar, and

'Out run the knights, out run the lords,
  And there was great ado;
  Some lost their hats, and some their swords;
  Then out run Burbage too.'

The impious fire, it was said, regarded

'Neither Cardinal's might
  Nor the rugged face of Henry the Eight,'

but happily there was no loss of life. One man had his breeches set alight, but with great presence of mind extinguished the fire with a bottle of ale he chanced to be carrying.

Among those who saw the conflagration were Sir Henry Wotton, the diplomat who offended James by declaring that 'ambassadors were good men sent to lie abroad for their country;' John Taylor, a Thames waterman who had taken to literature; and Ben Jonson.

Ben was not long home from France when he saw this exciting spectacle, and from Sir Henry Wotton he may have heard something of the splendours of Princess Elizabeth's wedding to the Palsgrave, that he had missed by his absence. It was Sir Henry who wrote for her:

'You meaner beauties of the night,
    That poorly satisfy our eyes
More by your number than your light,
    You common people of the skies;
    What are you when the moon shall rise?'

Or Sir Henry may have described the Queen's displeasure, who, thinking the match a poor one, scornfully called her daughter 'Goody Palsgrave' before her wedding-gown was off. But more likely their conversation turned on the intrigue that was growing between Rochester and Lady Essex.

In the marriage masque called *Hymenaei*, seven years before this, Jonson had prayed that the bride and bridegroom's ardour might endure till age remotely over-

204

took them; but prayed in vain. In vain did the masquers 'On Hymen, Hymen call,' for the god cast no smallest blessing on the union of Lady Frances Howard and the young Earl of Essex. She had been left alone shortly after the wedding, while the Earl went abroad, and in spite of her youth she took part in several major entertainments at court. It was possibly at a masque she first saw Rochester, and presently his handsome figure, his blue eyes and pretty complexion and auburn hair, seemed overwhelmingly desirable to her. She sent for Simon Forman, the alchemist, the magician, who provided her with philtres to alienate the love of her husband and compel the love of the King's favourite. Forman also made wax images of the principals concerned, and wrought upon them according to his skill. But Fanny found a more useful ally in her uncle, the Earl of Northampton, for so great was Rochester's power at court that the value of a possible family connexion with him was at once apparent to that aged vice. And so Northampton, to swell his iniquities, borrowed an opportune trick of Pandarus and did what he could to foster the intrigue. Rochester gratified him by falling violently in love. Like Troilus he looked at Pandarus' niece and thought:

'Her bed is India; there she lies, a pearl.'

So extreme became his passion that Fanny was able to persuade him of the inadequacy of adultery's intermittent joys, and inclined his thoughts to marriage. She intended to bring a nullity suit against Essex.

At this point Sir Thomas Overbury blundered with loud clamour into their plans. He and Rochester had been very close friends, and when he heard of these disastrous proposals he protested with all his vigour, which was considerable. He offered no great objection to the intrigue, but to the marriage he was vehemently opposed. It may be that, in spite of his improper hopes with regard to Lady Rutland, he nursed a sentimental regard for wifely virtue: *A Wife* is too dull a poem not to be sincere. Or perhaps he believed, if not in holy, at least in sensible wedlock, for now he did all in his power to keep his friend from so ill-omened a match. He protested too much indeed. He bellowed and blustered, called the girl a strumpet, which she was, and her relations bawds, which in fact they resembled. But he only succeeded in earning Rochester's enmity and Fanny's mortal hate.

They decided to get rid of him, and through Rochester's influence with the King, Overbury was offered an embassy in the Netherlands or Muscovy. He declined this convenient honour, however, with the excuse that he knew no foreign languages, and that writing letters made him splenetic. The King was offended. Overbury should have remembered that Wotton's *mot* about ambassadors had been rebuked with a reminder that foreign diplomacy was no jesting matter. And so as a reward for his contemptuous refusal Sir Thomas presently found himself, not in Muscovy, but in the Tower.

So much was known in June, when the Globe

burnt down and Burbage came running out in Wolsey's cloak. Much of what followed remained secret for another two or three years.

Fanny still felt unsafe. Her nullity suit had been postponed because a rumour spread that she had been conferring with a wise woman to bring about the death of Essex, and Overbury's strong hostility frightened her even though he was in prison. She was passionately in love with Rochester, and she looked for surer help than magic.

A new lieutenant had lately been appointed to the Tower, a man who was under some obligation to both Rochester and Northampton. When Overbury's health suffered from confinement he was attended by an apothecary and a physician's widow named Turner, who was famous for her invention of yellow starch. Both had been sent by Lady Frances. Overbury's condition grew worse, but his constitution proved unexpectedly resistant. Four months after his arrest he was still alive, and his physicians were compelled to use methods more violent than powdered glass.

His end excited no concern, for his unaccommodating manners had left him without friends, and Northampton circulated a story that he had died of the pox. Meanwhile the nullity suit went on. Donne, who had been seeking Rochester's help to enter the church, was fobbed off with legal employment, and made a compendium of the whole proceedings. He declared himself in favour of nullity, and was so sure of his patron's success that he composed, long before one marriage was dissolved, his epithalamium for the other. The King's influence was exerted on behalf of the petitioner. The King, softened by late sorrow, could deny nothing to those whom he loved. The royal family had grown small since Prince Henry died and Princess Elizabeth married, and kindness increased daily in the royal house. The Queen even escaped rebuke when, shooting at a deer, she missed her mark and killed Jewel, James's favourite hound. The King fell into a rage at first, but as soon as he learnt whose hand was responsible his anger vanished, and he begged the Queen not to be troubled by her accident. The next day he gave her a great diamond as a legacy from the dead dog.

Importunate Rochester could not be resisted, and the Essex marriage was dissolved. In November Rochester was created Earl of Somerset, being presented by his peers of Nottingham and Northampton, and Fanny came to court looking more beautiful than ever. She wore a robe of green velvet, lined with white satin, patterned with gold. Under her yellow ruff – stiffened with Mrs. Turner's starch – her breasts were almost bare, and their whiteness was made more white by the red beads about her neck. She had yellow feathers in her golden crisply curling hair (brushed from a smooth forehead) and she carried a yellow fan. Her mouth was primly closed, and her eyes, big, dark, unguarded by lashes, looked at the world with unrevealing calm. Her secret triumph lit her like a curtained room.

They were married on the day after Christmas, she

The portrature of Robert Car. Earle of Somerset Viscount Rochester. Knight of the most noble order of the Garter &c. And of the Ladie Francis his wife.

ROBERT CARR, EARL OF SOMERSET, WITH HIS WIFE,
FRANCES HOWARD

(previously the wife of the Third Earl of Essex)

with her hair unbound in the fashion of a virgin, and all the court attending. At night a masque of Campion's was shown, and on the following day there was a tournament preceded by Jonson's *Challenge at Tilt,* in which two Cupids prettily quarrelled for precedence, and he who served the bride defended his honour and hers with treble vehemence:

'Had I not lighted my torch in her eyes, planted my mother's roses in her cheeks; were not her eyebrows bent to the fashion of my bow, and her looks ready to be loosed thence, like my shafts? Had I not ripened kisses on her lips for a Mercury to gather, and made her language sweeter than his upon her tongue? was not the girdle about her he was to untie my mother's, wherein all the joys and delights of love were woven?'

That Johnson had no suspicion of the criminal prelude to the marriage is shown by the wedding poem he sent to Somerset, for there he refers, with the terrible irony of ignorance, to the murdered man:

'May she, whom thou for spouse to-day dost take, Out-be that *Wife* in worth thy friend did make,'

he wrote. Somerset himself, on his wedding-day, may not have known the whole truth of Overbury's death. Fanny and her uncle, Mrs. Turner, the apothecary and the apothecary's boy, kept their secret well.

Masques and feasting still went on. *The Tempest*

and *The Winter's Tale* were specially performed; Ben showed his *Irish Masque*, that the King liked so well he ordered it to be repeated; the City entertained the bride and bridegroom – and the ever-ready court – to a banquet and a masque by Middleton; and the gentlemen of Gray's Inn, under Bacon's patronage, presented their *Masque of Flowers*. Then festivities began to slacken, and there was little excitement till spring, when a parliament was summoned and the King made an eloquent speech in which he requested the Commons to show their good affection to him in such sort that this parliament might be called the Parliament of Love. But men were growing weary of the three-fold dominance of Somerset, Northampton, and Suffolk, and the Commons proved so contrary that the King, though his patience with them lasted two months, at last sent them packing. . . .

Jonson was busy with a new comedy. His last play, *Catiline*, had been a popular failure. Its audience, like Pepys when he saw it revived, had been wearied by its dull length, and though Pepys relieved his boredom by talking pleasantly to Betty Hall, those who saw it first expressed theirs in uproar that concluded the tragedy with untimely abruptness. But now the groundlings were to have a play that would make them laugh their bellyful and fill the Hope with cheering, for Ben was in labour with a whole world of jollity. He had gone to Bartholomew Fair, and seen huge comedy shining through rags, and like Cophetua fallen deep in love with the exciting stir, not of beauty, but of rascal life. For five hundred years the

Fair had been living on country credulity and the
holiday spirit of London, and from such loose abun-
dant soil had grown a teeming citizenry of bawds and
hucksters, cutpurses, ballad-mongers, purveyors of
bottle-ale and roast pig, and shouting puppet-show
impresarios. To squeeze so vast a background into
the theatre was a task for Hercules, but Jonson brought
it to the stage all alive, and held it fast together by a
cord of hilarious adventure.

Through the confusion of the Fair go Littlewit and
his pretty wife; her mother, Dame Purecraft, and
Busy, the Puritan preacher who courts her; Cokes,
a country squire, and Waspe, his tutor: Littlewit,
blissfully uxorious, Cokes with his arms full of gingerbread and drums and Catherine pears, and Busy
moralizing with the nasal inflection, the pious sniff,
and the unctuous roar of the dissenting pulpit. They
are cozened and robbed, they eat and drink at fat
Ursula's booth, that 'womb and bed of enormity.'
With a holy bellow Busy condemns the Fair as the
shop of Satan, but his nose is already tickled by the
savour of roast-pig, and he finds 'it were a sin of
obstinacy, great obstinacy, high and horrible obstinacy, to decline or resist the good titillation of the
famelic sense, which is the smell,' and so goes in to
gorge himself on young pork and bottle-ale, the 'diet-
drink of Satan.' Littlewit loses his wife, Waspe loses
Cokes. Those who have dignity lose that, and those
who nurse a fine conceit of themselves are robbed
of it. The Fair is always victorious. Hypocrisy is
unmasked, and it is no good pretending to be sophis-

ticated, or holding your silver tight. Horse-copers and pickpockets are too clever to evade, and it is better to waste your money on toys and gingerbread, like Cokes, than to keep it for a cutpurse. Nothing is proof against the vast unconquerable roguery of the Fair.

After all this jovial turmoil came, at Christmas, a masque fashioned to courtly measure, made with the whimsies and elegance of learning; and the following Christmas another, *The Golden Age Restored*, more nobly conceived, and conveyed in charming melody. More important than masques, however, was the folio volume of his works that Jonson's printer was busy with at this time. For several years Ben had been preparing and revising his plays and poems for a definitive edition, and now it was almost ready. But at the eleventh hour some excisions had to be made.

There was a masque called *Hymenaei*, bearing on its title-page the name of Lady Frances Howard; and the *Challenge at Tilt*, with Somerset's name on it. And now the truth about these two was known, and Overbury's murderers had been arrested. Hating his share in the two weddings, and unwilling that men should remember it, Jonson deleted from those pages dates, names, and the circumstances under which the entertainments had been given. The masques themselves he left, for poetry was poetry no matter where it had come into being. But so far as he could he did away with their commemoration of crime, and he burnt the wedding poem he had sent to Somerset.

Somerset kept his copy, however, despite its dreadful reminder of his friendship with Overbury, and it was found long after pasted into his volume of Ben's works.

Northampton had died in 1614, and after his death Somerset grew anxious. He looked feverishly for incriminating letters, and destroyed all he could find. He went to Sir Robert Cotton and persuaded him, out of his learning, to draw up a general pardon for all misdeeds, past and present, proved and unproved, after the style of that which Wolsey got from Henry VIII; but his influence was waning – the morning star of Villiers had risen – and the Lord Chancellor refused to sign it. By and by some one of the lesser agents in the murder confessed – the apothecary's boy, perhaps – and Somerset went to the Tower. Presently Lady Frances was sent to join him, and they were lodged in the apartment which Raleigh, newly released from his long captivity, had just vacated. Their trial was set for May.

In April Jonson left town to pay some visits in Warwickshire. He went to Polesworth in the north and Stratford in the south. Michael Drayton may have gone with him, for he had friends in both places. At Polesworth lived Sir Henry Goodere, Jonson's friend and Donne's, in whose father's household Drayton had been brought up as a page; while at Clifton Chambers, near Stratford, were Sir Henry Rainsford and his wife, she Goodere's sister and the *Idea* whom Drayton loved so long and blamelessly till he renounced his love, but not her friendship, in the sonnet beginning, 'Since there's no help, come let us kiss and part.' After her marriage he visited her regularly in her new home, and once while staying there gave her doctor the opportunity to cure him of a tertian fever. Her doctor was Shakespeare's son-in-law. Among his friends in Warwickshire Jonson found an almost family intimacy.

Shakespeare's work was done, and the doing of it had left him disillusioned with mankind and more than ever passionately in love with poetry: the poetry of escape. In the world were reeling Stephano, Leontes cankered to the bone with jealousy, and yellow Iachimo. The earth in her orbit was dominated by a bawdy planet. Men's flesh was foul, and their hands stank of mortality. But in poetry were Perdita and laughing rogues who sang of 'lawn as white as driven snow;' there were islands where fancy could make more sweet and certain melody than nature. It is said to have been a merry meeting that Shakespeare had with Drayton and Ben, but not easily, not at first, can we see their 'eyes in flood with laughter.' All, in their own way, were at enmity with the world. Drayton was happiest when he sang of English streams and rivulets scarce large enough to have a name. Ben, though his nose never shrank from the smell of human hands, hated the rank vapour of foolish brains. And Shakespeare heard through his last and sweetest music the earth's noise of lust and lies and jealousy.

They would have Beaumont's death to speak of, who had died a month before, and Henslowe's, that celebrated the New Year. They would scarcely grieve for Henslowe. Within three years he had five times bankrupted his company to his own profit, and at his dirty theatre, the Hope, he had defrauded his actors of more than £500 and sold their costumes for nearly as much. Only his creditors would mourn Henslowe; but Beaumont had died young, burnt out, with half his poetry unspoken in him.

The newcomers to Raleigh's old rooms in the upper story of the Bloody Tower must have given them conversation, and cannot have made them merry. 'Deformity seems not in the fiend so horrid as in woman.' Fanny Howard was such a character as Beaumont and Fletcher might have conceived, or started Webster's imagination to see

'Envy and pride flow in her painted breasts,
 She gives no other suck.'

There was truth in the most terrible fantasies of the stage. And Somerset, by the brilliance of his figure, the glitter of his power, had drawn into his service not Oswalds only and Sir John Daws, but men like Cotton and Donne. It was a baleful story. But Raleigh's release may with some happiness have set their fancies free. Perhaps he would see Manoa, perhaps recruit a Caliban from the Bermoothes. He meant to lie in wait for the Spanish plate fleet. He had told Bacon so, and Bacon may have told Ben how Raleigh had answered his objection that this would be piracy: 'Did you ever hear of men being pirates for millions?' said the last Elizabethan. Drayton at

this may have roused himself and recalled some of the
cheerful truculence in which he wrote –

> 'Arms were from shoulders sent,
> Scalps to the teeth were rent,
> Down the French peasants went,'

as King Harry lopped the French lilies. Raleigh
might shake the fatness of the times to action, and
Drake's old ship, rotten now, lend to new vessels
its proud fierce spirit. Did Shakespeare renew himself
at the thought? He who had been pleased to think of
England left to the guard of grandsires, babies, and
old women, while her men abroad conquered where
they fought and only sheathed their swords for lack
of argument: surely his blood grew lively to picture
Raleigh, old and reckless, setting sail to gamble his
neck against a million and a last knock with Spain?

If there was sack in Stratford they remembered the
Mermaid too and, as they had done before, warmed
themselves at the open hearth of Ben's spirit. Shakespeare lost his pallor, and when Ben mocked him for
his fancy islands and hag-born whelps, riddled him
once more with bolts of wit. But Ben, loving Shakespeare and honouring him this side idolatry, shook his
fat sides in mirth once more to be pinked and peppered
by that hand. True, he grumbled at its carelessness
and could see small merit in islands, but despite
these faults, despite, too, Shakespeare's lack of Greek,
he overtopped in Ben's eyes not only his contemporaries, but Aristophanes, Æschylus, Sophocles, the

giants of old time. And none knew better than Ben
the worth, none more esteemed the temper, of the
great classical dramatists. To be like them was to
come near perfection. But to Ben's thought, cruelly
critical, superbly generous, Shakespeare stood beyond
comparison alone, and stood for all time.

They spoke of their work, then. Though men were
liars and lustful, though fools vapoured and love
grew old or ran away, there was still poetry; and
friends were good. Even Lear had a Kent in his
house – a Kent not unlike Ben. It was good to have
heard the chimes at midnight, whatever morning
brought. And the inland petty spirits still mustered
to their captain the heart when sherris-sack called
them to arm. Shakespeare and Drayton and Ben
grew merry after all. . . .

Wearing a yellow ruff, Mrs. Turner came to trial
for her part in the murder of Sir Thomas Overbury.
She was condemned to death, and the hangman
wore a yellow band and yellow cuffs starched by her
invention. The Earl and Countess of Somerset were
both found guilty, but escaped execution for imprisonment. Yellow went out of fashion in London.

And Raleigh worked to equip his expedition for
Guiana. He told the King he had no intention of
turning pirate. He said the mine he knew of, the
'mountain covered with gold and silver ore,' was
neither in nor near the King of Spain's dominions.
He meant to explore in peace, and peacefully to
traffic with the river tribes. Had not his earlier deal-
ings with the Indians been impeccable? Raleigh was

a bold and fluent liar. With a vision of the plate fleet in his mind he could talk convincingly of trade prospects and colonial expansion. The King at last believed him, and with a final warning that conflict with the Spaniards would cost him his life, let him go. But because James acted in good faith, and because the friendship of Spain was the larger part of his peace policy, he told Gondomar, the Spanish ambassador, all Raleigh's designs (so far as he knew them) and the organization of his expedition.

Raleigh enlisted some old friends, his former shipmate Keymis, a relation or two, and some gentlemen adventurers whose relatives were glad to see them go. Most of the west country merchants held aloof. He was not allowed to impress seamen, and those he could recruit were mostly poor sailors or hard bargains. His own ship was the *Destiny*. He was sixty-five years old, and Plymouth cheered him when he sailed. His fleet encountered storms that scattered them and drove them into Cork to refit. He sailed again, and lay forty days in the doldrums, short of water, smitten by scurvy and fever. Raleigh fell to a calenture, and crews were mutinous. But in Guiana friendly Indians welcomed him, and had he wanted a savage throne would have made him their king. He wanted gold, however. He sent five small ships and four hundred men up the river, under his nephew George and the veteran Keymis. He was too sick to go himself. With the river force was young Walter, whom Jonson had once taken to Paris. This kind of work was more to his liking than theology.

The Spanish settlement of San Tomas halted the raiders and forced them to fight. The English, gaol-birds and harbour sweepings, had little fortitude and fled. Their leaders rallied them. Young Walter led a counter-attack and was killed. The attack was successful, but Keymis, like his leader grown old, was overcome by the boy's death and ordered a retreat. The Spaniards sniped at them as sullenly they drifted down the brown fever-smelling river, and Raleigh met them with bitter reproaches. Keymis had once written, in heroic tarry-handed pedantry: 'The chief commendation of virtue consists in action: we truly say that *otium* is *animae vivae sepultura*. And to kiss security is the plain highway to a fearful downfall, from which the Lord in his mercy deliver us.' Now, heart-broken by Walter's death and his captain's rebuke, he shot himself. Raleigh wrote to his wife: 'I never knew what sorrow meant until now. All that I can say to you is that you must obey the will and providence of God; and remember that the Queen's majesty bore the loss of Prince Henry with a magnani-mous heart. Comfort your heart, dearest Bess, I shall sorrow for us both. My brains are broken and it is a torment for me to write, and especially of misery.'

But he was not defeated. He would lead another expedition up the river, he would capture the Mexican plate fleet. If all else failed he would buy, with booty taken somewhere, an entry into French service. He spoke to his men. And they, with their smaller hearts, were afraid. They said it was time to go home. Then at last Raleigh knew his gallant knavery had failed, and he had lived too long. Brave as Regulus, he set his last course for England and death.

There is, perhaps, more significance in that beaten ship labouring homeward, bloody and ashamed, than in the *Golden Hind* come proudly round the world. For England has known defeat and too often forgotten the brave who were defeated. So much of conquest has dulled her memory, and all her battle-honours dazzled her eyes till she can hardly see the stubborn courage of the vanquished. Countries rise against her like giant tides; but the white cliffs stand still; slowly and sullenly comes the ebb, and peace behind the ebb, and England is again victorious. English history is a tale of nations who came proudly to war, fought well, and were driven home with bitter wounds. France and Spain and Holland, and France again, that incomparable enemy, and Germany that held the world in check but could not hold the sea – all are defeated. But between the paragraphs of glory are scarce-read lines that tell of mishap and private ruin, failure and botching, fool's-mate and utter repulse. So long as the island remains inviolate who cares for those little bits of England, the tumbling ships whose crews lived on wormy meal and green water and fought strange foes – ice and tropic heat and great galleons – till their seams gaped to sun and tide and turn they must for home, with one watch at the pumps and the other picking lice from threadbare shirts, with no treasure in the hold and no prisoners for ransom but the ghosts of their messmates who had died? Who would remember ghosts or welcome beaten men? Only the enemy. England has grown stronger and remembers those who lived for a while to share her magnificence. But the roots of her strength go down to the graves of beaten men from the Isthmus to Gallipoli; from Coronel to Khartum.

CHAPTER XIX

THE JOURNEY TO SCOTLAND

ABOUT the time of Raleigh's execution – the day of
the Lord Mayor's Show was chosen to prevent over-
crowding at the bloodier spectacle – Michael Drayton
received a letter from the Scots poet Drummond of
Hawthornden. Drummond wrote: 'Long since your
amorous (and truly Heroical) Epistles did ravish me;
and lately your most happy *Albion* put me in a new
trance – works (most excellent portrait of a rarely
endued mind) which, if one may conjecture of what
is to come, shall be read, in spite of envy, so long as
men read books.' Though his palate was not always
susceptible to the finest flavours, Drummond had a
great appetite for poetry, and his interest in poets
themselves was proportionate to their rarity in his
own country. That interest was soon to be gratified,
fed to excess indeed, by a visit from the *de facto* Poet
Laureate; for Jonson had arrived in Edinburgh.

He had left London in the early summer. He was
perhaps tired of town life, tired of uneventful journey-
ing from bookshelves to the court, from the court to a
tavern. He had published his poems, and all the
dramatic work he thought well of, in a scrupulously
revised and finally satisfactory edition, and he was in
no mood for more writing. He wanted to stretch his

legs and enjoy a little mild adventure before age came down to cramp and confine him; and at that time pedestrian travel might easily prove adventurous, with rogues and valiant beggars, bearwards and bands of gipsies and Abraham Men on every road. But there was a special reason why he should go northwards. In the previous year James had revisited his elder kingdom and found, with the zest of a returning native, much to interest him. He may have suggested that Jonson could find in the farther part of his dominions something to celebrate in verse or prose. For a year or two Ben had been drawing a pension of one hundred marks, so the King now had a warmer interest than ever in his activities. Or perhaps the mere fact of James's visit and the talk of his courtiers when they returned had been enough to stir curiosity, and wake in Ben a dormant desire to see the land of his grandfather's birth.

When he made known his intention of walking there, there was incredulity and mirth in London; for the idea of travelling for pleasure, at least in one's own country, was yet a stranger, and Ben was forty-six years old and weighed nearly twenty stone. Bacon, with a judicious frown, said he loved not to see poesy go on other feet than poetical dactyl and spondee; a hilarious scheme grew, it appears, to caricature Ben's journey by sending after him, also on foot, John Taylor the Water-poet, a cheerful vociferous drunken versifier who had forsaken his trade of rowing a Thames ferry to write bundling rhymes. And by the goblin humour of time, the sport of circumstance –

monkeys will escape a forest fire that devours the lion – we know more of Taylor's progress than Ben's; for Taylor's story of his journey, which he called *The Penniless Pilgrimage*, has survived, while Ben's more valuable account was burnt, with many other writings, in a fire that consumed his library.

Taylor travelled with a servant and a horse to carry his baggage; Ben probably went in like fashion. Taylor's initial progress was hampered by the excellence of the inns which surrounded London, and the speed of his first few days may be roughly estimated by his boast: 'Two miles I travelled then without a bait.' But as villages grew scarcer he stepped out more manfully, and after leaving the Saracen's Head at Whetstone he says, with a proud smack of hardship survived:

'My very heart with drought methought did shrink,
I went twelve miles, and no one bade me drink.'

Sometimes he slept in 'heaven's star-chamber' while 'sweet bawling Zephirus breathed gentle wind;' when it rained he built a pavilion out of green broom and hay, or sometimes lay in inns, where –

'for I found my host and hostess kind,
I like a true man left my sheets behind.'

With the exception that he was improbably tempted to remove his hosts' linen, that may pass for a description of the early part of Ben's journey also;

for it is likely that he found walking thirsty work to begin with. With his twenty stone and sedentary habits he must have larded the lean earth like Falstaff, watered the ground in knots like Dame Ursula. Like Chaucer's canon, it must have been 'joye for to seen him swete.' A vapour would rise from him, canary scented, pearly as evening mist sun-drawn out of fat meadows, and down his neck, down his great chest and the vastness of his back, would tumble a hundred streams to part in diverging floods to either side of his noble belly, and (drawing tributaries from that many-fountained Ida) wash faster to his knees. He changed his shirt, we may be sure, more often than Taylor, who did not find it necessary till his baggage horse had cast two sets of shoes.

Jonson travelled on the North Road through Yorkshire and Northumberland, but Taylor went by Manchester, where Lancashire hospitality impressed him—

'Nothing they thought too heavy or too hot, Can followed can, and pot succeeded pot,'

he remarks with lively satisfaction – and where rain fell steadily. He crossed the Border near Moffat, and found the chief difference between northern England and Scotland was that a Scotch quart equalled an English gallon. There were no inns such as the south boasted – those splendid inns where two hundred travellers might lodge, and find clean sheets, good furniture, various wines, and dine with their host for fourpence – but where there was a roof there was always shelter, and at the poorest, eggs and ale. He arrived in Edinburgh penniless, and without trouble or delay made friends who entertained him with lavish plenty and showed him all the sights.

Except by inference we know nothing of Ben's journey beyond his purchase of a new pair of shoes at Darlington. He was probably entertained in a score of country houses to which he bore introductions from friends in the City or at court. He may have seen 'poor pelting villages' terrorized by Abraham Men, or forced into charity by the Counterfeit Cranks, who with the help of a piece of soap could foam very fearfully at the mouth. He may have heard the beggars' canting tongue, seen the Upright Man with his mort, or the ragged Palliards who blistered their legs with spearwort to win a doubtful pity. A carrier's cart may sometimes have served to rest his sore feet, and Durham Cathedral have bred in his mouth sonorous phrases. The rascal fire that destroyed so much scholar's work burnt these more amiable details too.

In Edinburgh he was warmly welcomed and publicly honoured. His association with the Scottish King, his quarter of Scottish blood, his literary eminence, the genius of his personality – all had their special claim to favour, besides the traveller's normal reward of interest. And apart from friendship and acclaim he must have found Edinburgh worth his journey. London had its river, crowded with boats that blossomed in a dozen hues with the velvets and feathers of their passengers; London had its broad river, bright with swans, crossed by bridges on whose span reared venturesome houses; London had its theatres and the great church of Paul's. But Edinburgh's river was dark and narrow. It ran from a rock impregnable, crowned in the grim *hybris* of Scotland with a great castle, to the King's palace of Holyrood that bore his crest and its motto: *Nobis haec invicta miserunt 106 proavi* – 'One hundred and six forefathers left this to us unconquered.' Edinburgh's river, steep and turbulent, had banks of tall stone houses, high as cliffs, pierced as if for backwaters by lanes and closes in whose privacy light-sleeping nobles kept their feudal state. At night it ran darkly under the houses, lit by a faint window, freakt by a lurid torch, and as it flowed there came, perhaps, the clenk of steel, the noise of a scuffle, the shrill voice of Gaelic anger and the broader tones of Lowland ire. London spread its plumage in the sun; Scotland darkly bore its capital like a Gothic crest.

In September the Town Council of Edinburgh admitted Jonson as burgess and guildbrother, and shortly afterwards entertained him to dinner at a cost of £221 6s. 4d. (Scots.) He travelled westward, it seems, as far as Loch Lomond: did he find there a host so superb as the Earl of Mar, who in August had entertained Taylor with rude and spacious opulence? At Kindrochit Castle Taylor had found a great company of nobles armed for sport with all manner of weapons, bows and arrows, harquebuses, and Lochaber axes. To make his Englishry less kenspeckle

Mar put Taylor into a kilt, and with an army they set out to hunt deer, wild horses, and wolves. Fourteen hundred men made camp. Five hundred beaters drove deer into a blind glen, where two hundred Irish hounds were loosed on them, and their masters followed with dirks and daggers. Eighty fat deer were slain in two hours, and at night the hunters feasted on venison (baked, roasted, and stewed), kids, hares, fresh salmon, pigeons, grouse, capercailzies and ptarmigan; they drank good ale, sack, white and claret, alicant and most potent aquavitae; and Taylor, ravished, his stout Cockney soul in tartan like his middle, declared:

'If sport like this can on the mountains be,
    Where Phœbus' flames can never melt the snow,
    Then let who list delight in vales below,
Sky-kissing mountains pleasure are for me!'

Elsewhere the Water-poet encountered 'houses like castles for building; the master of the house, his beaver being his blue bonnet, one that will wear no other shirts but of the flax that grows on his own ground, and of his wife's, daughter's, or servants' spinning; that hath his stockings, hose, and jerkin of the wool of his own sheep's backs; that never (by his pride of apparell) caused mercer, draper, silkman, embroiderer, or haberdasher to break and turn bankrupt; and yet this plain homespun fellow keeps and maintains thirty, forty, fifty servants, or perhaps more, every day relieving three or four score poor people at his gate; and besides all this can give noble entertainment for four or five days together to five or six earls and lords, besides knights, gentlemen, and their followers if they be three or four hundred men, and horse of them, where they shall not only feed but feast, and not feast but banquet.'

This Utopia, set in such false economy, was perhaps the Scotland Ben meant to celebrate – but did not – in a pastoral play staged on the shore of Loch Lomond.

His friends in Edinburgh were Fentons, Nisbets, Wriths, Levingstones – disembodied names – and Sir John Scot of Scotstarvet, a striving man, something of a scholar, and a brother-in-law of William Drummond. At Leith Ben stayed with Mr. John Stuart, who owned a ship called *The Post of Leith*, and in his house he met Taylor when the Water-poet returned from the Highlands. Taylor was probably at some pains to make it clear that his journey to Scotland had not been undertaken to provide an irreverent footnote to Ben's, and Ben, either persuaded or tolerant, gave him a gold piece of twenty-two shilling to drink his health in England. Taylor was suitably grateful, and when he published the *Penniless Pilgrimage* protested his many obligations to Jonson, and assured his readers that he had left him 'amongst Noblemen and Gentlemen that know his true worth, and their own honours, where with much respective love he is worthily entertained.'

The concluding weeks of Ben's Scottish tour are the most important, for his last host kept a note-book.

It was about Christmas when Jonson went to Hawthornden. The house was walled by thick woods against the cold winds that scoured Edinburgh. From a little rocky promontory it looked down the twisting ravine of the Esk. It saw trees crowd in a dense company to the edges of the glen, bend over, step down, and find precarious foothold on the steep sides till they reached the narrow water that hurried over rocky ledges from pool to brown pool. The upper branches of the topmost trees, winter-bare, shivered in the wind, but in the glen even dead leaves lay still, and giant hollies kept winter at bay with their dark sheen. There is a legend, forgetful of Christmas weather, that says Drummond was sitting under a sycamore tree when Jonson arrived, and jumping up cried, 'Welcome, welcome, royal Ben!' – To which Jonson, rhyming trimly for the legend's sake, answered, 'Thank ye, thank ye, Hawthornden.' In silent assent the sycamore lives still, but the Esk to ribald pebbles chuckles on a sceptic note.

Drummond was thirty-three – thirteen years younger than his guest – when Jonson paid his visit. His appearance was agreeable. He had pleasant features set in a rather melancholy expression, and his eyebrows rose with a wondering arch into a smooth forehead. His eyes were ingenuous, his nose was long, and over a rather childish mouth grew a little thin moustache. He had lived a sheltered life. Making a pretence of studying law, he had kept his Sidney, Lyly, and some early Shakespeare quartos hidden under statute-books till he was twenty-four, when his father died. Then with a philosophical acceptance of sorrow and new responsibilities, Drummond put away his legal works and bought poetry to fill their place. His mother lived to look after his house, and the presence of some younger brothers and sisters reminded him that he was the laird. He read the *Faerie Queene* and wrote pleasant bookish verse of his own. Nothing disturbed the gentle sequence of his days till love, that he knew so well in duodecimo, appeared life-size in the person of a Miss Cunningham of Barns, and all his library fluttered to shed its poets' phrases, sweet epithets, and pleasant similes in her honour. He loved truly, though the language of his love was borrowed; but on the eve of their wedding Mary Cunningham died.

'O Pan, Pan, winter is fallen in our May!'

wrote Drummond in utter grief, and wandered inconsolable under the darkest trees and in the loneliness of the quiet glen.

And now, into this elegiac air, came the author of *Sejanus* and *Bartholomew Fair*. Beyond poetry Drummond and he had few interests in common, and their approach to poetry showed little likeness. One delicately bestrode a lady's palfrey, the other rode Pegasus to battle on an iron curb. Yet for his poetry Ben had been invited, and of poetry he stayed to talk.

Drummond with pride exhibited his library. He had a few Spanish authors to show, more Italian, and over a hundred French books. A dozen Hebrew volumes made forty Greek ones seem light reading,

while both were dwarfed, in number if not in difficulty, by a company of nearly three hundred Latin
texts. With a comfortable, almost a possessive
feeling, Ben considered the familiar titles. 'Quintilian'
he said, 'read Quintilian!' The *Institutiones Oratoriae*,
he declared, would teach Drummond all the faults
of his verse-making as surely as if Quintilian himself
lived at Hawthornden. Read Quintilian, he repeated.
Nay, not only read, but altogether digest the sixth,
the seventh, and the eight books of the *Institutiones*.
Juvenal, Persius, Horace, and Martial were there
for delight, and so was Pindar. But for education read
Quintilian. All one could wish to know about syllo-
gism and tropes, perspicuity and personations, was
in those invaluable sixth, seventh, and eighth books.
And if his health suffered from so much studious
amusement, and such engrossing toil, why worry?
There on the shelf sat Hippocrates, full of advice
about fresh air and epidemics, diet and regimen.
'Hippocrates for health,' Ben solemnly asserted, wink-
ing his inward eye in the solitude of an English joke;
and Drummond gravely nodded.

The classical authors provided their share of texts
when Ben sat down to talk, but they did not give
such an opportunity for mingled criticism, gossip,
and opinion as the English books in the library.
There were fifty or so, including the *Faerie Queene*,
Drayton's and Daniel's works, Sidney's *Arcadia*,
the King's *Basilikon Doron*, some plays by Greene and
Marlowe, and the early work of Shakespeare; and
Ben could talk for ever of these and their writers.

Night after night he talked; while Drummond listened, brought up another bottle, fixed with amazement in his startled mind some tyranny of judgment, or ventured with increasing diffidence his own opinion. For Ben rarely agreed with what his host would say.

Drummond, for instance, thought very highly of Daniel – compared him indeed to Petrarch – and laid himself open to Ben's double rebuke for two foolish enthusiasms. Why should Petrarch be praised for torturing poor verse into the narrow shape of a sonnet? The sonnet was like Procrustes' bed, in which short travellers were stretched, tall ones lopped of their feet, till they fitted its unyielding frame. Was the freedom of literary fancy bettered by dogmatic racking and pollarding? As for Daniel, he was a good honest man, but no poet. Nor had he any children, said Ben.

Then he told Drummond of the masque that Daniel made for the Queen, and the interruption of it when he and Sir John Roe were thrown out for laughing at the foolishness of the verse. Roe had seen campaigns and knew when it was wise to retreat. He was a soldier, and Ben loved that great profession, as once he had proved. He rehearsed his service in the Low Countries, his exploit at Nymegen. But Roe had fought farther afield than he, in Russia and in Ireland, and after their dismissal from the masque it was Roe who had rarely enunciated the soldier's philosophic acceptance of discipline in the line, 'God threatens kings, kings lords, as lords do us.' He had been a good friend, said Ben, and an infinite spender, protesting that when he had no money left he could die. And so he did, of the plague, and died in Ben's arms, who paid handsomely for his funeral. Twenty pounds it had cost him, but Sir John's relatives reimbursed him.

'But Daniel,' said Drummond, essaying to steer conversation farther from these barren rocks of war and plague –

'Is jealous of me,' said Ben complacently.

There was an awkward pause.

'Drayton's *Polyolbion*,' Drummond ventured, 'is one of the smoothest pieces I have seen in English, poetical and well prosecuted.'

'If he had performed what he promised, to write the deeds of all the worthies, it had been excellent,' said Ben. 'His long verses please me not,' he added truculently.

'He seemeth rather to have loved his Muse than his mistress,' said Drummond, trimming his sails to a dubious air of depreciation.

'And fears me,' finished Ben in a hearty voice.

At times he was unnecessarily rude to Drummond, but the temptation was great. With all his books Drummond was only an amateur of learning, and to the professional man, the artist conscious of his greatness, amateur criticism may be subtly exasperating; and amateur enthusiasm, especially for what he himself admires, wake in him a rowdy longing to squash it. There was a sweetish flatulence in Drummond's enthusiasm. The wavering treble of his

praise discorded with the sonorous choir that in
Ben's vatic thought were the only true celebrants of
poetry: poetry that was 'fit to be seen of none but
grave and consecrated eyes.' And so to discourage an
idolatry which irritated him, Ben sometimes took the
simple course of disparaging the idol.

Shakespeare, he gruffly said, wanted art. He was
careless too. No sea came within a hundred miles of
Bohemia, but Shakespeare had wrecked a ship there.
There were other things that Ben might have said
with equal conviction about Shakespeare. He might
have set him, as elsewhere he set him, in his place
above Æschylus and Euripides. He might have
called him, as at another time he called him,

'Soul of the age,
The applause, delight, the wonder of our stage!'

He might have told the high and loving reasons why he

'would not lodge him by
Chaucer or Spenser, or bid Beaumont lie
A little further, to make him a room.'

Shakespeare lived in his works and had no need of
monument or tomb. But Drummond was told he
wanted art and thought Bohemia had a beach,
because Drummond knew no better than to praise
him in the same breath with the Scotch poet Sir
William Alexander. Praise indeed, in Drummond's
estimation, but –

'Pouf!' said Ben. 'He wanted art.'

Nor in company so given to indiscriminate rapture would he confess his love for Beaumont. 'Beaumont,' he said, and thrust him out of the conversation, 'loved too much himself and his own verses.' With equal abruptness he dismissed Spenser, saying neither his stanza nor his allegory pleased him.

Drummond, veering again to a new breeze, eagerly professed his dislike of the *Amoretti*. They seemed so childish he could hardly believe that Spenser had written them.

Promptly Ben went on the other tack and told a sad story of Spenser's misfortunes: how the Irish had robbed him and burnt his castle of Kilcolman with a little child new-born in it; how he and his wife and four small children escaped the rebels and fled to Cork; and afterwards, despite his service to England and to poetry, he died of starvation in London, refusing on his death-bed twenty pieces, that Essex sent him, with the cold reason 'He was sorry he had no time to spend them.'

There were small inaccuracies, perhaps a little colour for story-telling's sake, in this narrative; but it served very well to rebuke ignorant depreciation. And Jonson, growing thirsty, also remembered some admirable lines in the *Shepherd's Calendar*, and quoted with appreciation:

'For Bacchus' fruit is friend to Phœbus wise,
  And when with wine the brain begins to sweat,
  The numbers flow as fast as spring doth rise.'

Not numbers only flowed when wine had produced its beneficent diaphoresis on Ben's cortex, for with that amiable extension of sympathy that drinking gives, he remembered various anecdotes of a humorous nature, and Drummond, who had refilled his own glass, listened with obvious enjoyment to the story of the tobacco-smoker who lit his pipe with a ballad, and suffered the next day from a great singing in the head.

But out of this mild jest Ben drew some critical severity, for he added: 'A poet should detest a ballad-maker.'

There was, however, no apparent moral to the story of the man who let his hair grow long, and when a bald acquaintance unpleasantly asked him why, answered, 'To see if it will grow to seed, that I may sow it on bald pates.' Nor did any purpose beyond entertainment attach itself to the history of a packet of letters that fell into the sea, and a fish swallowed it, and the fish was caught by a boat out of Flushing, and the letters were safely delivered to their address in London.

How unconquered by time are the wonders of the deep, and how static the sense of humour! 'What,' asked Ben – there was little oil left in the lamp and less wine in the bottle – 'What is that, that the more you cut it, groweth still the longer?' Drummond could not say. He taxed his brains and scissored tails in his imagination, but none would grow by cropping. He gave it up. 'A ditch!' said Ben triumphantly. Drummond was delighted. How cogent the solution, and yet how impenetrably veiled by the obfuscating paradox of the problem! A charming puzzle. Lest he should forget them, he repeated question and answer, and when Ben had gone to bed carefully committed the riddle to his note-book. It would entertain his sisters.

He wrote down other stories that were less suitable for such an audience: stories of Flesh the clown who so comically trips the proud ringmaster Man; and side by side with simplicities an occasional morsel of sophisticated humour, such as Ben's delight in the picture of Ahasuerus surprising Haman while the latter is courting Esther (very competently in bed) and a caption inadequately remarks, 'And wilt thou, Haman, be so malicious as to lie with my wife in mine own house?' But Ben's appreciation of the joke may have been heightened by recollection of a similar incident in his own life, when the unfortunate husband's remonstrance was hardly more forcible.

In most of his moods Ben was frank as daylight. What he liked he praised, what amused him he laughed at, and what he hated heartily condemned. He boasted of his exploits and cheerfully confessed his sins. Often he brusquely contradicted Drummond, but more often was kind; and patiently read his poetry with all its academic glimpses of enamelled skies, harbingers of woe, lutes and pearly streams and golden bowers. There was *Tears on the Death of Mœliades* for instance, Drummond's elegy on Prince Henry:

'Mœliades, sweet country nymphs, deplore
From Thule to Hydaspes' pearly shore;

Chaste Maids which haunt fair Aganippe's well,
And you in Tempe's sacred shades who dwell,
Let fall your harps, cease tunes of joy to sing;
Dishevelled make all Parnassus ring
With anthems sad!'

It was good, said Ben, though it smelt of school too
much, and was hardly in the fashion of the time. But
it was good, he declared. And of *Forth Feasting*, in
which Drummond had begged the King to remain in
Scotland, promising

'The Tritons, herdsmen of the glassy field,
Shall give thee what far-distant shores can yield' --

such as Ethiopian plumes and Antarctic parrots --
Ben said he wished (to please the King) he had written
it himself.

But sometimes in the midst of his reading a savage
melancholy took him, and bitterly he demanded what
profit was to be got from all this writing. Poetry
had betrayed him, and it would betray Drummond
too. What had he gained by all his long toil? With
far less exertion he might have been a rich lawyer,
physician, or merchant; but he had chosen to be a
poet and poetry had beggared him. All his plays
together had not brought him £200, yet he was
better versed and knew more Greek and Latin than
all the poets in England. Yes, and quintessenced
their brains! Who was there to compare with him?
Middleton was a base fellow. Owen was a poor

pedantic schoolmaster, sweeping his living off the posteriors of little children. Sharpham, Day, and Dekker were rogues, and so was Minsheu. Beside himself only Fletcher and Chapman could make a masque. Yet he was so poor that more than once stark penury had compelled him to pawn every book he had.

Things had been different in the olden world. Then writers had been honoured, not, as in these degenerate times, scorned and neglected. The age was rotten, and men matched their century. Base wits and cowardly fops crowded the court, villainy prospered, and virtue starved. He wished he had been a church-man, so that he might preach one sermon to the King, careless of consequence; for he would not flatter though he saw death!

The boast restored his spirits. He had spoken his mind and lived bravely often enough to keep his loudest brag from being meaningless. Had he not put Salisbury to shame for his meagre hospitality? Had he not told Duperron, the French cardinal whose learning everyone praised, that his translation of Virgil was naught? Had he not said to the King his ear was corrupted by Scotch education, so that he sang verses instead of reading them? True, he had flattered James in his masques, but a masque was no place for preaching. Were he in Donne's position, now!

There was much talk of Donne at Hawthornden, for Drummond thought his lyrics second to none, and far from all second; and Ben accounted him the

WILLIAM DRUMMOND OF HAWTHORNDEN
Engraved by Gaywood (*Scottish National Portrait Gallery*)

first poet in the world in some things, though he believed much of his verse would perish by its obscurity. He knew by heart Donne's poem *The Bracelet*, and repeated that other poem of a ship stayed in a calm so motionless that

> 'in one place lay
> Feathers and dust, to-day and yesterday.'

But he disliked the *Anniversaries* on Elizabeth Drury's death, and had told Donne they were profane and full of blasphemy. 'Had they been written of the Virgin Mary,' he said, 'they had been something!'

And now Donne's wife was dead, of her twelfth child, and Donne had repudiated the world and dedicated his last act to God. With impassioned beauty he preached of God, and with awful terror of separation from God. At court and at Paul's Cross he preached of sin, and the worm that devours, and death that makes all equal: 'When a whirlwind hath blown the dust of the Churchyard into the Church, and the man sweeps out the dust of the Church into the Churchyard, who will undertake to sift those dusts again, and to pronounce: This is the Patrician, this is the noble flower, and this the yeomanly, this the Plebeian bran. So is the death of *Jesabel* (*Jesabel* was a Queen) expressed; *they shall not say, this is Jesabel;* not only not wonder that it is, nor pity that it should be, but they shall not say, they shall not know, this is *Jesabel.*'

Undoubtedly Ben had heard Donne's sermons, and

seen him weeping for his audience or with him. Perhaps like Lady Bedford he felt suspicious of his new calling, and remembered with inconvenient clarity the manner of his early life. More likely he too wept, and for a minute leaned on misery, as now he did to think of poetry's hard service. But Ben was ballasted like a great ship, and though he might bend to a rare squall he swung always upright, and so, if one night at Hawthornden were dark and gloomy, the next would be loud with laughter or cheerful gasconade.

Like Henry V's old soldiers who, to the wearying of their neighbours, would strip their sleeves and show their scars and say 'These wounds I had on Crispin's Day,' Ben remembered the feats he had done at Nymegen, and beside the Globe when he beat poor Marston, and in Hogsden Fields when he killed Spenser, though the actor's sword was ten inches longer than his own. All these exploits sounded again in Drummond's library, and with equal candour Ben described the blasphemous trick young Raleigh (dead now in Guiana) had played on him in Paris. Sir Walter, he added, had abominated the story, but Lady Raleigh was delighted, saying her husband's own youth had been full of such wicked pranks. Then gleefully Ben told how he had deceived a lady who was looking for an astrologer to tell her fortune. She was a friend of a friend of his, and the friend made an appointment for her at a certain house in the suburbs. There she went, and climbed by a ladder into a little attic lit by dimly burning candles. The astrologer was waiting for her. He wore a long robe, and half his face was hidden by a white beard. Skilfully he cast her horoscope, and she left well satisfied. And the joke was this, that the astrologer was Ben disguised in false whiskers and a gown from a theatre's wardrobe.

Poetry too had its humours. Had Drummond read Davies's *Orchestra?* It began:

> 'Where lives the man that never yet did hear
> Of chaste Penelope, Ulysses' Queen?'

And Sir Richard Martin, to whom it was dedicated, read this and called at once his cook, of whom he asked, had he heard of chaste Penelope? 'No,' said the cook.

> 'Lo, there the man that never yet did hear
> Of chaste Penelope, Ulysses' Queen!'

said Martin to the discomfited author.

Then from others' verses, good or bad, Ben would return to his own, and repeat with murmuring Esk for accompaniment 'Drink to me only with thine eyes,' or one of his songs to Charis:

> 'For Love's sake kiss me once again,
> I long, and should not beg in vain.
>   Here's none to spy or see;
>   Why do you doubt or stay?
>   I'll taste as lightly as the bee,
> That doth but touch his flower and flies away.

'Once more, and faith, I will be gone,
Can he that loves ask less than one?
Nay, you may err in this,
And all your bounty wrong;
This could be called but half a kiss;
What we're but once to do, we should do long.'

That reminded him – it may be – of Twickenham
Park, and Twickenham Park of Lady Rutland's
house, and so the night passed with talk of those
charming great ladies who kept a court for poets,
and Drummond, listening, might think his own life
lean and colourless; or hearing the soft stream beneath
his windows be glad that he lived alone and far from
the bruising tournament of life and striving wits.

So from small things to great things talk ranged in
freedom, now bawdy, now oracular, and between
empty bottle and idle rumour the names of Roman
poets jostled living men. Gossip of London, gossip of
Raleigh, Queen Elizabeth, Sir Philip Sidney, stirred
the dust on Drummond's old books, and pungent
abuse of Inigo Jones was succeeded by the mellow
judgment that it was better to eat dinner without the
accompaniment of music. Sometimes, no doubt,
Drummond took his visitor walking in the woods,
or by the steep path through the glen to the castle
of Roslin, half-ruined on its rock, and the little chapel
beside it whose windows and arches were so exquisitely
carved; and often Ben, with lively interest in what he
heard or saw, would besiege his host with questions
on Scotland's history and Scottish customs. He

wanted information about Loch Lomond, to use in
the pastoral play he meant to write; he wanted,
perhaps for a present to Cotton, a copy of the oath
taken by Knights of the Thistle; he wanted to know
the system of education at the Scottish universities;
he wanted a copy of Edinburgh's municipal laws; he
wanted a full description of the emblems and im-
presas embroidered by Mary Queen of Scots on a
Bed of State.

But Ben's visit came to an end, and, with so much
to talk of, there had been no time to marshal such
detail and collect these divers items, so Drummond,
like a good host, undertook to make a full report of
all Ben wished to know and send it after him; while
for his part Ben promised that if he died on the road
home everything he had already written about
Scotland should be brought back to Hawthornden.
With this amiable agreement, and with expressions
of mutual esteem, they parted. A strange stillness
fell on the house when Ben had gone.

In a few days he sent his host a couple of poems,
one *On a Lover's Dust, made Sand for an Hour-glass,*
with the sad conclusion 'Even ashes of lover find no
rest;' the other more cheerful, called *My Picture left
in Scotland*:

'I doubt that Love is rather deaf than blind,
    For else it could not be
      That she
    Whom I adore so much, should so slight me,
And cast my suit behind.

I'm sure my language to her is as sweet,
And all my closes meet
In numbers of as subtle feet
As makes the youngest He
That sits in shadow of Apollo's Tree.
Oh, but my conscious fears,
That fly my thoughts between,
Tell me that she hath seen
My hundred of grey hairs,
Told six and forty years,
Read so much waist, as she cannot embrace
My mountain belly, and my rocky face,
And all these, through her eyes, have stopped her
ears.'

Drummond read it a little sourly. He was suffering
from the reaction of a strenuous fortnight. Jonson's
robustness had tired him, yet with Jonson gone his
house had no life, and was empty – especially the
cellar. The havoc of entertainment appalled him.
And now Ben's gaiety about his monstrous girth and
rough cheeks was strangely irritating, for Drummond
had never been able to laugh at himself. Distaste-
fully he remembered Ben at table, vastly eating,
drinking deep, loudly declaring his likes and dislikes;
querulously he thought of his imperturbable arrogance,
his huge chest shaken by masculine laughter: and
Drummond's fastidious mind was suddenly repelled.
He took a pen and wrote: 'He is a great lover and
praiser of himself, a contemner and scorner of others,
given rather to lose a friend than a jest, jealous of

every word and action of those about him, (especially after drink, which is one of the elements in which he liveth,) a dissembler of ill parts which reign in him, a bragger of some good that he wanteth, thinketh nothing well but what either he himself or some of his friends and countrymen hath said or done.'

Then a fairer impulse checked his petulance, and slowly he added: 'He is passionately kind and angry, careless either to gain or keep, vindictive, but, if he be well answered, at himself.'

No guest of such a stature, or near it, ever came again to trouble Hawthornden with the domination of his genius. For many years nothing interrupted Drummond in his peaceful interests, but with sober pleasure he added new books to his library, and wrote new poems with melancholy culture. By and by he obtained a patent to invent certain instruments of war – a kind of revolver, a shooting pike, and something like a tank – whose hypothetically bloody use he concealed under Greek names. And in 1632 he met a young woman who reminded him of Miss Cunningham of Barns, his first and only love for seventeen years; and her he married for this gentle reason.

When civil war broke out Drummond published a tract that counselled both sides to use moderation; and when King Charles was executed, died of grief.

CHAPTER XX

PLEASANT EXCURSIONS

THE Queen who had danced in so many of his masques lay dead when Jonson came back to London. She had died on March 2nd, but she was not buried till May, and it was believed the exequies had been deferred because there was no ready money in the royal purse to buy mourning. Her funeral procession dawdled on its long walk from Somerset House to the Abbey, and the ladies grew tired under their twelve yards of black broadcloth. Countesses, who had to wear sixteen yards, were still more weary, and the lagging tail of two hundred and eighty indigent women was not a crowd-compelling sight. A far more popular spectacle was provided on the following day by the funeral of Richard Burbage, the actor.

On neither occasion was the King present. A shrewd fit of the stone kept him at Newmarket, and though he recovered, his legs (which for some time had not been very strong) were left so weak that he could walk only with difficulty, till he discovered an ingenious cure. So long as he could be tied on a horse no disability kept him from hunting, and now, when he superintended the brittling of a deer, he always took advantage of the opportunity to bathe his legs in its warm entrails, and derived great comfort from the fomentation. His strength and spirits so happily returned that when he made his formal re-entry into London he wore a new suit of pale blue satin, with a white feather in his cap; and a week or two later he invited all his Privy Councillors to take the sacrament of the Lord's Supper with him, to show mutual kindness.

In this mood of convalescent amiability he received Jonson with great friendliness, and warmly commended his proposal to write a description of his journey to Scotland. He listened with unfeigned interest to Ben's impressions of Edinburgh, and was doubtless gratified to hear it described as

'The heart of Scotland, Britain's other eye.'

Had Jonson encountered there that remarkable boy, Andrew Ker, nine years old, who had greeted the King on his Scottish visit with a speech in Hebrew? Or Mr. Wiseman, the schoolmaster of Linlithgow? who when James included that town in his progress had encased himself in a plaster lion and from that curious pulpit saluted his Majesty in the verses:

'Thrice Royal Sir, here I do you beseech,
Who art a Lion, to hear a Lion's speech.
A miracle – for since the days of Æsop
No Lion till these times his voice dared raise up
To such a Majesty: then, King of Men,
The King of Beasts speaks to thee from his den;

249

Who though he now enclosed be in plaster,
When he was free was Lithgow's wise Schoolmaster!'

But perhaps Jonson had not encountered the ingenious
dominie. Had he occupied any part of his time with
theological discussion? That was fertile ground
for conversation in Scotland, and so simple an act as
kneeling to receive communion could provoke the
liveliest argument; though opinion was so stubborn
as often to make good debating impossible. A
Scottish bishop had totally refused the Cup because
James had knelt for it. And when one of his guard
died and was buried in Edinburgh there had been
a most unfortunate squabble at the graveside because
the Dean of St. Paul's desired those present to recommend with him the soul of their deceased brother
to Almighty God. The Dean had been obliged to
retract his words and profess he spoke them in a
kind of civility rather than according to the perfect
rule of divinity. On the same occasion very rude
exception had been taken to Dr. Laud for putting
on a surplice.

And, of course, Jonson would have seen no pageants
or masques in Edinburgh. They were considered
idolatrous. No one, incidentally, had liked the last
New Year masque. It had been very inferior to those
the court was accustomed to see, so Jonson's return
in ample time for the next Christmas entertainment
was particularly welcome.

But neither Ben nor his King were in a mood to

stay at home and work. The King went to look at Stonehenge, and was so interested that he commanded Inigo Jones to find out all he could about it; with the result that Jones informed him it was a Roman temple built after the Tuscan order to the god Cælus. And Jonson went to Oxford to see his friend Richard Corbet, a jovial man, then senior Student of Christ Church and afterwards Bishop of Norwich. Corbet had wit and humour, he laughed loudly at the Puritans, and wrote very engaging verse. Better jokes than that conundrum about the ditch were made at Oxford, but Corbet unhappily kept no note-book. A pleasant light on Ben, however, is thrown by the eptitaph he wrote there for Corbet's father, a famous gardener of Twickenham, who had died not long before at the near-age of eighty:

'Dear Vincent Corbet, who so long
Had wrestled with diseases strong,
That though they did possess each limb,
Yet he broke them, ere they could him,
With the just canon of his life,
A life that knew nor noise nor strife;
But was, by sweetening so his will,
All order and disposure still.
His mind as pure and neatly kept,
As were his nurseries, and swept
So of uncleanness or offence
That never came ill odour thence!'

Ben saw the merits, the grave sweetness of his peaceful

life. He could be moved to most affectionate admiration for the old man among his trees, whose placid holy demeanour was in itself a rebuke to folly. And yet he knew the temper of such men was an alien thing whose calm walled him from the secret of their strange happiness. With a sigh he admitted

> 'Much from him I profess I won,
> And more and more I should have done,
> But that I understood him scant.'

During his visit to Corbet he was formally inducted into the degree of Master of Arts which the University had long before conferred on him. The ceremony took place in full Convocation. It was gratifying, no doubt, but it happened too late to have the significance it might have borne. Ten years before, when the battle for honour was yesterday's memory, such recognition would have had the splendour of coronation. But Ben's throne was warm and comfortable by now, and the honour that Oxford offered was no more than a graceful tribute to his reign. His royal pension had made him virtual Poet Laureate, and as though he had no wish for further conquests he now wrote nothing for the stage. Why should he spend his strength in endeavours to amuse an audience that could never be depended on to understand the scope and aim of his work? Their condemnation was the noise of beasts, and their praise the voice of children who were equally tickled with a straw. How much more congenial to work in the silent company of books, and find one's thoughts echoed back by the solid perfection of Latin, the felicitous surface of Greek enunciation; and how much happier to be with one's friends than to compel a two hours' attention in strangers! The ripest fruit of success was that Mahomet had now no need to go to the mountain, for the best of it came to him. The flowers of the mountain, poets in the pied April of their early brilliance, sought Mahomet's company in his favourite taverns, The Old Devil, The Sun, The Dog, and The Triple Tun; the rich earth of the mountain – the London Livery companies – came to ask his help in the presentation of their occasional addresses to the King. Sometimes an opportunity occurred to assist old friends: when Selden had drawn the anger of James by denying the clergy's divine right to tithes, it was the stalwart intervention of Jonson that diverted that anger. Perhaps it is even more significant of his power that he was armed against dubious honour as well as anger; for the King, whose sword was seldom idle in a civil way, wanted to make him a knight, and Jonson, thinking how many thin or greasy shoulders that blade had already touched, made shift to escape it – and succeeded, though with some difficulty.

The King's genial temper was now softening into a kind of sentimentality. Sometimes it looked like a tolerant gentle understanding, as when Dr. Abbott, the Archbishop of Canterbury, so unhappily shot a beater while hunting in Lord Zouch's park; and James refused to hear any ill report of the accident, declaring

an angel might have miscarried in that way. Sometimes it resembled a fatherly benevolence, as when,
to the people crowding about him while he rode to
the parliament he had summoned after a seven
years' interval, he said so kindly, 'Bless ye, God bless
ye,' – and not 'A pox on ye!' that was in earlier years
his more usual remark if the unwashed many came
too near. And sometimes there was no disguise, as
when he interested himself in the teething troubles
of Buckingham's youngest child. He was suffering,
not only from stone and frailty in his legs, but from
sentimentality, the malady of Scotland that is a
reaction to early hardships, poverty, dull food, harsh
grandeur in the rain, and a biological necessity for
courage.

On occasion, however, James could still live up to
the advice he had given Prince Henry: 'Where ye
find a notable injury, spare not to give course to the
torrents of your wrath.' With fine energy he made
known his anger, for instance, when a riot grew out
of an apprentice's insult to Gondomar, the Spanish
Ambassador. Gondomar, being the exceptionally
able representative of England's natural enemy,
was sincerely hated by the lower orders, and once,
while he was passing through Fenchurch Street in
a litter, one apprentice called to another, 'Sirrah,
knowest thou what goes there?'

'Why, what?' said the other.

'The devil in a dung-cart!'

A member of the Ambassador's party objected to
this rude identification, and for his protest was knocked

down. The apprentices were arrested and sentenced to be whipped at the cart-tail, but the punitive procession was stormed by a roaring mob, and the victims rescued by three hundred of their indignant fellows. Immediately he heard of this disgraceful riot the King posted in from Theobalds and took charge of the situation. He threatened to put a garrison into the City, to take away the City's charter and sword; and under the stern spell of his displeasure exemplary measures were taken. A brewer, chosen for sacrifice by reason of his prominence in the riot, was whipped through the streets, guarded by a hundred halberdiers, while every constable stood in his precinct and every householder, halberd in hand, watched his own door. The City was quiet, but in its stillness continued to hate Spain.

And the King, with obstinacy equal to the City's – though tinctured by a sentimental optimism – continued to believe that Spain could be the friend of England, and with England the agent of peace in Europe. The fact that Europe was already at war made no difference to this curious faith, for he expected to smother the noise of battle under a connubial counterpane. He trusted to handcuff Mars and hobble his horse with family ties.

Elizabeth, his debonair light-hearted daughter, was married to the Palsgrave, who was the leader of the German Protestants. The Palsgrave had recently been elected King of Bohemia, in opposition to Spanish interests, and was no sooner elected than a Spanish army boisterously defeated him in the

battle of Prague. In England there was an immediate
impulse to defend his English queen, 'that most
princely maid,' as Jonson called her, by force of arms.
When news came of the disastrous battle thirty
gentlemen of the Middle Temple swore on their
drawn swords to live and die in the service of Diana
of the Rhine, their Queen of Hearts; and James
tolerantly permitted a regiment of volunteers to
proceed to Germany in her service and the Palatinate's.
But there would be no official war. He declined to
believe that his daughter and her husband had any
business to be in Bohemia, and declared that his
subjects were as dear to him as his children, and he
would not embroil them in an unjust and needless
quarrel.

His own plan was much better. If his conscientious
and solemn son Charles were to marry the Infanta of
Spain, then surely the Protestant lamb could in safety
lie down with the Catholic lion while he, in a grand-
fatherly way, observed their innocent sporting from his
throne of peace in Whitehall. With this end in view
Prince Charles, accompanied only by the family adviser
Buckingham, set off in a solemn romantic disguise
to ride, in a romantic way, to his wooing in Madrid.
But his solemnity was only a light-hearted gipsy
compared to the astutely grave, the ponderously
dignified Spanish court. Nor was the Infanta a
Rosalind to be wooed in gay hurry. She had a charming disposition, but her chief pleasure was in meditating on the Immaculate Conception of the Virgin,
and preparing lint for the use of hospitals. So Charles's

wooing tarried, though the King sent more and more jewels to the two adventurers, to bedeck their persons and purchase the friendship of Spanish ministers.

He was lonely without them, for Charles was a good son and in all the world there was no one like Steenie. On what countless occasions had Steenie saved him from boredom! There had been a masque two or three years before in which Jonson's invention had seemed duller than usual, and Jones's scenery had been really disappointing; and the dancers had lagged till James, losing all patience, shouted, 'Why don't they dance? What did they make me come here for? Devil take you all, dance!' And who but Buckingham saved the situation? At once he sprang forward and cut a score of such admirable high capers that he soon appeased the King's anger and won for himself the applause of all beholders. Steenie was wonderful. And Charles had survived a trying infancy to become an excellent young man. As a child he had been grievously disappointing, able neither to walk nor talk at an age when other children were chattering like starlings, skipping like lambs. James had wanted to cut the string under his tongue, and put him in iron boots to strengthen his ankles. But he had been overruled, and seemingly with reason, for now Charles danced very gracefully – though he was a little short of breath to emulate Steenie's speed – and the Venetian Ambassador had warmly praised the formality of his bow. He took an interest in graver matters too, and had diligently attended the last parliament.

The King sighed and called for his pen. 'God bless you both, my sweet babes, and send you a safe and happy return,' he wrote. They replied affectionately, but Charles doubted if a collar of ballas rubies and knots of pearl, sent as a present for the Infanta, was quite good enough for her. The King was troubled, and told them not to waste it on anybody else, but bring it home again. He invited Steenie's wife and Steenie's sister to dine and sup with him, and they discussed the weaning of Steenie's child, and its four small teeth. For a little while they were not unhappy together, despite the absence of their dear boys. A chain of two hundred and seventy six Orient pearls was sent as a more fitting gift for the Infanta, and the Spaniards were astonished at its magnificence. They in their turn offered gifts, and Steenie wrote to say he was sending his dear dad and master some camels, a Barbary horse, and an elephant. The King was delighted, and in his next letter suggested that some good strong mules might be added to the menagerie, for they would be useful and economical when he went visiting.

But in defiance of these amenities the match fell through, for Spain demanded too much that savoured of militant Catholicism for even a peacemaker to concede, and so Charles came home without his bride, and London, wild with delight, had bonfires lit, tables spread in the streets, hogsheads tapped and butts of sack, for all to be merry at this rebuff to Philip and the Vatican.

Charles and Steenie hurried to Royston, to the old

King, and knelt before him. He fell on their necks and they all wept together, forgetting their disappointment in the joy of this happy reunion. A few weeks later the Count Mansfeld, General of the Protestant army in Germany, arrived on a diplomatic visit and slept in the bed prepared for the Infanta.

CHAPTER XXI

THE ORACLE OF THE BOTTLE

BEN had a motto *Tanquam explorator*, whose significance was twofold. As those who travel with a spade
for buried cities, he travelled and dug in the ancient
classics; and like a pioneer he planted seed in un-
tilled places. His later experiments are differentiated
from his early ones by an easy geniality, but they are
none the less experiments, and under his direction
the masque developed an astonishing strength and
variety. Before Jonson's time it had been a dull
charade, mere dressing-up with a few lofty common-
places done into verse, and a dance or two to finish
it off. To make much of so restricted a vehicle might
well have seemed impossible. It was hopelessly
artificial, it was local to the court, its purpose was
flattery, its aristocratic nature made it sterile. But
Jonson gave it the nerves of poetry, gave it a dramatic
structure by means of antimasques, stiffened its
artificiality with realistic characters, and envigorated
its anaemic pomposity with comedy.

On comedy he relied more and more as he grew
older: wearied by the futility of allegorising virtues
and drawing dull processions out of mythology, he
gave Venus a habitat in Pudding Lane, made her
son Cupid a London apprentice, and introduced

a greedy Comus whose attendants welcomed him in
galloping rhymes:

'Room, room! make room for the Bouncing Belly,
First father of sauce and deviser of jelly;
Prime master of arts and the giver of wit,
That found out the excellent engine the spit!'

Ben was no longer impressed by the duty of entertaining a court, and flattery, if one had to flatter,
came more easily with accompanying laughter than
under a top-dressing of exalted sententiousness. He
brings in Cockney clowns where none but queens and
faery knights were used to show themselves. He
makes a Poet debate his craft with a Cook, and the
Cook puts down the Poet. He uses the King's money
and the King's time to lampoon a fellow-writer, one
Wither, who had set himself up in a Puritanical way
to scourge the iniquities of the age. Sometimes he
boldly introduces pure nonsense – that literary nonsense which is almost exclusively an English taste –
and catalogues the topsy-turveydom of dreams as
Lear (the other Lear) might have done:

'If a dream should come in now to make you afeard,
With a windmill on's head, and bells at his beard,
Would you straight wear your spectacles here at
     your toes,
And your boots on your brows, and your spurs on
     your nose?'

But when enough nonsense had been gabbled a picture
of spring was disclosed:

261

                              'Behold
How the blue bindweed doth itself infold
With honeysuckle, and both these intwine
Themselves with bryony and jessamine,
To cast a kind and odoriferous shade.'

Winter has all gone, and now

                        'the shining meads
Do boast the paunce, the lily, and the rose;
And every flower doth laugh as Zephyr blows.
The seas are now more even than the land,
The rivers run as smoothed by his hand;
Only their heads are crisped by his stroke.
How plays the yearling with his brow scarce broke
Now in the open grass! and frisking lambs
Make wanton salts about their dry-sucked dams!'

How essentially native is this impertinent juxta-position of a lyrical delight in nature with nonsensical stuff about windmills and beards! Jonson had made of the masque, that expensive cumbrous half-Italian court toy, something as English as the Wakefield Shepherds' Play. Brocaded commonplace was thrust out by comedy, as comedy had elbowed off medieval pietism; and when comedy made a gap in the hedge, poetry followed. A masque called *The Gipsies Metamorphosed* was shown to the King at Buckingham's country house. Most of it is comedy rough and rude. Hilarious personality alternates with tongue-tripping rhymes, and gipsy knavishness foxes the village copu-

latives. But in the middle of this wild green stuff
grows a lyric of pure enchantment:

'The faery beam upon you,
The stars to glister on you;
 A moon of light
 In the noon of night,
Till the fire-drake hath o'ergone you!
The wheel of fortune guide you,
The boy with the bow beside you
 Run aye in the way
 Till the bird of day
And the luckier lot betide you!

'To the old, long life and treasure,
To the young, all health and pleasure;
 To the fair, their face
 With eternal grace,
And the soul to be loved at leisure.
To the witty, all clear mirrors,
To the foolish their dark errors;
 To the loving sprite,
 A secure delight;
To the jealous his own false terrors.'

Despite the labour of innovation, the burden of
experiment, it is quite clear that Jonson enjoyed
himself in these later entertainments to an extent
unthought of in his earlier years. He was free at last,
and powerful in his freedom. The concluding years
of King James's reign gave him almost all he wanted,

and in his two hundred and seventy-eight pounds of robust and happy manhood poetry found a seat very different from her more wonted tenement of lean anxiety. The gaunt pugnacity of his younger days was lost in jovial flesh, and while the shabby hunger of his early manhood had made others mock him, his roundness he laughed at himself. He won bets that he could tip the beam to within two pounds of twenty stone.

There was, however, one disastrous accident that marred the contentment of this period. In 1623 Jonson's library was burnt and a great quantity of manuscript destroyed. There was part of a play; the account of his journey into Scotland; a history of Henry V; notes compiled during more than twenty years of learned reading, and 'humble gleanings in divinity;' an English grammar that he had written; and three books of an epic poem on Persephone. It was an appalling loss. The grief of Shylock for his ducats, the sorrow of Niobe for her children, may well have been blent in the dismay with which he regarded the ashes of so much labour: coils of paper on which burnt lines showed faintly white; leaves curled and crackling still, and sooty fragments that fluttered in the air; thick greasy bundles of blackened pages with crumbling grey edges. It was a catastrophe to stupefy a man, but Ben survived the shock and with wry humour eased his feelings by lustily cursing the Fire God. Vulcan had always been a blunderer. Think what reams of paper there were, fit only to be burnt: lewd rhymes, defamation of Church and State, nonsense about Amadis de Gaul, senseless anagrams, verse idiotically written in the shape of a pair of scissors or a comb, heathen legends, catchpenny Rosicrucian recipes, and news-sheets full of lies and rubbish. These would have been a proper meal for Vulcan, and kept him from ravening on Ben's good writing. But the lame god was malicious and a fool –

> 'Pox on thee, Vulcan! thy Pandora's pox,
> And all the ills that flew out of her box,
> Light on thee! or if those plagues will not do,
> Thy wife's pox on thee, and Bess Broughton's
>   too!'

The last item of the curse has weakened with time. Now we can only surmise the extent of Bess's ability to blight her lovers, and as surmise is unsubstantial so Vulcan's possible affliction is vague. But in the hour of writing there was probably enough urgency in the malediction to relieve Ben's wrath. Power over words and the dominion of apt allusion are comforting things, and enlargement on paper is more sovereign than parmaceti for an inward bruise. Nor is the ointment of conversation to be despised, and Ben's loss was assuredly mitigated by the discussion it engendered among his friends and in his favourite taverns. He had many friends, and there was a sufficiency of good taverns.

The Mermaid was deserted now – Shakespeare and Beaumont were dead, Camden died in 1623, Jones had become insufferable, Donne was Dean of St.

Paul's – but Jonson's love of good company and equal wine was unimpaired, and the solid loadstone of his personality drew to him, under new inn-signs, a coterie of young poets who proudly named themselves the Tribe of Ben.

Herrick was the most famous of them. Others were Randolph, Carew, Mayne, and Howell. Most of them saw, in the deluding clarity of their morning light, the obvious connexion between writing poetry and drinking. The poet's frenzy, the illumination of poetic madness, were so pleasantly induced by a pint or two of Canary that drinking seemed almost a duty, and his bottle was as much part of a poet's equipment as his mistress. With typical extravagance Herrick defines this attractive view in his *Farewell to Sack:*

> "'Tis thou, alone, who with thy Mystic Fan,
> Work'st more than Wisdom, Art, or Nature can,
> To rouse the sacred madness; and awake
> The frost-bound blood, and spirits; and to make
> Them frantic with thy raptures, flashing through
> The soul like lightning, and as active too.
> 'Tis not Apollo can, or those thrice three
> Castalian sisters, sing if wanting thee.'

But though wine and good company might rouse the sacred madness, none knew better than Jonson, and none was more certain to shout the truth abroad, that there was a great deal more to be done before creditable poetry was actually written. A man, he said, must not 'think he can leap forth suddenly a poet by dreaming he hath been in Parnassus, or having washed his lips, as they say, in Helicon.' Inspiration might be the first step, but others as necessary were exactness of study, multiplicity of reading, mastery of matter and style, and then, when all the materials were ready, one thing still remained before the stair could be properly built, and that was art. Only art could lead a man to perfection, and leave him safely in possession of it.

So the Sons of Ben were chastened in their drinking, and with the taste of sack in their mouths reminded of library dust and lamp-oil and the inward sweat of scholars. Wine was a cult, not a vice, and Ben was the high priest, the Oracle of the Bottle, speaking wisdom under the vine and lavishly casting abroad the fertile surplus of his wit:

> 'Ah Ben!
> Say how, or when,
>   Shall we thy Guests
> Meet at those Lyric Feasts,
>   Made at the Sun,
> The Dog, The Triple Tun?
>   Where we such clusters had,
> As made us nobly wild, not mad;
>   And yet each Verse of thine
> Out-did the meat, out-did the frolic wine.'

More famous than The Dog or The Triple Tun, however, was The Old Devil, a room in which, called the

Apollo, became Ben's Tavern Academy. Over the door hung verses:

> 'Wine it is the milk of Venus,
> And the poet's horse accounted:
> Ply it, and you all are mounted.
> 'Tis the true Phœbian liquor,
> Cheers the brains, makes wit the quicker.
> Pays all debts, cures all diseases,
> And at once three senses pleases.
> Welcome all who lead or follow,
> To the Oracle of Apollo!'

Like any reasonable society the academy had an abundance of laws, and these, in fine Latin, in fine gold letters on a black ground, were clearly written round the walls of the Apollo Room. They were twenty-four in number. Some of them echo the inscription on the great gate of the Abbey of Theleme, that classified wanted and unwanted guests; others, mistrusting the anarchy of *Fay ce que voudras*, that Gargantua thought sufficient for men who were free, well-born, well-bred, and conversant in honest company, declare certain restrictions and embargoes. So admirably do they recognise all the potential enemies of good fellowship that only long experience of conviviality could have dictated them. The first commandment was that everyone, unless the guest of a member, should be able to pay his share of the night's entertainment; the second forbade the intrusion of the ignorant, the foolish, the doleful, and the wicked; while the third more positively insisted that members should be learned, witty, gay, and honourable. Others enjoined the cook to study members' tastes and make his dishes choice rather than extravagant; while the drawers must be quick, attentive, *oculati et muti*. Such beastly exuberance as breaking windows or glasses was loudly forbidden; but it was right to stir one's companion with moderate cups. If the wine was found to be poor or adulterated, then the host should be beaten – but that was a joke, for the host was famous old Simon Wadloe, brave Duke Wadloe, Old Sim the king of skinkers, and Sim respected wine as much as he despised ale and beer.

The twenty-third commandment forbade the publication of anything said or done in the Apollo Room. This was undoubtedly a wise rule, for the circumstances of the time provided an abundance of personal and political gossip, and the political atmosphere was so tense and irritable that public comment was hardly safe except in strictly private circles . . . The Puritans were gaining ground, and Puritan morality was becoming a political force. The last Parliament had been very unaccommodating, and Bacon had been impeached and ruined only to satisfy its prickly conscience. The *Mayflower* had sailed with an indignant cargo, and many other dusty shoes were ready to be shaken in England's degenerate face. Buckingham was playing at war without Parliament's authority, and the Prince of Wales was about to make himself unpopular by marrying a French princess. A large depression was moving into the political sky.

In the way of personal gossip an amusing story had been provided not long before by an argument between the King, Dr. Andrews the Bishop of Winchester, and Dr. Neile the Bishop of Durham, who were at dinner with him. The poet Waller, eighteen and already a Member of Parliament, was also present. The discussion went like this:

The King: 'My lords, cannot I take my subjects' money when I want it, without all this formality in Parliament?'

Dr. Neile: 'God forbid, sir, but you should; you are the breath of our nostrils.'

The King (to Dr. Andrews): 'Well, my lord, what say you?'

Dr. Andrews: 'Sir, I have no skill to judge of Parliamentary cases.'

The King: 'No put-offs, my lord; answer me presently.'

Dr. Andrews: 'Then, sir, I think it's lawful for you to take my brother Neile's money, for he offers it.'

The King and his guests were pleased with this answer, and found it witty. Presently a certain lord came in.

The King: 'O, my lord, they say you lie with Lady ——?'

The lord (in confusion): 'No, sir, but I like her company because she has so much wit.'

The King: 'Why then do you not lie with my Lord of Winchester there?' . . . .

Then there were still in circulation anecdotes about the Spanish adventure of Charles and Buckingham, and it was related that Archie Armstrong, King James's fool, had offended Madrid with some tactless jokes about the Armada. In spite of this, however, and in spite of Buckingham's sometimes insulting behaviour, the Spanish court had very honestly returned all the jewels – worth about £100,000 – that Charles had distributed in anticipation of his wedding. But no one knew what became of the suits of perfumed leather, embroidered with pearls and gold, that the Infanta (leaving the hospitals scarce of lint) had been preparing for her English husband. . .

And the family affairs of Dr. Donne were interesting, for Constance his eldest daughter, who was twenty, had recently married Edward Alleyn the actor, who was seven years older than her father; and already the noise of domestic altercation about the loan of money, the ownership of certain bed-linen and so forth, was echoed abroad. . . . .

There is no reason to believe that nothing but poetry was discussed in The Old Devil; and to publish some of the lighter conversation might easily have been imprudent.

There was a rule against the admission of fiddlers except on special occasions when there was singing or dancing, but selected female guests were not refused; there was indeed a special corner for lovers' debate. Women who took advantage of this privilege may not always have been socially elect; some of the professional ladies of the town were very distinguished, however. The chaplain of the Venetian Embassy was once accosted, at the Fortune theatre, by a

271

charming person in a mask, who showed him her fine
rings and asked him for his address. She wore a yellow
satin bodice, a petticoat of gold tissue, a robe of red
velvet, an apron of point lace, a delicate ruff, a perfumed head-dress, and no less than three pairs of
gloves, one on top of the other. The chaplain, being
a chaplain, rebuffed her; and yet remembered these
interesting details. The female guests at The Old
Devil may have been very decorative.

Urban Dianemes and Electras of Herrick's choosing,
Lalages of Randolph's, Carew's Celia – these may
have heard the Oracle of the Bottle and the loud
choir of his Tribe. Some Julia with black and rolling
eye –

> 'Double-chinned, and forehead high,
> Lips she has all ruby red,
> Cheeks like cream enclareted' –

some London Julia listened to Ben's adventures on
the road to Edinburgh (told again with unfailing
zest) and grew jealous – her eye more blackly rolling –
when her Herrick swore:

> 'Candles I'll give to thee,
> And a new altar,
> And thou *Saint Ben* shalt be
> Writ in my psalter!'

They were learned poets. There was verse in harder
tongues than English read at The Old Devil, and the

Julias, the Corinnas, and Perillas may have yawned and pouted when wit began to clothe itself in Latin – unless indeed they were *cortisanae Romanae, dignae tanto nomine* even to a knowledge of the language – which is unlikely. They would hardly be interested when Ben was challenged to describe a Puritan so that the ghost of a Roman senator (if one by chance were about) would understand him. Without interest they saw him look round for paper and find none. Bored they watched him take from his pocket a new Amsterdam edition of Lucretius and, mustering his wits, write on the inside of the back cover:

> '*Surge Musa*
> *Non confusa*
> *Non est labor sanus*
> *dic percite*
> *& polite*
> *Quid sit Puritanus*'

They knew very well what a Puritan was. He was a gloomy fellow who saw sin in pleasure, virtue in none but himself, merit in tears, and punishment for everything except his own hypocrisy. It was plain enough in English, so why obscure it in dog-Latin? –

> '*Semet praebet*
> *quod non debet*
> *tollit magistratum*
> *caenam vorans*
> *unquam plorans*
> *precibus ingratum*'

273

But if Perilla or Dianeme knew the poet George Wither – a fair enough poet, but tainted with Puritanism and no friend of Jonson's – they might well be pleased when Ben took up his defiance of female authority. For Wither had written petulantly:

> 'Shall a woman's virtues make
> Me to perish for her sake?'

With a querulous affected shrug of the shoulders he had demanded:

> 'If she be not so to me,
> What care I how good she be?'

And Ben had answered in a rollicking mood:

> 'Shall a woman's vices make
> Me her virtues quite forsake,
> Or her faults to me made known
> Make me think that I have none?
> Be she of the most accurst,
> And deserve the name of worst;
> If she be not so to me,
> What care I how bad she be?'

At The Mermaid Ben had sat among his peers; at The Old Devil he was enthroned, and his subject poets believed his words and obeyed his laws. When he said *Neminem reum pocula faciunto* there was no abuse of freedom or wine; but when he proclaimed *Focus*

perennis esto he was no wiser than Canute forbidding
the running tide. While he was there to feed it the
fire burnt brightly, giving heat and light, but already
there were ominous noises in the chimney. For a
storm was brewing over England that would quench
Apollo's hearth, and scatter the Tribe of Ben.

CHAPTER XXII

INIQUITY JONES

On January 9th, 1625, King James saw Ben's masque of *The Fortunate Isles*. A melancholy student, 'shrouded under an obscure cloak and the eaves of an old hat,' comes in to sigh, like Troilus for his false love, for the infinite knowledge that magic offers. An airy spirit mocks him, offers him the customs paid at all the ports of the air's intelligences, promises him a secretaryship to the stars, will summon for his pleasure spirits of the great dead. The enraptured student asks for Plato, Pythagoras, or Archimedes. But they are busy, says the spirit. Pythagoras is herding asses from a field of beans, Archimedes is making a mouse-trap. Will not the old English makers Skogan and Skelton do instead? With a clatter of rhymes and quick-trot of verse Skogan and Skelton come in and summon for the antimasque a dozen nursery figures: Howleglass and the Four Knaves, Elinor Rumming and Mary Ambree, Tom Thumb and Doctor Rat and Long Meg of Westminster. Cheerful rhyme, good clowning, and the lover-sigh for learning were all to the King's liking. Then the nursery-figures danced and were dismissed, and the student, deluded in his search for wisdom, vainly pursued them. There followed a show of Proteus, the Shepherd of the Seas, and ships beside an island where no sickness nor old age were known. Here was no hunger nor grief nor envy, but soft winds blew to perfumed flowers, and happy islanders made feasts and sport, and danced the Graces' hay while old musicians sang. . . .

Did the King look at Ben's rocky face and great body swelling (like ancient Comus or a Border county) to its round belly, and marvel that such gay nonsense, such summer sweetness, could come from that huge Christmas figure? Did Ben look at the old King, and think that after all his flattery might have found less worthy heads to crown than that nodding one, a little too heavy for its neck to hold quite still? The King's mouth was loose, and his lips were wet with wine. But he was a merry man, kind and generous to his friends; nor had he sacrificed armies to ambition, but with a stubborn heart maintained peace in his kingdom till the concluding months of his twenty-two reigning years. Did Ben see him helped to unsteady feet by silken supple courtiers, and guess this tale of the Happy Isles was the last that James would listen to?

By March the King was sick of a fever that he and those round him recognised as fatal. He took the physic his doctors ordered and composed himself to die like a Christian. He suffered the old Countess of Buckingham to wrap plasters of her own concoction on him, and grew worse because of them without complaint. He took the Sacrament with zeal, and having recited the Creed, said earnestly: 'There is no other belief, no other hope!' He forgave his enemies and desired to be forgiven of them; but through this charity spoke once more the dogmatic voice that had wearied bishops' ears and shouted against the Assembly, for when he was asked if he would hear the Absolution, he answered, 'As it is practised in the English Church I ever approved it, but in the dark way of Rome I do defy it!' Then the chaplains about his bed spoke pious sentences, and though the pangs of death were on him the King lay still and took comfort from their words. '*Mecum eris in Paradiso*,' said one of the bishops. The King's tongue was swollen so that he could hardly speak, but those close to him heard his faint whisper, '*Vox Christi!*' and twice or thrice he repeated, '*Veni, Domine Jesu, veni cito.*' The last prayer was recited, and when the words were spoken, '*In manus tuas, Domine,*' the lords on the left hand of the bed, and the bishops on the right, saw with equal eyes that his lips were still, and Solomon slept. . . .

His funeral, like his reign, was extravagant and untidy. His coffin was placed in a tall and magnificent hearse designed by Inigo Jones. It threw a shade on the watching crowds – a transient shade. But on Ben Jonson the shadow of the catafalque so designed, so burdened, was to lie long and darkly.

The new King had neither his father's faults nor his father's intellectual ability. Charles was a grave fastidious young man, nervously intent on preserving his dignity. He had artistic tastes, but preferred painting to poetry, a nicely tooled binding to the heavy content of a book. Neither Ben's scholarship nor his capacious Chaucerian humour (that James had so happily laughed at) attracted him. He had taken a keen interest in the court masques, but rather for their scenic quality than their literary foundation, and when he succeeded to the throne he discarded Jonson and retained the service of Inigo Jones.

While Charles was still Prince of Wales, Ben had once said to him: 'When I want a word to express the greatest villain in the world, I call him an Inigo.' Jones was a great artist, and for posterity that is all that really matters. But under cover of his Palladian scenery lived for his contemporaries' benefit a social success. He won constant applause by his imitations of celebrities, and such was his store of amusing gossip and tales of foreign travel that a party was hardly considered complete without him. To present company he was gaily complimentary, and he always knew something to the discredit of unpopular absentees. And then he sang, and was equally willing to explain the science of mathematics, and he had an amusing trick of jumping over chairs. He had good hopes (under Charles) of elevation to the peerage.

But he had never agreed with Jonson. Their regular association on competitive terms – one brilliantly appealing to the eye, the other brilliantly to ears – had been attended with considerable friction, and though in the early days of their partnership Ben had always acknowledged the importance of Inigo's share in their productions, and repeatedly described his scenery in language of superb appreciation,

Inigo had not been satisfied. He thought himself entitled to highest place in the masque-making combination of poet, painter, composer, and choreographer, and this opinion Ben had naturally declined to encourage. They were, perhaps, essentially incompatible. Jones had a delicate stomach and suffered, between social engagements, from what was known as vomiting melancholy; while Ben, both *gourmet* and *gourmand*, did credit to his palate and his appetite. The thought of his meals had probably caused Inigo as much heart-burning as his domination of the masque. And then Jonson, some of whose standards were simple, was contemptuous of Inigo's lack of physical courage. Inigo's sword was purely ornamental.

Their mutual dislike was not hidden. Jones, jumping over chairs, paused in his social flight to utter his meditated depreciations of Ben, and Ben replied with a couple of pounding epigrams. Whoever threw a hat into the ring found Jonson ready. He wrote with bare fists, as if for the championship of England, and every line was attack, every phrase a measured swing to the ear or sudden straight left to the heart. He was poetry's Jem Mace, a bruiser on deft iambic feet, loving the glow of combat and always fighting to win. Inigo took his punishment and waited for revenge. He wrote some verses in which he complained that listening to Ben's recital of his adventures on the road to Edinburgh made him as tired as walking must have made Ben. But his lines were muffled and without weight. Nor, while James was king, could intrigue displace the firmly established Laureate. But when Charles succeeded it was Inigo's turn for favour, and Inigo used it. For five years Ben wrote no more New Year or Twelfth Night entertainments for the court. Iniquity Jones ruled the revels like a vizier jealous of his own shadow's nearness to the throne.

It was nine years since Ben had written for the theatre, but now, his pleasanter occupation gone, he returned to his old trade philosophically and with sturdy good humour. A novel kind of roguery had providentially appeared in London – the commercial possibility of newspapers had been discovered – and to this invitation he energetically responded with *The Staple of News*.

Admitting first of all the prime importance of a busy inquisitive restless temper in the age, there were three people mainly responsible for the birth of periodic journalism. One was the Queen of Bohemia, another was a stationer called Nathaniel Butter, and the third was Captain Gainsford, a veteran of the Irish wars. Elizabeth of Bohemia was London's darling, and when her kingdom was stolen by the detestable armies of Spain, European politics became a matter of poignant interest. For some time the chief source of news was Amsterdam, and the Dutch bulletins were so sensational that they greatly stimulated England's thirst for information without wasting time on educating its palate to the taste of authenticity. By 1623, however, the Amsterdam monopoly was broken, and a weekly news-sheet was published from Pope's Head Alley whose reckless omniscience compared very favourably with the encyclopaedic assurance of Holland.

Butter had already shown his enterprise by publishing *King Lear*, a pamphlet protesting against Dutch boats fishing in English waters, part of Chapman's *Homer*, and the account of an interesting murder in Yorkshire; while Gainsford had written a life of the Earl of Tyrone, and a gossiping account of England's natural superiority to all other countries. The Captain had travelled far and wide, and wrote with the authority of one to whom the Golden Horn was familiar, the Grand Canal a friendly waterway. He was an admirable man for Butter's purpose, for he had an easy prolific pen and the proper courage of a soldier. Sitting in his room in Pope's Head Alley he conquered towns, crossed the Rhine, invaded provinces, repelled a flank attack, and with unfailing aplomb made history of dubious inference. The *Weekly Courant* became very popular.

Gainsford and Butter had genius. They knew when the iron was hot, and they knew how to strike it. But Ben's genius was rarely tactful, and he failed to remember, or did not trouble to consider, that pouring cold water on a red-hot surface causes a violent reaction. He played a cheerful hose on a glowing occasion for satire, and the result was a lot of very angry vapour.

The third act of Ben's comedy showed a newspaper office conducted by a staff that included an unmistakable caricature of Butter, a barber, a court parasite, and one or two other semi-professional gossips. Distinguished visitors arrive and are treated to samples of the day's latest news. They are told that the King of Spain has been elected Pope, that Galileo has invented a fatal ray to burn up enemy shipping, and the Dutch possess a mechanical eel for submarine warfare. Then the office is invaded by a throng of Puritan customers eager for ecclesiastical news, and they are told, for sixpence an item or so, that the coming of the prophet Baal is now momentarily expected, and that the Grand Turk will shortly celebrate his conversion to Christianity by a visit to the Reformed Church in Amsterdam. All this was good hilarious travesty of the *Courant's* pages. To-day it may seem wild travesty, but actually it was too close and pointed. Most of the audience did not quite recognize the burlesque and were angrily unsure how much they were meant to believe. Nathaniel's stage-news sounded so very like Butter's Pope's Head Alley news, and yet . . . The King of Spain might perhaps be elected Pope, and his general Spinola made commander of the Jesuits – anything about Jesuits was credible – but they refused to believe in the Dutch submarine. Jonson, they concluded, was gulling them, deliberately inventing falsehoods, fooling them and filling them with fraudulent information. They became indignant. Their virgin credulity was being outraged. They shouted, they protested, they interrupted the impertinent scene. And when the play was published Ben found it necessary to prefix an explanation that the 'news' in it was not meant to be real news, but only a burlesque of *Courant* news.

The satire on contemporary journalism (which was only half the play) did little, therefore, to restore Ben to the popular favour which he had forfeited by his ten years' desertion of the stage. But the management and picturesque vigour of the satire showed that he had lost none of his old power, and there seemed, despite a doubtful start, every prospect of a succession of new plays not incomparable with his earlier masterpieces. It is true that half the comedy consisted of allegorical matter reflecting too much the influence of the masque, but good realistic characters kept breaking out of the double meaning, and sitting on the stage throughout the action was a chorus of four gossips whose tongues clacked so truly, whose comments were so admirably racy, that they effectively redeemed any *longueurs* in the scenes. They showed too that Ben was far from being cast down by his misfortune at court, for his gossips grumbled at the play and poked fun at the author with such happiness he seemed instead to be rejoicing in his recapture of the stage's freedom. The theatre was his proper place, and he was glad to have returned.

So it seemed; and doubtless his friends predicted a new *Alchemist*, a second *Fox*. But the months passed and Ben wrote nothing more. His ability to manage a play had not failed him, but invention was grown tardy with long years of ease. Unlike other drama- tists he had always devised his own plots, and now that first conceptual gust was weakening. A poem, inspired by occasion, was still easy, and all his scholarly faculties were strong. He wrote verse epistles to his friends, and did something to refashion the fragments of his English grammar that the fire had destroyed. He read and digested his Greek and Latin authors. But for a long time he could not find a story good enough, in his hard judgment, to fill two hours on the stage. He could have written masques, but Inigo was powerful at court and Christmas came and went, and came and went again, and the King's entertainment was provided by men who would let Jones take all the credit he wanted.

Ben, however, was not unhappy. There were The Old Devil, The Sun, The Dog, and The Triple Tun; and wherever he sat the young men surrounded him – Herrick, Carew, Randolph escaping from Cambridge, a dozen others – for though he never wrote another word he had written *The Alchemist* and *The Silent Woman*, and no one else in all England had his gift of conversation that taught and stirred enthusiasm and woke great laughter. He was Ben, and life flowed from him. He gave the whole air vitality – and in his head the germ of a new play was now slowly growing.

At this time, then, Jones was merely a negative enemy. He helped to keep Ben out of court employment that would have maintained his fortunes, but for the present he was powerless to do anything more definitely injurious. In similar fashion Ben's other enemies – the poet Wither, the offended journalist Nathaniel Butter, and a covey of jealous inconsiderable scribblers – were for lack of opportunity hostile only in intent. But a positive enemy, blind, unpointed, and invisible, was growing in the circumstance of the times.

In 1626 the Duke of Buckingham had been saved from impeachment only by the dissolution of Parliament. With the help of forced loans he was now endeavouring to conduct against France a war that his personal displeasure had precipitated. He had no military sense or education, and his efforts were ludicrous and bloody. A year or two earlier, when he had been at war with Spain, he had contrived a naval fiasco in Cadiz Bay, and in 1627 he sent an equally ineffective expedition against La Rochelle. Half the force died to no purpose, and the remainder came home in a state of semi-starvation. Meanwhile men of wealth who had resisted the forced loan lay in gaol or had their houses filled with conscript soldiers. The country was getting tired of Buckingham.

In August 1628 national resentment leapt to a single fanatical point in John Felton, a Suffolk man. He was crazy, but patriotic, and he had a dagger. He killed Buckingham. He was, of course, hanged; but few except his judges condemned him. While he lay in prison verses praising his heroic altruism circulated in London.

Such a poem, of considerable superficial vigour, came into the hands of Jonson's old friend Sir Robert Cotton. It exhorted Felton to enjoy his magnificent doom. With a lofty spirit it bade him:

'Farewell! for thy brave sake we shall not send
Henceforth Commanders Enemies to defend;

Nor will it ever our just Monarch please
To keep an Admiral to lose our Seas.

'And I dare boldly write, as thou dar'st die,
Stout Felton, England's ransom, here doth lie!'

Sir Robert considered it carefully and thought that he recognized Ben's voice in these energetic lines. Sir Robert had had no cause to love Buckingham, and he was perhaps not unwilling to believe that his friend Jonson had felt as he did about the Duke's death; though he knew how dangerous it was to express such feelings. He left the poem on his table so that Jonson, a neighbour and frequent visitor, might see it when he came in. Ben came, and dined, and after dinner Sir Robert showed him the verses with a pleasant suggestion that perhaps he knew the author. This Ben very definitely denied. He had assuredly not written them himself, nor had he ever seen them before. He condemned the sentiment in them – it was certainly too rhetorical to be convincing – and protested his entire ignorance of their origin.

Yet other eyes than Cotton's must have seen in the perilous eulogy a fancied resemblance to Jonson's hand, for in October he was taken before the Attorney-General to be examined on his knowledge of it.

He affirmed his complete innocence, protested it upon his Christianity and hopes of salvation, and swore that no copy of the verses had ever been in his possession. He had seen them in Sir Robert Cotton's house, and that was all. He was asked if he knew the author, and he answered 'No.' He was asked if he had ever heard it rumoured who wrote them, and he answered by common talk it was Zouch Townley, a parson and Student of Christ Church in Oxford. And Townley had now fled to Holland.

Then the law took a curious turn. The Attorney-General asked Ben whether he had not once given a dagger to Zouch Townley? Ben admitted it. It was a dagger with a white handle that he customarily wore at his belt, and one Sunday, after Townley had preached at St. Margaret's in Westminster, Townley had taken a fancy to it; so a couple of nights later, after supping with him and finding that he still admired it, Ben had made him a present of the weapon. But what a dagger had to do with a poem about Felton he did not know.

This concluded the examination, and Ben was exonerated from the suspicion of authorship or complicity in authorship of the lines that expressed such vigorous contempt of court. In his youth he had suffered often enough the inquisition of hostile judges. He had known the inner smell of Marshalsea and Newgate, and on his thumb was the white scar of a Tyburn T. But in those turbulent years he had been proof against all misfortune. Now he was less resilient. The shock of detention, the strain of examination, were too much for him. In his surcharged brain a small artery burst.

The stroke was not fatal, but when he recovered he shook with a palsy, and his legs would not carry him.

CHAPTER XXIII

THE LOSING BATTLE

In his house in Westminster – over a passage leading
from the churchyard to the old Palace – Ben worked
doggedly at his new play. . . .

Tanquam explorator: for there was a new current in
the air, and his nose was not too old to appreciate its
savour. Charles's French queen had brought refine-
ment with her, and under her influence the court was
gingerly experimenting with novel ways in gallantry.
The jocular rude licence of James's reign was frowned
on now, and its stead something called Platonic love
most palely flowered. Clearly to define it would
probably have puzzled most of its protagonists, but
it was characterised more by discussion than action.
It quickened the imagination, but it did not spoil the
figure. It was very important, but poetical rather
than procreative.

'I was the laziest creature,
The most unprofitable sign of nothing,
The veriest drone, and slept away my life
Beyond the dormouse till I was in love!'

says the hero of *The New Inn;* but his now engrossing
passion seems quite as inane as the idleness it had
displaced:

'I oft have been too in her company,
And looked upon her a whole day; admired her;
Loved her, and did not tell her so; loved still,
Looked still and loved; and loved, and looked, and
    sighed:
But as a man neglected I came off,
And unregarded.'

Here surely was prey for satire. This pink and
pretty affectation was born to wake laughter, Ben's
laughter, that could blow it up like a balloon and burst
it. It was a new kind of alchemy, false in theory,
propped-up on its own dialect, rich in its chance of
roguery. The search for Platonic ideal love could
have been built into a comedy brilliant as that made
by the quest of the Philosopher's Stone. But Ben
refused his opportunity and treated the subject
seriously. He drew his romantic hero with a strange
and almost passionate sympathy.

He wrote of love with high and loving seriousness,
and sympathy that would not let young love be
disappointed. The adored unyielding lady yields
at the proper time.

'O speak, and speak for ever! let mine ear
Be feasted still, and filled with this banquet!
No sense can ever surfeit on such truth,'

she cries when her lover has talked an hour about the
spiritual coupling of two souls. It is the nearest
Ben ever got to Juliet's voice; and he was almost

sixty and half-paralysed when he got so near – and stood so distant.

Now like Shakespeare in his last years Ben began to make of his poetry a way to comfort and escape from life. The Platonic troubadours at court had shown him a way, and their example revived the romantic strain that he had so determinedly buried in his mind, and was so loth to be buried. As Shakespeare begot Perdita in a world of turbulent brutality, Ben got Lovel in a town full of clamouring Puritans. Both sought relief from tired life and ugly age in a youth of shining impossible grace. But the difference between them was that Shakespeare's poetry could still make a comedy, and Ben's was no longer able.

The equipment for a play was still at his command, and some of the scenes in *The New Inn* were done with his wonted command of vivid and forceful language; but others were little more than senile chattering, an old man's talk that showed the palsy like his hand. The plot, moreover, was involved and foolish, and the comedy had no life, no whole organic life, but moved its separate limbs spasmodically like a beast whose back had been hurt.

The actors of the Blackfriars Theatre, where it was presented, openly showed contempt for parts that could do nothing to enhance their reputations, and played with studied negligence. A further misfortune lay in Ben's choice of a name for one of his principal characters, a lady's maid. He had called her Cis. It seems harmless enough, but some Cicely of the time must have made the diminutive extraordinarily offensive, for the audience loudly objected to it. The play was damned. It had indeed no hope from birth, but bad acting and this innocent unfortunate allusion overdamned its self-defeat, and few of the audience waited for the last act. Those who stayed heard a brave and pitiful epilogue:

'If you expect more than you had to-night,
  The maker is sick and sad. But do him right;
He meant to please you: for he sent things fit,
In all the numbers both of sense and wit;
If they have not miscarried! If they have,
All that his faint and faltering tongue doth crave,
Is that you not impute it to his brain,
That's yet unhurt, although set round with pain,
It cannot long hold out. All strength must yield;
Yet judgment would the last be in the field
With a true poet.'

The dramatist might be dead, or nearly dead, but the poet could still fight fiercely in a losing battle. Even the small self-pity of the epilogue is shot through with warm defiance of fate, and when news came of his play's disastrous failure all Ben's fearless arrogance mustered to cover the retreat of his genius. The old lion, chained by disease in his narrow den, would not admit his weakness, but roared his hatred of the vulgar world in the *Ode to Himself:*

'Come leave the loathed stage,
  And the more loathsome age;

Where pride and impudence, in faction knit,
    Usurp the chair of wit!
Indicting and arraigning every day
    Something they call a play.
     Let their fastidious, vain
     Commission of the brain
Run on and rage, sweat, censure, and condemn;
They were not made for thee, less thou for them.

  'Say that thou pour'st them wheat,
    And they will acorns eat;
'Twere simple fury still thyself to waste
    On such as have no taste!
To offer them a surfeit of pure bread
    Whose appetites are dead!
    No, give them grains their fill,
    Husks, draff to drink and swill:
If they love lees, and leave the lusty wine,
Envy them not, their palate's with the swine.'

This braggart ode woke a company of echoes.
Randolph and Cleveland came in with hot-headed
gallantry to the defence of their Father, and Carew
wrote wisely and comfortingly. But a rhymer called
Feltham mocked openly in a parody of Jonson's verse
that charged him:

    'Come leave this saucy way
     Of baiting those that pay
   Dear for the sight of your declining wit!'

Ben's failure was far more momentous than another

man's victory. Nearly all his plays had stirred dispute, but out of dissension he had built a reputation – buttressed by his personality – that was already a kind of fabulous monument. His name stood for something unique. He had outlived competitors and peers, and his twenty-years-old achievements had the half mythical distinction of Roman triumphs. Their glory had mellowed by being half-forgotten. And now the monument had collapsed. A landmark had gone, a myth had been destroyed, and many were troubled. But some, like thieves at the taking of a city, were full of glee.

The noise of the disaster reached the King's ear and moved his pity. Charles was not unkind, and he could sometimes be generous; but he had always disliked the confidence of Ben's manner. Now, knowing him sick and humiliated, he was more willing and he found it easier to make friendly overtures. In his ranting ode, moreover, Ben had disclosed a suggestion of celebrating 'the glories of his King,' now that he had apparently done with the stage. A gifted historian would be valuable to an exponent of absolute monarchy, thought Charles; and sent Ben a hundred pounds.

This was undeniably handsome, and Ben was properly grateful. But he had never learnt to save money, and the gift was soon spent. His income now consisted of his Laureate pension of one hundred marks, and a salary, that he had been drawing for a year or so, of a hundred nobles as Chronologer to the City of London. His duty in this post was to record in suitable language memorable deeds and occurrences in the City. It had been paltry occupation had he done it; but he took the £30 without chronicling the small beer and so saved half his dignity. If his tastes had been simple he could doubtless have lived in decent comfort on these emoluments; but his tastes were not simple. His table in the house behind the Abbey showed food and wine as good as Sim Wadloe's while the money lasted, and many visitors came, and not seldom stayed to dinner. Before the end of the year Ben petitioned the King to enlarge the marks of his pension into pounds, and Charles, still generous, consented. He added too, of his own free will, an annual tierce of Canary from the royal cellars. And still his benevolence was not exhausted, for after five years' neglect Ben was invited to make a masque for Twelfth Night and another for Shrovetide.

For a moment his decline was checked. His fortunes had even risen a little, but their rise was brief and ill-omened as a see-saw's. Jones grumbled sourly at the return of his enemy whom he thought defeated, but the King had willed it and he had to control his displeasure till the masques were made. Ben's strength was still sufficient for this smaller work, and the masques he wrote were not much inferior to those the old King had seen. But Jones had more to do with their invention than formerly, and when they were printed he expected his name to precede Jonson's on the title-page. He was disappointed, however. The caption read:

'*The Inventors*, Ben Jonson; Inigo Jones.'
Inigo shouted his indignation. That a decayed and
ancient half-dead poet, an old fat palsied man, should
precede him in honour! Was he, who might at any
moment become a peer of the realm, to run second to a
decrepit drink-sodden wreck of a playwright, mumb-
ling in his bed the stale crust of wit and dull orts of
learning? Should Inigo, the King's architect, the
Palladian deviser of magnificence, follow meekly a
grey rhymer too lame and short of breath to hobble
into his grave? It was impossible, unthinkable, and
Jones blustered and raved to see the unthinkable so
calmly set in print.

Nor was the bedridden fat and ancient poet
content to hear in silence such rude and violent
attacks on himself and his sacred craft. Inigo might
shout from the bed-end, but Jonson roared as loudly
from the pillow. The poet came first by right divine,
and always would come first, whatever claims Inigo
made for his painting and carpentry. Did he think
deal boards and a dab of vermilion made a masque?
Because he dressed his actors in costumes of wild
irrelevance, and hid the orchestra where it could not
be heard, should he be honoured for this sacrifice to
something he called design? Because he got paid
three times over for the same scenery, was he worthy of
precedence? Did the ass bray because he wore rich
trappings now? Let him run puppet-shows where
he could be his own artist, musician, author, and
scene-shifter, and bray as loud as he liked with no one
to interrupt him.

Then, having uttered such abuse as he could readily think of, Ben discovered that a contemptuous silence would suit him best. 'Sir Inigo,' he said, 'doth fear that I should write some sharp verse upon him, able to eat into his bones? He is too ambitious. His forehead is too narrow for my brand!'

The quarrel did Ben no good, for Charles, who was only a fair-weather friend, swung back to Jones's side, and the following Christmas was convinced, by Jones's arguments, that Ben was no longer fit to provide a royal entertainment. In his place was chosen a court scribbler called Townshend, who wrote what Inigo told him to write and modestly stood aside to let Inigo take the credit.

1631 was a sorrowful year, for old friends died – Drayton, Cotton, and Donne – and in November the City withheld its wretched salary on the poor mercantile excuse that Ben had done nothing to earn it; and Ben went hungry. The author of *The Alchemist* had failed to describe the Lord Mayor's Show and the aldermen's fur gowns, so the Lord Mayor put his hundred nobles back into the till. Jonson had spent his time writing for the sinful players, that nest of pernicious birds roosting in the godly Puritan tree of Blackfriars. Why should the City subsidise a poet whose profane comedies had helped to fill those colleges of transgression, the theatres, where nothing but the seven deadly sins were studied? Why, indeed. The Puritans were gaining ground faster now.

Out of his extremity Ben wrote to the Lord Treasurer:

'Poor wretched states, prest by extremities,
Are fain to seek for succours and supplies
Of princes' aids, or good men's charities.

'Disease the enemy, and his engineers,
Want, with the rest of his concealed compeers,
Have cast a trench about me, now five years,

'And made those strong approaches by faussebrayes,
Redouts, half-moons, horn-works, and such close
      ways,
The Muse not peeps out, one of hundred days;

'But lies blocked up and straitened, narrowed in,
Fixed to the bed and boards, unlike to win
Health, or scarce breath, as she had never been;

'Unless some saving honour of the crown,
Dare think it, to relieve, no less renown,
A bed-rid wit, than a besieged town.'

He had had another stroke. And still his spirit,
though sometimes it cried for help, was undefeated.
With incredible fortitude he summoned all that
was left of his strength, all the tired companies of his
practised skill, and began to write another play that he
called *The Magnetic Lady*. He was like those Spanish
veterans of Gonzalo's regiment whose valour had
stirred such talk in the Lowlands when, forty years
before, he had carried his pike and killed his man
under the walls of Nymegen. Victory was in his

blood, and lifted on by that vital essence old soldiers could march, and march, out-pacing green youth, and fight at the last with solid unyielding ranks.

It was a solid play he wrote, but his old hand had lain too heavily on it. The lines no longer leapt, the action moved steadily but without plumes to grace its progress. It was competent, and as a defiance of the paralysis and poverty in which it was written it was magnificent. But as a comedy it was dull. The actors tried to enliven it with extempore oaths, which incurred everybody's dislike.

A fashionable audience attended its *première*. Jones and Nathaniel Butter, the newspaper proprietor, had their stools in a prominent position on the stage. They had come to show their scorn of Ben's labouring wit, and they laughed at the slow lines. They laughed ostentatiously, cackled at each indomitable small sally, guffawed in their neighbours' ears. They succeeded in attracting the audience's attention but failed to infect them with the desire for destruction. The play went on, and was more fortunate than its predecessor in that it was heard to the end. But a successful rear-guard action can only by courtesy be called a victory.

CHAPTER XXIV

THE TRIBE OF BEN

IN a tub in the yard of Ben's house a fox barked suspiciously at the noise coming from its master's room. The beast had been given to Ben by Sir Thomas Badger, who, curiously enough, was Master of the King's Harriers, because its smell was considered a very good remedy for palsy and the apoplexy. With petting and stroking Ben had done something to tame it, partly by its proximity hoping to mend his disease, and partly for pleasure in speculating on a fox's nature. But when company came, to whom its odour was unpalliated by therapeutic virtue, the fox was removed to the yard.

There were many visitors to the house behind the Abbey, for despite the weakening of their Father's power the Tribe of Ben had increased its numbers. Its most brilliant member was lost indeed – for Herrick, gloomy as Ovid setting sail for Tomi, had gone to his Devonshire exile – but in Herrick's place were younger men: Digby, Falkland, Marmion, Mayne, and Cleveland. Young playwrights who might be expected to have shrugged their shoulders at the old dramatist eagerly sought his company, and sometimes followed his teaching. Nabbes and Cartwright,

Davenant and Rutter, were sealed of the Tribe. Ben's old servant Brome had caught the spilt surplus of his master's strength and taken to writing plays himself – successful plays – as Field, the boy actor whom Ben taught for his amusement twenty years before, had also done. There was virtue in his presence, so that even in his bed, palsied and a little tipsy, young men came to him not only for the long-garnered wisdom of his years, but to borrow something of his unquenchable vitality.

When with great hauling and heaving he was got out of bed, dressed, and set in his chair by the fire, he had a massive shapeless look, though he had shrunk a little since his illness. His belly drooped and his ponderous shoulders stooped towards it, as if pulled earthwards by its compelling weight. His hair had turned white, and under it his swarthy red face was stippled with scarlet venules, and on his temples big swollen veins showed clearly. There was a tight uncomfortable feeling in his head, that always kept him reminded of the possibility of another stroke, terrifying in its dull obliteration of life. Much talk and drinking made the discomfort worse, but sack and lively friends were worth a little pain and a little danger.

Sometimes he talked too much of the past, and rather insistently recalled the triumphs of his youth. He sprinkled his conversation now with military metaphors, as though his brief adventure in the Netherlands had been half a lifetime of campaigning. It grew in his memory, and he liked to think that he had been a soldier. With rich familiarity he spoke of quartermasters and trench-masters, of tertias and ramparts and tactics, and smacked his lips on a *maestro del campo.* He had enemies now, but there had been a time when with his long sword he would made them skip.

He talked of dead poets, Shakespeare and those wild pioneers of the trade, Marlowe and Greene. He told stories of that old rascal Henslowe, and of Burbage, and of Burbage's father, who built the first theatre in London out of money he borrowed from his brother-in-law, a grocer, who had sold his currants and spice, his house, and even his clothes, to speculate in this brave new venture. He spoke of Lady Rutland, and through her gave the young poets a link with that perfection of his age, Sir Philip Sidney. He remembered Queen Elizabeth.

His roots were in the solid past, and thought of that solidity gave his audience a kind of comfort, for there was nothing stable about their own age. The monarchy had become absolute, and everyone with a smattering of English history knew that such rule was short-lived. The noises of dissatisfaction were already loud, and growing bolder. Members of the last contemptuously used Parliament nursed their resentment, and political opposition was joining its force with the Puritans.

Often Ben spoke like a Puritan himself, and cursed the vice and folly of the times. Men were not as they had been. Taste was degenerate and the people followed false gods. Theatres, that should be the home of stately tragedy and comedy that taught true things, pandered now to base appetites. At The Red Bull the Queen's Men acted always to crowded houses, growing rich on mere noise, vile plots, and trumpery verse. Plays at the Blackfriars theatre were social occasions only, and of an afternoon the streets were so crowded with coaches that there was brawling and bloodshed, and shopkeepers stood in empty shops because the congestion of traffic kept customers away. No wonder the Puritans in Blackfriars hated the theatre.

'And yet,' said Ben, 'I cannot think Nature is so spent and decayed, that she can bring forth nothing worth her former years. She is always the same, like herself; and when she collects her strength, is abler still. Men are decayed, and studies: she is not.'

He might complain and condemn, but his complaints were not pessimism and his condemnation had not the bitterness of failure. He had no inclination to curse God and die. He was not optimistic, for optimism is a light and gaseous thing, but he knew that a capacity to survive was life's chiefest quality. He knew that life was undefeatable. The world went on, and that was a good thing. A limited survival was possible even to individuals, for though change was certain, ill-fortune could not crush those whom good fortune had not deceived. Nature was invincible, and men, who were Nature's heirs, could claim a life-lease of their heritage.

It was this heroic temper that kept the Tribe about him. Palsy might sometimes sour its utterance, age make it garrulous, wine raise its voice; but the intrinsic bravery was always there. Some of his friends were gallant as well as lettered men, and they found this soldierly confidence very sympathetic. Lord Falkland was one who thought swords and poetry good company; ten years later, when the Puritans had put their cropped heads into steel and were sweeping England with their pious fury, he threw away his life for a cavalier's gesture in the fight at Newbury. The Earl of Newcastle, Ben's most faithful patron at the last, wrote plays and poetry before he commanded an army for the King, and charged with Rupert at Marston Moor. Davenant and Marmion were to see service on the Royal side, May on the other. And Suckling brightened a campaign by the fine uniform in which he clothed his troopers. But the flower of the company was the poet and adventurer, the philosopher and privateer, that scholarly man of fashion Sir Kenelm Digby. He had written his romantic memoirs on the island of Melos; he had escaped the love of the Queen-Mother of France only by spreading a rumour of his death; he had secretly married Venetia Stanley, who by her beauty, her intellectual attainments, and her scorn of convention, was the scandal and jealous topic of London; he had taken the King's licence to voyage in the Mediterranean for the increase of his knowledge, and first putting letters of marque in his library had fitted two ships in a very warlike fashion, and defeated a mixed fleet of French and Venetians in the gulf of Scanderoon.

Digby stood high in Ben's favour, who thought:

'In him all virtue is beheld in state;
And he is built like some imperial room
For that to dwell in, and be still at home.
His breast is a brave palace, a broad street,
Where all heroic ample thoughts do meet.'

And in Digby's opinion Ben's work was second only to the *Faerie Queene* – a curious juxtaposition, perhaps, but the victor of Scanderoon was not bound to a particular school of thought any more than he lived in the circumference of one vocation.

Still dearer to Ben was Venetia Digby. She was a little older than her husband, and before her marriage she had flouted convention with the independence of one who sets her own high standards and lives by them in calm assurance of their sufficiency. Ben wrote:

'She had a mind as calm as she was fair;
Not tost or troubled with light lady-air,
But kept an even gait; as some straight tree
Moved by the wind, so comely moved she.'

Her intellectual abilities were linked with Christian charity, and her physical beauty gave to both an uncommon distinction and a rare endearment. Ben called her his Muse, and indeed she inspired the vast ruin of his genius (in which song must have seemed far-buried) to something of its old lyrical felicity. He thought her

'voice so sweet, the words so fair,
As some soft chime had stroked the air;

And though the sound had parted thence,
Still left an echo in the sense.'

But she helped him more actively than by the loan of an inspiring presence. Sometimes perhaps she wrote to his dictation, and criticised, suggested, amended, as she wrote. She talked to him and comforted his sickness. Her sudden death, in 1633, was one of those tragedies that stagger the mind with their unexpected and senseless brutality. It drove Sir Kenelm to a hermit's seclusion and brought Ben the likeliest vision of despair he had ever seen.

"'Twere time that I died too, now she is dead,
Who was my Muse, and life of all I did,'

he wrote, and found for once no consolation in the swings of life for the plunder of the roundabout. In the passion of his grief he cursed all nature and saw no comfort in humanity. A new paralysis had visited him and held him powerless to reach for any earthly lenitive. With an old man's nearness to death he turned instead to the imminence beyond the grave, and in the very simplicity of belief cried out that only in Heaven was solace, but there indeed it was, and all happiness with her, robed now in light, who shone with her Redeemer's gladness. His elegy is shaken with sorrow, it trembles with the fervour of his faith and hope in God; and then in a sudden peace he sees that calm and fruitful beauty which poets of an elder day, hemmed in with the rigours of savage life, prophesied for their ultimate beautitude in Christ. It was a pagan hope, simple and splendid, dressed in the passionate weeds of the early Church.

The tragedy of Lady Venetia's death obscured the small triumph he won by the presentation of a masque at Lord Newcastle's house of Welbeck, where King Charles and his Queen halted on a visit to Scotland. It was a gay little piece, and their Majesties liked it so well that they asked for another of the same sort when, in the following year, they made a second progress to the North. In this, his final entertainment, Ben flaunted his last audacity and revenged himself on Iniquity Jones.

A few months before he had patched up an old play called *A Tale of a Tub*, and inserted a villainous caricature of Jones in the likeness of a rural joiner making a wedding masque for the constable's daughter. Inigo heard of the coming attack, and, seized with trepidation at the thought of Jonson's unsparing pen, used all his influence to have the material scenes suppressed. His succeeded, and the play, made insignificant by their excision, was produced without excitement.

But the masque of *Love's Welcome*, shown to Charles and his Queen at Bolsover Castle in Derbyshire, gave Ben the opportunity he wanted, and having abbreviated the caricature he boldly made it a *divertissement* for the King. The Earl of Newcastle, as the King's host, took a risk in permitting it, but his friendship for Ben was justified and his royal guests were amused at the picture of Inigo, ever busy and yet seeming busier than he was, drilling plumbers, carpenters, and masons to dance before them. When they returned to London the King spoke seriously to the City authorities about their stoppage of Ben's salary, and ordered them not only to continue it but to pay what arrears were due.

When this windfall arrived Ben sent to Sim Wadloe for wine and gave a dinner to his friends. That was the advantage of money. It could be turned into boiled capons, a shield of brawn, a venison pasty, a marrow-bone pie sweet with raisins and white wine and cinnamon; it brought friends to your table; mere six shillings got a gallon of the best Canary. So the City's chandlery pension, paid so grudgingly, was turned to good use, and the fox in his tub – carried into the yard for the company's sake – was startled again by laughter and the gay noise of friendship. He barked eagerly at the smell of cooked food, for he had been hungry for the last week or two.

When the visitors had gone he was taken up to Ben's room, and snarled suspiciously to feel Ben's fumbling hands smoothing his harsh red coat. Ben drank a little more sack. The woman who lived with him took some too. However bare the house might be they were seldom without wine, for both loved it, and neither took much thought for what next week would bring. In his corner the fox crunched loudly on fat capon-bones.

CHAPTER XXV

POET'S DEATH

In 1634, at Ludlow Castle, the house of Lord Bridge-water, President of Wales, a masque was shown which sang in verse of amazing beauty the swan-song of its kind. Its theme was the serious doctrine of Virginity, its principle the holy dictate of spare Temperance. Its author, John Milton, a young man of twenty-six, was not a little indebted for his art to Ben Jonson's practice of poetry, but he had no intention of following in Jonson's steps and writing for the entertainment of a court. The principal figure in his masque was Comus – not now an honest glutton, as Ben had once drawn him, but a monster who would cajole Innocence into the debaucheries of a Sensual Stye – and to Comus Milton gave his loveliest verse: willy-nilly, for poetry has predilections of its own: but far more matter he gave to the enemies of that sinister creation, and their concern was the grave doctrine of Chastity and the pious Puritan commandment to be temperate. The masque was stretched to contain a sermon; the masque perished, and sermons multiplied.

Ben had outlived his age. All his old friends – and there had been so many of them – were dead, and some of his young ones also. Randolph had died, and

Lady Venetia; Digby was conducting mystical experiments in a hermit's gown, and Herrick was far away in Devonshire. In 1635 Ben's surviving son died, a shadowy figure. Once he had collaborated in a play with Brome, his father's servant; but he was a slight creature with nothing of inherited character. Fewer visitors came as Ben grew less able to talk, and those who did come brought gloomy and affrighting news: Dutch ships and Spaniards fought without let or hindrance in English waters, and in the Channel Moorish corsairs plundered coastwise shipping at their ease. England under Charles's personal rule was no longer a power in Europe, scarcely a power in her own territories. Ireland was at war in a confused way, partly domestic and partly against Strafford, who was trying to impose unity. Archbishop Laud was railing-in altars, and would have the clergy clad as he ordered, stand or kneel as he bade them. He said that every man must worship in his own parish church and on his knees take communion from a railed-in table set in the east end of that church. But the Puritans were uttering defiance of all authority in the matter of religion. Why, they asked, should men do or believe what was repugnant to their own understanding? Insubordination was growing in church and state – John Pym, lately Member for Tavistock, had denied the very existence of sovereignty – and church and state sought to quell it by ever-narrowing laws. Hundreds of Puritan families were emigrating to New England to escape an obedience that had grown intolerable. . . .

'The vulgar are commonly ill-natured, and always grudging against their governors,' wrote Ben in his old age. But he added, 'he is an ill prince that so pulls his subjects' feathers, as he would not have them grow again.'

There was abundance of such wisdom in ancient writings. Greek and Roman authors had seen their countries torn by internecine strife, and made their estimates of human nature in its midst. The Acropolis stood beneath a bluer sky, and Tiber was a different colour to Thames, but politicians in Greece and Rome were curiously similar to English politicians, and a London mob had many likenesses to an Athenian one. The ancient wisdom kept its savour in a modern air, and Ben, re-reading his familiar authors, found much that was pertinent to his own time and some things that might comfort a philosopher. There were not only general resemblances to be discovered, but even individual applications.

He began to prepare a collection of *pensées*, Lilliputian essays, miniature homilies, that he called *Timber* or *Discoveries*. These were not exactly translations, for much he remodelled to his own design, and all that he copied was so like his own thought that the Greek and Latin authors seemed merely to have anticipated his expression of it so happily as to make further explication superfluous. 'Truth is man's proper good: I know no disease of the soul but ignorance.'– There is Ben's natural voice, though the words were written when his ancestors thought woad a pretty sign of civilization. Men had spoken with his tongue before, and where he recognized the accent he made the passage his own. Sometimes his Latin book was like a mirror in which he saw an image of himself, as when he read in Seneca of a man 'that knew no mean, either to intermit his studies, or to call upon them again. When he hath set himself to writing, he would join night to day, press upon himself without release, not minding it, till he fainted; and when he left off, resolve himself into all sports and looseness again, that it was almost a despair to draw him to his book; but once got to it, he grew stronger and more earnest by the ease.' So in his youth and noon had he lived.

Sometimes he found portraits of his friends, of Shakespeare and Bacon, and sometimes the stuff that his enemies were made of. In Quintilian there were many sensible rules of composition that appealed to him by reason of their closeness to his own practice. He and Quintilian were as one in believing that 'for a man to write well, there are three necessities: to read the best authors, observe the best speakers, and much exercise of his own style.' Care and industry were all-important, and so was a good model. Ben made a kind of schoolroom for poets and dramatists, and filled it with classical precepts useful, he believed, in a world that was fundamentally unchanging. Ignorance was still a cancer of the soul, and comedy had still a nobler end than laughter.

So on his pillow was Ben removed from life far enough to see time as a bond and not a barrier, and still his brain was eager to teach some particles of truth to men who had, he knew, learnt nothing from history, but were like children occupied with toys.

He too had his toys, that pleased him well enough: not others' books only, but his own. In a fine large folio volume that lay comfortably on his knees were the plays of his genius, and as he turned the pages the mannikins of his creation jeered and strutted, paraded their foppery or rebuked it in others, clothed their vice in glittering jewels and adorned their rags with wit. Here under a drooping plume was Bobadill putting Moors pell-mell to the sword, with nothing but a bunch of radish in his stomach; there was Dol Common (Subtle half-strangled by her useful hand) bullying her fellow-rogues into friendship. Here was Clerimont listening while his page sang 'Still to be neat, still to be drest,' and there Sejanus boasting that only fear made gods. Now Hedon played parlour-games in Cynthia's court, now Volpone sold patent medicines at a street-corner in Venice. A world of freaks and crazy egotists lived in those pages – a world that was everywhere if satire's eyes were sharp enough – and with what rare economy was its earth built, with how splendid a dress its creatures clad! How admirably they spoke all that they were intended to speak! Deft and muscular, easy-sounding with the ease that comes of hidden effort, packed with meaning and ripe with allusion, trimly fitted to character – such was the speech of every citizen in that folio world. . . .

Echoing in the perfect lines were the voices of the actors who had spoken them: the clear high voices

313

of the Children of the Chapel, Salathiel Pavy's voice, and Nid Field's; here was an echo of Burbage, there of Shakespeare. The ghosts of Marston and Dekker slipped through the scenes of *The Poetaster*.

To the poems and the masques clung whole troops of memories. In their pages Charis and Sir John Roe returned to life, Lady Rutland and the Earl of Salisbury and Fanny Howard walked again with all the pageantry of James's court like a crowded tapestry behind them. In a room thick with tobacco smoke and the brewing of his Great Elixir, Raleigh spoke of Punic wars, and down palace corridors came slinking that old grey fox Lord Henry Howard. Now the large splendour of Inigo's masquing stage filled Ben's eye, and out of a scene obscure and cloudy, in which nothing was visible but a dark cliff, and shadowy wild trees above, came over the lip of the rock the rising moon, and in her yellow light a satyr put forth his head and shrilly called.

His feathered hat a little too small for his massive brow, the old King sat watching, and when his lords danced a galliard made good jokes in his comfortable Scots voice. Had it not been for James there would have been fewer masques for Ben to read, and hardly so much familiar recollection of a court to make him philosophical.

Day after day Ben studied his own writings, and peopled them with memories. Night came heavily to shut them out, and sometimes he was loth to wake. Time on its heavy feet went curiously fast. . . .

He closed the book. It was good, and it would live.

314

He had worked for posterity's applause as much as his contemporaries', and he knew that posterity would praise him. He had lived in honourable competition with the greatness of past time, and by gigantic labour earned his share of the immortality that Virgil and Aristophanes wore by like title. He had built no barns except his book. He had not sought, like Shakespeare, the visible honour and security of a mansion house, but dwelt in a precarious Bohemia where tavern signs were the household deities, poetry and scholarship the greater gods. In their service he had worked, and his work would live. . . .

He lay half-dead, like an empire whose distant provinces have fallen to invaders or wasted in civil strife, but still its capital lives, and is still subject to its former faith, still dominated by its young ambition. Half his body lay inert and useless, but in his unconquered brain was still a handful of living seed, and, emulous of increase yet, it started once again to grow. In sight of death Ben began to write another play, and its green quickening concealed for a little while the ruins of his strength.

He called it *The Sad Shepherd*, but typically redressed the weakness of pastoral affectation by giving his flocks a grazing on the fringe of Sherwood, and bringing into his shepherds' company Robin Hood and the merry men. The sturdy naturalism of folklore stiffened his Theocritean idyll, and in this lively air he found miraculous health. Never before had he written with such natural sweetness and vigour so

315

unstressed; never before had his imagination been so lyrical. At last, with death creeping up his limbs, he found the freedom that he had shut himself out of nearly forty years before, when he so resolutely determined to write a new kind of comedy fast-bound to realism; and he entered his freedom with the knowledge that came of living so long with realism. Under the green boughs of Sherwood his poet-people truly lived, and thickets that waved in leafy beauty hid useful deer for Scarlet and Scathlock.

In the depths of the forest dwelt Maudlin, a witch. Her home was a gloomy dimble overgrown with briers and sheltered by a ruined abbey. There she crouched like a hare in its form. Her son Lorel, a swineherd, had stolen a fair shepherdess, and till she would accept his love imprisoned her in a stout oak-tree. Meanwhile Robin Hood made preparations for a feast to all the woodland folk, and the sad Shepherd Aeglamour haunted the forest rides looking in vain for his lost Earine:

'Here she was wont to go, and here, and here!
Just where those daisies, pinks, and violets grow:
The world may find the Spring by following her;
For other prints her airy steps ne'er left.
Her treading would not bend a blade of grass,
Or shake the downy blow-ball from his stalk!
But like the soft west wind she shot along,
And where she went the flowers took thickest root,
As she had sowed them with her odorous foot.'

– Lorel has wooed her with a present of badger cubs

316

and boasting of his wealth in swine and cattle and twenty swarms of bees, but Earine has again refused him and been thrust back into the oak. Aeglamour thinks she is drowned in Trent, pulled under by the treacherous river-nymphs, and has no heart to mix with Robin's huntsmen in the proffered solace of spring.

'A Spring, now she is dead! of what? of thorns,
Briers, and brambles?'

he asks.

Greedy Maudlin steals the venison ready for the feast, and tries to stir trouble between Robin and his Marian; but Alken, a wise old shepherd, warns them of her malice. Alken knows her tricks and all her court of luckless owls and fire-drakes, flitter-mice with leather wings, and span-long elves that dance about a pool with changelings in their arms. With the old shepherd to help them, Scarlet and Scathlock and Little John set out to hunt the witch, and Alken promises:

'I will find her for you,
And show you her sitting in her form; I'll lay
My hand upon her, make her throw her scut
Along her back, when she doth start before us.
But you must give her law: and you shall see her
Make twenty leaps and doubles; cross the paths,
And then squat down beside us.'

The hunt is up, to ride and run through Sherwood. . .
But no horn sounded. Ben's strength failed at last,

and he lay helpless for anything but to wait. Before his eyes the forest emptied and the bright turf grew dull. The shepherds stopped their singing, and the hunters faded into tree-darkness. Trent's waters sank.

The mocking crest that he had chosen for himself mocked him now for the last time. It was a compass with one arm broken, and the motto *Deest quod duceret orbem*.

He could not draw it whole. Life was too short to go on equal terms with art, and the circle would never be complete. *Tanquam explorator* he had written in his pride, but – *deest quod duceret orbem* – like Drake he had fallen on the equator.

All the provinces of his body were captive now, and only the inmost citadel of his brain held out. His eyes were bright, and travelled over his long row of books. He heard the noise of London come through his window. But he could not speak. A spoonful of sack lay in his mouth unswallowed, and still his dark eyes shone. Judgment was last in the field.

In August, 1637, a vast throng followed his body to its grave in the Abbey. Peers and poets went, the Sons of Ben, players and potboys, scholars and the unlettered many whose dull minds were stirred by the death of someone whose name meant greatness. How great or why they did not know, but great he had been, and he was dead. They jostled the mourning poets and stared at his coffin as though it held a dead king.

318

A flag of blue marble covered the grave. Some little time after the funeral, a man called Young was walking in the Abbey and saw the stone being fitted into position. He stopped, and gave the mason eighteen pence to carve an inscription. The mason's hammer and chisel rang boldly, cheerfully, and presently he blew away dust, and in the marble deep letters read: O RARE BEN JONSON.

INDEX

INDEX

An index conscientiously including every reference in this book would make a very tedious long procession of names. I have therefore noted only people living at the time of the narrative and generally sustaining a part in it; a few subjects of special interest; titles of contemporary poems, plays, and masques; and occasional place-names.

Cotton, Sir Robert, 98, 104, 105,
152, 176, 213, 245, 286, 287, 297
Cunningham, Mary, 231, 247
Curtain Theatre, 30, 57–59, 64
Cynthia's Revels, 75, 76, 78, 79,
83, 185

DANIEL, SAMUEL, 122, 124, 125,
127, 181, 232–234
Davenant, William, 301, 304
Davies, Sir John, 98, 152, 243,
Dee, Dr., 189
Defence of Poesie, A, 27
Dekker, Thomas, 45, 68, 78, 83–87,
92–96, 120, 131, 163, 240, 314
Denmark, King Christian IV of,
159–161
Digby, Sir Kenelm, 300, 304–306,
310
—— Lady (Venetia), 304–307, 310
divine right of kings, 133, 134, 270
Donne, John, 42, 50, 98–100, 104,
152, 170, 171, 176, 180, 181, 183,
199, 207, 213, 240–242, 265, 271,
297
Drake, Sir Francis, 10, 31, 50, 123,
216, 318
Drayton, Michael, 163, 176, 181,
213–217, 222, 232, 234, 297
Drummond, William of Hawthornden, 23, 43, 44, 159–161, 168,
183, 222, 229–247
Duperron, Cardinal, 201, 202, 240

Eastward Ho! 145
Edinburgh, 17, 108, 109, 112, 114,
159, 222, 226, 227, 229, 230, 245
249, 250
Elixir, the Great, 169, 197, 314
Elizabeth, Princess Palatine, Queen
of Bohemia, 204, 208, 255, 256,
281
Elizabeth, Queen, 10, 13, 30, 31,
47, 50, 75–77, 105, 108, 109, 116,
123, 140, 189, 244, 302
Endimion, 29
Essay's Bacon's, 50, 163
Essex, Robert Devereux, 2nd Earl
of, 76, 99, 118, 236
—— —— 3rd Earl of, 166, 204, 205,
207, 208

Essex, Countess of, *v.* Lady Francis
Howard

Faerie Queene, The, 13, 33, 231,
232, 305
Falkland Lord, 300, 304
Fawkes, Guy, 154, 156, 157
Featley, Daniel, 199
Feltham, Owen, 293
Felton, John, 286–288
Ferrabosco, Alfonso, 165, 166
Field, Nid, 81, 102, 301, 314
Finsbury Fields, 11, 22, 58, 87, 163
Fletcher, John, 163, 215, 240
Forman, Simon, 189, 205
Forth Feasting, 239
Fortunate Isles, The, 276, 277
Fortune Theatre, 271
Fox, The, 150, 151, 153, 159, 164,
173, 184, 186, 187, 284
France, 137, 141, 142, 161

GAINSFORD, CAPTAIN, 281, 282
Garnet, Father, 154, 156
General Assembly, 114, 153, 278
Gipsies Metamorphosed, The, 262,
263
Globe Theatre, 70, 71, 89, 203, 206,
242
Gondomar, Diego Sarmiento de
Acuna, Marquis of, 218, 254
Goodere, Sir Henry, 183, 194, 213
Gray's Inn, 210
Greene, Robert, 50, 51, 232, 302
Greenway, Father, 154
Grenville, Sir Richard, 30, 31, 50
Guiana, 217, 218, 242
Gunpowder Plot, 153–156, 179

HALL, JOSEPH, 50, 53
Hampton Court, 124, 125
Hannam, Captain, 94
Harington, Sir, John, 136
Hartshorne Lane, 14, 152, 179
Hemmings, John, 57, 58
Henrietta, Queen, 269, 289, 307
Henry, Prince of Wales, 111, 129,
130, 169, 187–189, 197, 208, 219,
238, 254